WRITERS & COMPANY

Writers & Company

ELEANOR WACHTEL

Alfred A. Knopf Canada

PUBLISHED BY ALFRED A. KNOPF CANADA

Copyright © 1993 by Eleanor Wachtel

All rights reserved under International and Pan American copyright conventions. Published in 1993 by Alfred A. Knopf Canada, Toronto. Distributed by Random House of Canada Limited, Toronto.

Canadian Cataloguing in Publication Data

Wachtel, Eleanor.
    Writers & company

ISBN 0-394-22738-7

1. Authors — 20th century — Interviews.   I. Title.
PN453.W33 1993   809'.04   C93-093237-4

10 9 8 7 6 5 4 3 2

Printed and bound in Canada.

Toronto, New York, London, Sydney, Auckland

To the Snowdon branch
of the N.D.G. Boys & Girls Library

Acknowledgments

My first thanks go to Anne Gibson, Executive Producer of CBC Radio Arts, for giving me opportunity and encouragement—an indispensable pairing that comes along only rarely and for which I am grateful. Also to Damiano Pietropaolo, now Head of Performance for CBC Radio, who supported "Writers & Company" from the beginning.

Making radio is a team sport, more like volleyball than tennis; there are many people who keep the ball in the air. I would like to acknowledge, in particular, the talent and generosity of the program's producers. Sandra Rabinovitch is principal producer, a key role I will elaborate upon in the Introduction. Richard Handler and Greg Kelly have also acted as producer on a number of occasions. The indefatigable Lisa Godfrey functions as program assistant, which means doing everything in a small unit such as ours. We work with many technicians in actually recording and broadcasting interviews—too many to name here—but I am happy to mention our once regular studio engineer, Joe Mahoney. The CBC's London and New York studios provide frequent assistance in contacting and welcoming guests. I would like to thank in particular Judith Melby, Linda Perry and Donna Gallers.

Also, I have the pleasure of having as colleagues Shelagh Rogers, Liz Nagy, Susan Feldman, Angelica Fox, Rosemary Bates and Sandra Jeffries.

Outside the CBC, I am indebted to Greg Gatenby and his

Harbourfront Reading Series and International Festival of Authors for bringing to Toronto many of the show's favourite writers, and for introducing us to many, many others. His initiative enhances the experience of living in Toronto.

And I'd like to thank my friend Irene McGuire, of Writers & Co, the Literary Bookstore, for allowing me to use the name for the show, and hence the book.

In turning radio interviews into a book, a number of other people have been very valuable to me. First, of course, the writers themselves who agreed to have their conversations appear between covers. Then, the ongoing enthusiasm of Boris Castel of Queen's Quarterly, Linda Spalding and Michael Ondaatje of Brick: A Literary Journal and Douglas Fetherling enabled me to pursue this process. The keen interest and enterprise of Catherine Yolles, Louise Dennys and Jan Whitford provided the means. Special thanks to Donya Peroff and Hedy Muysson for attentive transcribing and to Caroline Christie for ever-altruistic research.

Personally, I have been sustained by a reliable cheering section that might be dubbed Marlene and Frank Cashman & the Beautiful Boys. Also by my Toronto buddies Beth Kaplan, Barbara Nichol, Connie Guberman and Linda Hossie. My professional life was shaped by the timely and extraordinarily generous participation of Andy Wachtel. Finally, for help in the preparation of this book with editing, "keyboarding" and the pursuit of puffins, my thanks (in neon) to Gayla Reid.

Contents

Introduction

I was going to start by quoting Saint Teresa: "Words lead to deeds.... They prepare the soul, make it ready, and move it to tenderness." I showed this to a friend who said, "Yes, that's sweet, but words can also move people to other things, to despair, or even violence." And of course that's true, but it made me realize how much I rely on words, on literature in particular, to understand how other people live and have lived, and how they work through the pain and joy of being alive. "What are you going through?" is all we need to ask, wrote Simone Weil.

I think the audience's connection to the CBC Radio program "Writers & Company"—often a remarkably personal connection—comes from their pleasure in hearing a writer talk about ideas and feelings with intelligence and candour. And here, "writers" embraces not only novelists and poets, but also essayists, playwrights, biographers, critics and film-makers. It is perhaps reductive (even naïve or romantic) to see compassion as the currency of human exchange, but if I were to add curiosity or a keen interest in imagination, could I get away with it? Oprah and Geraldo and American confessional exhibitionism notwithstanding, I am still Canadian enough to be moved when two middle-aged male movie directors talk to me about love: Henry Jaglom details ecstatically how he met the woman he has fallen in love with, as he counsels me—and everyone—"not to settle [for less]." And Volker Schlondorff sadly recounts the end of his twenty-year marriage and partnership with actress and film-maker Margaretta von Trotta, acknowledging how, ultimately, the working relationship superseded the intimate.

Some writers are surprising in other ways. The South African J.M. Coetzee pulls out a small notebook and thumbs through the thin pages. I think to myself that he's tactfully looking through his appointments to retrieve my name. Wrong. He asks if I mind if he jots down my questions during the interview. Then, never looking up at me, he very slowly and carefully frames his responses. He's thoughtful, impersonal and compelling in the most halting manner. At one point he declares that he's lost his voice, though no hoarseness is perceptible. I urge water; he continues. At the end he stays and talks longer than arranged and says how much he's enjoyed the exchange.

The flamboyant American writer Marianne Wiggins comes into our smallest and shabbiest studio (this is pre-Broadcasting Centre). Studio temperatures veer unpredictably between sauna and icebox; on this occasion it was the latter. Wiggins, who sported rings on every finger, including a Mandarin-style wraparound on her fingertip, was wearing a leather mini-skirt, silk blouse and jacket, with spike heels. When she remarked on the cold, I suggested she keep her jacket on. "But what about my tootsies, honey?" she said.

And I don't suppose I'll ever be able to start an interview the way Carrie Fisher began hers with Madonna: "We go to the same therapist…"

While I always prefer to interview face to face, the luxury of radio is that "Writers & Company" can contact virtually anyone in the world who speaks English and is near a telephone. In London, Paris or New York we invite our guests into a CBC studio; elsewhere in the United States, into the studio of an affiliate of National Public Radio. In some instances—Nadine Gordimer in Johannesburg, Andre Dubus in Haverhill, Massachusetts—we send a reporter to hold a microphone in front of the guest while I talk to her/him over the phone. Then, we "mix" the two sides of the conversation—that recorded at the home of the writer, while talking to me, and that recorded in the studio in Toronto. This way, the broadcast is always "studio quality" and is easier to listen to over the extended period that many of the conversations run.

If the world is more or less our oyster, how do we (not the royal but the collective we of producer, program assistant, executive producer and host) choose our guests? We are influenced by the arrival of new work and authors' tours, but even more by personal enthusiasms or the development of a theme in a series of specials. After the guest has agreed to be interviewed, our researcher (a.k.a. program assistant) ferrets out background information, including reviews, previous interviews if available and articles. The producer and I read these, along with as many of the author's books as we can manage, starting with the latest. We talk, and then the producer prepares a detailed line of questioning. These may be discussed with the executive producer, and amended by me, but this is the roadmap I will follow in the studio. Naturally I try to listen and respond to whatever is happening conversationally during the interview, but I rely on those original questions to get me where I think I want to go.

Then the producer deftly edits the tape for broadcast, attentive to pace and coherence while ensuring the conversation continues to sound natural. This is where, to my relief, my own hesitations are "cleaned up." I listen, add my two cents' worth and write the introductions.

In preparing this book, in virtually all cases I have gone back to the original, uncut interviews, and I've edited for print, unfettered by program time constraints (or considerations of how things sound), and thus I've been able to include new material. (The most difficult task, of course, was choosing which twenty-one conversations to include from the over one hundred interviews recorded.) One thing that interviewing for radio, as opposed to print, has taught me is to react noisily—that is, audibly. When I wrote author profiles for magazines, I tended to fade into the wallpaper. I'd transcribe the tapes and then shape my article later.

Radio forced me to try to be present in a more immediate way, but in editing these interviews I've cut some of my interjections where they merely served as prompts or where they break the flow. My hope is that, even without radio, the sounds of the voices come through.

More about the power of words. The Quechua-speaking Indians of the Andes look at time differently from the way we do. We tend to view the past as behind us and the future as ahead, as in "Let us go forward into the future." The Quechua, more logically perhaps, recognize the past as what is already known, so it's right in front of you. The future is behind your back because it's what you can't see, unless you catch a glimpse of it out of the corner of your eye, over your shoulder. Our whole conceptual framework is based on a metaphor. A good writer can turn your head around.

WRITERS & COMPANY

Cynthia Ozick

In the spring of 1991, when *The Shawl,* Cynthia Ozick's
novella about a Holocaust survivor, was published in England, she was hailed as one of America's most underrated
writers, "a writer of exquisite slivers," or, as another critic
put it, "a master of the meticulous sentence and champion
of the moral sense of art." I think Cynthia Ozick is not so
much underrated as relatively unknown; people who
know her work tend to rate it very high. Whether she is
writing fiction—stories, novellas, novels—or essays about
other writers or about life and art, such as *Art & Ardor*
(1983) or *Metaphor & Memory* (1989), Ozick writes with
intelligence, precision and passion.

Cynthia Ozick was born in New York in 1928 and grew
up in the Bronx, a child of Russian-Jewish parents. She
studied at New York University in Greenwich Village.
Ozick was thirty-eight when her first novel, *Trust,* was
published in 1966. "For a long time," she said, "I didn't
feel I could honourably call myself a writer, because I
didn't have any of the accoutrements. Readers, mainly."

Both *The Cannibal Galaxy* (1983) and *The Shawl* (1989)
appeared first in *The New Yorker* magazine. Reviewers of
The Messiah of Stockholm (1987) compare her writing to
that of Isaac Bashevis Singer, Henry James, Vladimir
Nabokov, Franz Kafka and Evelyn Waugh. Cynthia Ozick

not only writes with enormous imagination, wit and virtuosity, but clearly she's a writer not easy to categorize.

———————

WACHTEL First, I should thank you for agreeing to talk to me at all, because I've read about your wariness of giving interviews. When you spoke to *The Paris Review* you insisted on what must be a unique arrangement, in which you met with the interviewer, who asked you questions, and then you typed your answers in response.

OZICK I don't think that's unique. In fact, I think I swiped it. I'm not positive, but I may have read that it was Saul Bellow whom I was plagiarizing in this activity. It wasn't my idea, but it was very comfortable to do that.

WACHTEL Why are you wary of conversation as a form of communication?

OZICK Well, in general it seems to me that conversation is air. One can't control it; foolish germs escape one's lips and contaminate the air and one cannot draw them back. Whereas if you write you can change, reflect—re-reflect—and in general erase your nonsense. But all that is spoken escapes forever.

It escapes in another way, too. It can't be contained. I think of all the wonderful telephone conversations, literary conversations I've had with friends over the years, and they're lost forever. I find that the oral is not as satisfactory as that which can be nailed down forever, like print.

WACHTEL So you're conscious of both the plus side and the negative side of speech. What you're worried about in the first instance is that something that's not completely thought out will escape; at the same time, it's ephemeral so you can also lose something that's really good.

OZICK Yes, isn't that strange. It's a total contradiction, which I've never noticed until you just pointed it out. The two should cancel each other out but they don't. The ephemeral sits there side by side with the embarrassment. I suppose the good point is that it's the embarrassment that is the ephemeral. But if you do an interview which is spoken and then is put into print, you're stuck.

WACHTEL You get the worst of both worlds.

OZICK Precisely, you get the worst of both, yes.

WACHTEL There is a line in one of your stories that was published in *The New Yorker*, "Puttermesser Paired." The story is about Ruth Puttermesser, a lawyer in her fifties, who, despite her parents' urging, has never married. The line is, "For the first time it struck her that her mother was right. It was possible for brains to break the heart." How do brains break the heart?

OZICK In my view they don't, but in the view of mothers and other normal people they probably do, since a passionate concentration on intellect and intellectual life in someone as obsessive as Puttermesser certainly is gets in the way of normality, of ordinary life. And ordinary life—getting married, having children, sitting with the other mothers at the sandbox, going to work, office politics, all of this growth and decay—is the opposite of what intellectual obsessives, intellectually possessed people like Puttermesser, are involved in. Puttermesser would give away her soul for a historical or philosophical idea. Her mother wants her to get married and have children and be normal.

WACHTEL Let's talk about this character of yours, Ruth Puttermesser. An unmarried lawyer, a civil servant is how you always identify her, and you've written about her before—Puttermesser at thirty-four years old, at forty-six and now at fifty plus. Tell me about her.

OZICK I think I'm going to carry her to the grave. In fact, I wrote down in my journal the other day a possible name for the last in what has turned out unexpectedly to be a series. The title I wrote was "Puttermesser Brained." In this case I think she's going to be attacked by a mugger in New York and meet her end in this unfortunate way. I don't know if I will actually carry through this plan, but I do intend to carry her right down to her funeral.

I guess she's a kind of alter ego. She's much more obsessive than I am. She's lonelier than I am. But I think I'm almost as obsessive and almost as isolated as she is. So we are sisters under the skin in a sense, Ruth and I. And I never call her by her first name, though other people do. Her name, if it were German, would be Buttermesser, a butter knife—and Puttermesser is the Yiddish version. She's a butter knife because she is totally ineffectual, diffident, reckless; those are opposites but she contains them. She wants to hide away and yet she wants to control pieces of the universe. I suppose this is what's characteristic of writers. They want to be hermits and they want to imagine being directors of some vast stage of humanity.

WACHTEL But are they necessarily ineffectual?

OZICK Writers, I believe, are ineffectual, yes. I don't agree with Shelley—though I certainly used to when I was an adolescent— that poets are the unacknowledged legislators of mankind. We've seen writers as threats in the former Soviet Union, where they were considered important enough to imprison. Writers all over the world are in prison. But I believe that's the illusion of dictators who fear ideas. Of course ideas are powerful, but writers are not, even though they carry ideas, writers are not. The power of a writer is when the writer is most powerless, when there's no pressure on the writer to take a position. Once you belong to some institution, some bureaucracy, some foundation, then you've traded away your freedom. You might have traded it away for something as benign as gratitude; nevertheless, even gratitude is a pressure, and I believe a writer should live without any kind of pressure, which includes getting up in the morning and making breakfast for somebody else.

WACHTEL Before discussing ideas and writers, I want to return to Puttermesser for a moment. I'm intrigued by a couple of things common to your most recent fiction—this story "Puttermesser Paired" and your last novel, *The Messiah of Stockholm.* It's the idea of doubleness and mimicry. In both works your fictional character wants to merge with an actual dead writer. In "Puttermesser," it's George Eliot; in *The Messiah of Stockholm*, it's the Polish-Jewish writer Bruno Schulz, who was shot by the Gestapo during the war. It's like mirrors within mirrors. Also in *The Messiah of Stockholm*, Lars Andemening, who works as a book reviewer, reviews a book about a double, who masquerades as someone else. What is it about this doubleness that attracts you?

OZICK That's a curious question. I've never made the connection between one piece of fiction and another in relation to this doubleness that you speak of. Probably it has something to do with the seduction of impersonation, which itself probably has something to do with why one is a writer in the first place. It may be the desire to hide an intense shyness that drives one to impersonate, to be somebody else, to imagine oneself in another being. And at the same time one is oneself, so one is double, as you say. I do believe writing is related to the notion of impersonation. This is a famous fact about actors, that they have the need to impersonate; I'm not sure that writers are very different from actors in this sense, except that actors are given a script, and they create an impersonation only to a limited extent, whereas writers invent the fever of a whole world.

It is mirrors within mirrors. It's the passion for impersonation, or the passion to escape the self one has been given. Now, why one seeks this escape is an oddity. One would want to travel in a time machine and ask Charles Dickens that question, since he was a very grand impersonator and did it, in fact, on the stage with great lustiness and gusto. In a much quieter way, sitting at home, I suppose I want to do the same thing. And I suppose all writers want to do the same thing—pretend to be somebody else so one doesn't have to be oneself.

This leads to the question, Why don't you want to be yourself? I don't know the answer. You may have given it to me a moment ago when you spoke of merging. Perhaps one wants to merge with the landscape, with another society or one's own society. Merge with the moon, merge with the universe, merge with the mind of God. The lust to merge is, I suppose, the secret of impersonation.

WACHTEL For someone like you the readiest person at hand to merge with is an author. You described once how, at twenty-two, you lived like the elderly bald-headed Henry James. Was that another kind of merging?

OZICK I think you're right. That was one of the follies of my youth. It does seem to me a rather common folly. As does merging, wanting to get mixed up with ventriloquism or just commonplace imitation. Young writers sometimes believe that because they read writers they admire, they can begin with the powers of the great simply from the perfume of the reading. The fumes seem to enter the pores of the young writer and the young writer is deluded into thinking that those elderly powers have entered youthfulness. Actually one has to suffer one's way towards those powers.

WACHTEL You began writing early. In fact, you have said that you knew from the moment you first formulated a sentence that you were going to write, you were going to write novels. You started writing full-time after college and for years worked on a long novel that was never published, and you have said you regret all those years you invested in that novel.

OZICK Yes, I do. I probably will never erase the scar of what I regard as a life error. I feel that I ought to have thrown myself into the world of the literary stewpot, as I describe it in *The Messiah of Stockholm*. That stewpot where young writers run around and try to get themselves reviewing assignments, essay assignments, article assignments; do interviews; try to scale the ladder; feel the world pressing in on them. Don't do what I did, which was to imagine that I could reproduce *The Ambassadors* at the age of twenty-two, with no knowledge of the world and with insufficient skill at a simple thing like writing dialogue. Dialogue has to be honed. That's something that needs to be learned; it takes time, and apprenticeship.

I had a very long apprenticeship of about seven years on a work

I called "Mercy, Pity, Peace and Love," after a line by Blake. It got abbreviated, as the years went on, into MPPL. My husband began calling it "Mipple" for short, and I regarded it finally as a nipple on which I had sucked too long. But it was the wrong thing to do. One cannot be the elderly Henry James, bald-headed and paunchy, at the age of twenty-two, especially if one is a skinny, near-sighted young woman. One has to wait to develop the baldness. One has to wait to develop, period. And in the meantime one must scramble. I failed to scramble.

WACHTEL I find it enviable to cloister yourself away and hone your craft and read books. Why is scrambling good?

OZICK Scrambling is good because it's not the cloister, because in the cloister one remains arrested. During that period I would go to the New Rochelle Public Library, and before that to the Westchester Square Public Library in the north-east Bronx, and come home with piles and piles of books. They were fiction, the novels that I was catching up with; also literary criticism, history—lots of history—philosophy; and I would read sometimes sixteen hours a day before sitting down to write. And I lived this way for a very, very long time. It was certainly an education—but only a half-education. I think one does need to scramble. One has to scratch like a squirrel up a tree trunk. One has to learn to be wounded. One has to learn to be rejected; and one has to learn to write quickly and briefly for periodicals. Periodicals are a great school. They're as great a school as my own lonely apprenticeship, or perhaps even greater.

WACHTEL I'd like to talk to you about being Jewish and being a writer, and I want first to perhaps annoy you by combining the two. I understand you don't like being called a Jewish writer because to you that's an oxymoron.

OZICK The reason I regard the phrase "Jewish writer" as an oxymoron, in which each half of the phrase is at war with the other, is that in my mind a Jew is a citizen bound to a moral tradition, bound to a view of history which impresses on you the highest standards of humaneness and decency between human beings.

Jewishness insists on an ethical standard which has been honed through history and is rooted in an ideal—a monotheistic ideal, very stringent because it's very easy to worship all the wrong things all the time. There are idols everywhere; the state is an idol, oneself can be an idol; but monotheism means no idols, no false gods, don't make mistakes in that direction. Be a good citizen and pay attention to your responsibility as a human being in a world with other human beings. That's the Jewish part. I'm sure that members of other traditions can identify fully with that, though they would give it another name. Nevertheless, that's the Jewish part.

The writer part, by contrast, is a wild animal. The writer is responsible to no one. The writer derives extraordinary glee when inventing villains. The writer's an axe murderer, easily. Slashes, hurts, mutilates, acts out the evil impulse at every turn. The writer can invent an evil world and participate in it, which the good citizen must never do. Now, it's true that a writer can also invent a moral world. How do you invent a moral world without being Pollyanna? You've got to have a villain or two, and the writer enters into every cell, every grain of villainy, of wickedness, even while insisting that the goal is a decent vision of humankind. Nevertheless, the writer's not a good citizen, by definition.

WACHTEL Let me back up for a moment. How would you describe your own Jewishness, or do you consider yourself a practising Jew?

OZICK I am enamoured of tradition. I suppose one would say that there is a conservative temperament at work here in the sense of prizing what has been valued over several thousand years, an intellectual tradition of great brilliance.

I define Jewishness as a series of intellectual movements. I define Judaism as intellectual history, or the history of a series of philosophies, some of them in conflict with one another. Nevertheless, they are all attached to the central tree trunk of uncompromising ethical monotheism, and I'm fascinated by this philosophical centre. I adhere to it. I find it very freeing, the opposite of constraining. It's philosophically freeing.

And then, of course, the history of a people that has been around for such a very, very long time is intriguing. I feel very centred as a Jew. I feel centred in the West as a Jew; I feel centred in the Enlightenment as a Jew; it gives me a sense of being a part of the great mainstream. We live in a dual civilization with two strains or forks, the Hellenic and the Hebraic, and, of course, Christianity participates in both. So, incidentally, does Judaism. The Socratic view, or mode, of teacher and disciple, so to speak, has entered Judaism through Greece and through Greek models. The classroom is a Greek model. The study of text is a Greek model. There is a great intermingling of these great strands and streams, and I feel very much a part of both forks, but curiously enough through ancestral pressures a part of one of them inexorably.

WACHTEL You've elaborated how you feel centred as a Jew culturally and intellectually; what about as a writer? I'm going back to your statement that to be a Jewish writer is an oxymoron because to be a Jew requires a certain kind of behaviour and monotheism and morality and to be a writer requires its opposite. How have you functioned as a Jew and as a writer? How do you, as it were, bridge the oxymoron? I'm intrigued because even the language you use to describe literature has religious overtones. You talk about literature as "my single altar." One of your characters says he would have thrown himself on "the altar of literature." You've talked about literature as a false god. How have you reconciled that?

OZICK I think those "altars" of literature are ironic and satiric and dismissive. I don't take them seriously. I don't mean them. Not those altars. I don't, to use your words, bridge the oxymoron. The oxymoron is unbridgeable. When I am a Jew I am not a writer, and when I am a writer I am not a Jew, and when I'm sitting at my desk and dreaming up some fiction or some idea ... well, but ideas are different. Ideas and essays belong, I think, to the civic, that is, to the citizenly self, to the Jew. But fiction and the imaginative life are free of any kind of constraint, any kind of allegiance. I think

I'm least Jewish when I'm writing fiction. I know I am not a Jew when I am writing fiction.

Now, I know there are people who may quarrel with this and say, well, your characters are Jewish, and some of them have Jewish ideas. This may be true, but that's because one dips into the well in which one finds oneself. One lives on the planet into which one is born. But insofar as it's possible for a writer to be extraterritorial, I am, you might say, a Martian, an alien visitor to the planet, when I'm a writer. When I'm a Jew I'm certainly endemic, intrinsic to the planet, anything but marginal.

WACHTEL Do you still think there's something idolatrous about the act of creation itself?

OZICK Well, you know, writers and people in general go through what you might call states—feverish states or ideational eruptions. And it is true that at one point—and I suppose this fever was fairly long-lasting—I did carry on quite a bit about the idolatry of writing. I was struck by the fact that the writer is a creator of a universe and that this might put one—it's a very grandiose notion—in competition with the Creator of the Universe, and that therefore what the writer was doing was something idolatrous, intending to vie with God. I think Chaucer had this notion. I believe T.S. Eliot did, and I think at one time even Auden did. I regard this now as a fever through which I passed. The idea is no longer of any importance to me.

The difficulty, though, is that one really should not write down one's fevers because then one is stuck with them forever, and so this fever comes back, even though I'm cured of it, it comes back to haunt me.

WACHTEL But the line you use, I think, still percolates through— in the expression "the redemptive ardour of literature."

OZICK Yes. It's true that everything I've said so far denies the redemptive in literature. There are writers who do offer us redemption and I have to confess that they are closest to my heart. These are the great nineteenth-century redemptive writers, such as George Eliot, Chekhov, Tolstoy. Conrad has been an influence.

E.M. Forster. And on and on. In these writers one finds the redemptive.

I suppose, if one tries very hard, one can make a case, a theoretical case—I'm not sure I'm smart enough to make it—that all the best writing is redemptive. I'm not sure of that. I think of another writer, whom I do regard as redemptive, and most people would not—that's the late, and much mourned by me, Jerzy Kosinski, who wrote what many people have called a depraved art. And yet it seems to me that what he meant by showing degradation and depravity was that this is not how it ought to be; it was a kind of anti-ought. This is true also of Isaac Bashevis Singer, whose demons and imps steal souls and lead human beings away from the paths of decency. Singer's point was that in order to show the redemptive you must show the sin. You must show the depravity, you must show the anti-ought, in order for the ought to be implied. That, I suppose, is the theoretical argument for the redemptiveness of art. But I'm very unwilling at this latter point in my life to be dogmatic, to issue principles, to take stands. I think I want now to be on the side of flexibility, relaxation, tolerance. I've been dogmatic and intolerant for so many decades I'm looking perhaps for some paradisal relief.

WACHTEL You're a writer who believes that ideas are emotions. What do you mean by that?

OZICK Oh yes. That's a principle that I certainly don't want to relax. Literary critics tend to make a distinction between psychological realism and what they call the literature of ideas, but it strikes me that nothing is more participatory, more allied to psychological realism, than ideas. Ideas make your heart beat; ideas turn your stomach upside down; ideas are the most emotional stimuli there are.

The world may be divided between writers who believe in experience as stimulus and writers for whom ideas are the stimulus. In other words, do you start with a character, and the event is your germ, to use the Jamesian phrase: is your germ an experience or is your germ an idea? Very often for me the germ is an idea, and the idea creates the character, and the character and the idea are fused—they cannot be pried apart. The psychological and the idea are entwined. But then you may say, well, which comes first? For me, the idea comes first. There's nothing more emotional than certain notions.

WACHTEL Is this a position you have to defend against aesthetes or storytellers or people who would argue—as you pointed out in one of your essays—that the Holocaust carries the same weight as a corncob, in other words that you don't have to have a morality or an idea behind what you write?

OZICK The very distinguished writer who made that statement at a party I attended didn't at all mean that he wouldn't respond like any decent human being to the coming of Nazism. What he meant was that in writing a story, morality is irrelevant.

Very recently I've finished, as an Elderly Novice, the writing of a play. The issue of the play is so-called revisionism, the lies disseminated by those neo-Nazis (which is precisely what they are) who claim that the Holocaust never occurred. I have as a central character one of these neo-Nazis, and I was determined not to allow him any moral space at all, any aesthetic space, any glimmer of pleasantness or attraction. That was the first version of the play. I wanted to do that because I was not thinking of theatre, I was thinking of citizenship, I was angry at the so-called revisionists and their outrages. But it was pointed out to me—and I finally became persuaded—that the devil must be seductive in art. So in the latest version the same character is indeed seductive, even erotically seductive. Unfortunately, the devil is seductive in and out of fiction.

Now, that was an instance, I think, where the moral overtook the aesthetic to begin with, then I reversed myself and allowed the aesthetic at least equal space with the moral.

WACHTEL You have written a novella, a book called *The Shawl*, about a Holocaust survivor who lives in a perpetual and wretched state of mourning, dreaming of her lost daughter, writing letters to her, imagining the life her daughter might have had, had she survived, and rejecting any attempts to live a life now. I've heard that this is a book you're not happy with, even though it's a very powerful, strong book. Why are you no longer comfortable with it?

OZICK I suppose I was not comfortable with it even before I wrote it, during, and certainly after. The reason is that I did undertake to turn this event, this cataclysm, this great destruction, into a lyrical piece of writing, into a poetic artifact. I turned it into fiction and at least an attempt at making art, and it seems to me I did it because I couldn't help myself; it was done to me, so to speak. That doesn't mean that I approve of it, because I believe that if we spent five hundred, a thousand years simply ploughing through the documents of the Holocaust, there still wouldn't be enough time to learn in every detail what happened.

I don't believe that the Holocaust was a mysterious event. I believe that it's an event comprised of known and knowable data, and these data are in a thousand, two thousand, a million books. These books are growing generation by generation, decade by decade, and it seems to me that our responsibility is to pay attention to the documents and not to indulge in myth-making. I believe that's what I did, in a sense, in *The Shawl*; I approached the mythopoetic. I also believe that it is becoming dangerous to write Holocaust fiction. When we are surrounded by people of depraved imagination who say that the data are false, that what happened never happened, that what happened is in fact fiction, and we ourselves then participate in making these events into fiction, in some way we become complicit in that depravity.

WACHTEL Is this a variation on what the Frankfurt philosopher Adorno once said—that after Auschwitz there can be no poetry?

OZICK If Adorno meant that in a very generalized way, which I think he did, no; if he meant it specifically as to these events, then yes. But I believe he felt that the great mourning should never end, and so it would be impossible to write poetry of any kind afterwards.

I don't think that is either practical or in consonance with human nature, and probably not even in consonance with what we require to be moral persons—namely, in God's world, so to speak, we should not be mourners exclusively; we should also be celebrants. We should make new life and pursue new efflorescence with hope. In other words, we should not only be in mourning forever; we should also have poetry and wedding songs.

WACHTEL   But Rosa, in *The Shawl*, is unable to do that.

OZICK   She is unable because she is a direct victim. And yet even she—as a survivor—is less a victim than the murdered. Primo Levi points out in *The Drowned and the Saved* that nobody has drunk the Holocaust to the lees unless he went through the gas, and anyone who has been very close to that and yet survived cannot be said to have drunk the dregs.

WACHTEL   Writers from Sylvia Plath to D.M. Thomas have used the Holocaust in their writing. Would you ever give yourself or another writer permission to write about it, to write fiction?

OZICK   I certainly would not give myself permission to do it again. And yet I seem to be doing it again and again. Lars Andemening, in *The Messiah of Stockholm*, defines himself through identification with Bruno Schulz, who was murdered by the SS. I seem to go in pursuit of that. This may be because I am Rosa's generation; it may be because for my generation it is inescapable. Had I been there and not here I wouldn't *be*. I wouldn't have a child. I would be less than ash, I would be a plume of smoke. I'm the right age; I am Anne Frank's contemporary, and therefore for me the fact of murder can never go away. My sense of that fact is much more than a memorial; it's part of experience itself, and this is Rosa's view. Rosa is an exception. She will never enter normality. By definition she has been made abnormal—by being singled out by the Nuremberg Laws; she carries that mark. However, it's not a mark of her own making but a mark of the death of civilization.

WACHTEL   You are a fiction writer who also writes wonderful essays. You once wrote that writing essays is looking for trouble. What kind of trouble?

OZICK   Since the essays by and large represent the good citizen, the rational thinker, and the fiction represents the wild, untamed, loose creature, it becomes problematical when the essays are used as a measure for the fiction, or the fiction is used as a yardstick for the essays. The essays are citizenship and the fictions are wildness, and the two don't mix. When I'm an essayist I'm a good citizen by and large, a rational thinker, somebody who makes sense, and when I'm a fiction writer I'm not to be trusted; I'm dangerous. The difficulty—and this happens all the time—is when someone reads the essays and begins to distil out of them a kind of value system, which, I suppose, can be found in them, even a "moral" value system, and then starts interpreting the fiction according to what has been distilled out of the essays. It won't do; it can't be.

WACHTEL What about a hierarchy of values? Do you, like so many people, exalt the making of fiction, or regard it as a superior literary activity to essay-writing?

OZICK Oh yes, no question. With an essay you have your goal in your pocket; you know where you're going. At least you know what it's about. For instance, I'm in the process now of reading *The Awkward Age* by Henry James, which I've never read before, and I intend to write an essay on it. Well, I know what the essay is about. It's about *The Awkward Age*. I don't know yet what I'm going to say, what I'm going to discover, and I will surely make discoveries. Nevertheless, there's a premise, there's something to work with, there's something already pre-existent. But in fiction the challenge is an abyss. You don't know where you're going. You don't know what you're going to discover. You start out with empty pockets. You have no notion about whom you're going to tell your story, or what will happen, and so your heart is in your mouth. It's a great, great peril. You're walking on the edge of a very narrow road over a boiling crevice and you might fall in; and, in fact, you will fall in.

The essay goes on a highway, with civilized pastures on either side and houses, too, with cozy smoke coming out of their chimneys. The essay is an easy form compared to fiction. Poetry, of course, is higher than fiction. Poetry—for that you need wings.

WACHTEL You've said that while writing teachers say you should write about what you know, in fact you should write about what you don't know. That, I would think, is harder. How do you get to know what you don't know well enough to write about it?

OZICK Well, that's the work of the imagination. The imagination has resources and intimations we don't even know about. As I once wrote, it seems to me that the imagination has powers to think us into the leg of a mosquito or the leg of a chair; we can become a Tibetan; we can certainly, if we're women, become men or, if we're men, become women. The imagination is a species of knowledge, knowledge that takes the form of discovery. I have a kind of mystical faith in the nature of discovery. Sometimes discovery assumes a kind of physical response, or rather, an antiphysical response. I find when I write I am disembodied. I have no being. Sometimes I'm entranced in the sense of being in a trance, a condition that speaks, I think, for other writers as well. Sometimes I discover that I'm actually clawing the air looking for a handhold. The clawing can be for an idea, for a word. It can be reaching for the use of language, it can be reaching for the solution to something that's happening on the page, wresting out of nothingness what will happen next. But it's all disembodied. A state where you have no sex, you have no history, you have no prior experience, you belong to the task itself.

WACHTEL As you know, the issue of how disembodied a writer can become, or what happens when the writer returns to his or her body, is increasingly discussed. I'm referring to the idea of identification of ethnicity or gender in writing. How do you feel about that?

OZICK Oh, I feel that it's extraordinarily limiting for a writer to take on such circumscribing identities. It seems to me a total limitation of imagination to say to a woman who writes well, you must write about women, you must write about what women feel, you must write about women's issues. Why must I? Why can't I write fairy-tales? Why can't I write anything I goddamn please? There are ideas abroad, ideas which I may not reject at all, ideas to which I may even declare passionate allegiance. But as a fiction writer I will declare myself free. I will not be limited by my body or by my history. I may be enriched at times by my history and by my body, but to be limited by them, no. I refuse.

WACHTEL You've written about what you call the Age of Eliot, T.S. Eliot. Do you mourn the loss of the Age of Eliot, the power and prestige of high art?

OZICK I do mourn the demise of high art. I realize that in this mourning I'm probably a fossil among other fossils. This may be true! Yet philosophically there is a difference between blurring and distinction-making, and I believe that making distinctions is a higher intellectual act than fusing. There are movements now in literary criticism in which the line of demarcation between the high and low is thoroughly annihilated; there's no trace of respect for it. To me it's a great loss. When you follow the impulse to blur, everything is levelled and there is no difference between, let's say, a poem by Yeats or a novel by Proust and McDonald hamburger ads or "The Honeymooners" on television—then we really have achieved erasure of distinctions. We've achieved generalization in the debased sense.

Seeing the difference among what Proust aspires to, what Yeats aspires to and what a television sitcom aspires to seems to me to be really one of the bedrock bases of a rational civilization. High is not low and low is not high. This may be a shockingly elitist point of view unacceptable in an age of egalitarianism, and if so I plead guilty to it. This doesn't mean that as a social creature I'm against pluralism, against equality—God forbid, not at all. But in terms of art I believe we ought to remain on the side of distinction-making.

WACHTEL You once said you've spent each decade regretting the one before. You're sixty-three now and I wonder if you still do?

OZICK I suppose I regret all the decades. I wish I had written more. I wish I had been more prolific. I wish I had had less fear of writing, more self-confidence, less terror of it. And in that sense I regret all the decades. There are writers who are quite fearless, and they are prolific. But I'm a fearful writer and I don't know how to become brave. At this age I ought very quickly to find out. I haven't found the key to that secret.

WACHTEL Do you know what it is you fear?

OZICK What do I fear? I fear the act of writing because it is so exquisitely, supremely demanding. I fear not arriving at a standard that I admire. I fear falling short. I probably also fear entering that other world; the struggle on the threshold of that disembodied state is pure terror. Once one has been living in it for a while, though, one wants never to quit that atmosphere; one wants to stay in it forever. It takes quite a long time to push oneself over the threshold and to start breathing the air in the vestibule, then to move forward into the first corridor. When one enters the great central living room, so to speak, or the grand parlour of the work, one loses all fear, and then one is thrust into that freedom I spoke of before.

January 1992

interview prepared in collaboration
with Richard Handler

Russell Banks

Russell Banks is one of the most compelling and authentic voices of poor, white, blue-collar America. His writing is sometimes associated with "dirty realism" because of the harshness and sense of disappointment in the lives of his characters. *Affliction* (1989) concerns an unhappy, desperate and violent man who watches his family and his life fall apart. His frustration and alcoholic despair draw him inexorably into further brutality. Here and in other novels, Banks portrays his often unappealing and alienated characters with impressive sympathy. It's a world Banks knows intimately.

Russell Banks was born in Massachusetts in 1940 and grew up in New Hampshire and eastern Massachusetts. His father was a plumber, a sometimes violent alcoholic who abandoned the family when Banks was twelve. When he was seventeen, Banks won a scholarship to an upper-crust college, but finding it too alien an environment, he stayed only a couple of months before returning home one cold November night. He left again a year later; this time he got as far as Florida, where he married. Banks has been married four times and is the father of four daughters. Despite his travels, he always returns to the American Northeast, to the area where he grew up and the source of much of his fiction. He is now a tenured professor at

Princeton University, drives a Mercedes and summers in the Adirondacks.

Russell Banks has written seven novels, including the critically acclaimed *Continental Drift* (1985) and *The Sweet Hereafter* (1991), and four collections of stories. *The Sweet Hereafter* is also about a small town and working class lives, but unlike *Affliction*, Banks starts with a disaster, rather than ending with one. One winter morning, a school bus goes off the road, killing fourteen children. How does the town deal with such a catastrophe? Telling the story through the voices of four characters, Banks explores fate and responsibility in the absence of answers. As in so much of Banks' writing, there is pain and there is also redemption.

WACHTEL You once said, "It seems like it's the hardest thing in the world to become an adult who isn't the same adult as your parents were." What does that mean for you?

BANKS That was a couple of years ago, in the context of *Affliction*. It was a pressing question for me then, because that book is written from the point of view of a child, or a man, Wade Whitehouse, who thinks of himself as a child, and his destiny is shaped by this; that is to say, he is shaped by his parents—particularly his father. That's the struggle the novel is involved with: his attempt, and his failure, to avoid becoming what his father was. It was an insight that was driven by my own attempt not to duplicate my father's life. I don't think that's a peculiar experience. All of us are trying not to be our parents. Whenever we talk to our children, we hear our mother's or father's voice coming back to us, and it makes us cringe. We're all struggling to avoid that.

In Wade Whitehouse's case, of course, it was particularly useful for him not to duplicate his father's life, insofar as it would make him kinder to other people. The same is true in my own case. My father's life was, in a sense, tragic. He was a very bright man, a gifted man, who was destroyed, really. His life was radically restricted, by neurosis and social circumstances and alcohol. It's very important for me not to let that happen to me, because my initial social circumstances weren't all that different from my father's, and I'm certainly neurotic. I haven't had a particular struggle with alcohol, but it has been a matter of some importance to me, personally, that's true.

WACHTEL You dedicated *Affliction* to the memory of your father, though in some ways the father in that book is not a very heroic man.

BANKS No, but my father had a father, too, and his father before him. In fact, after that book was published, a number of people—including family members—made the assumption that it was about my father, that Wade Whitehouse was somehow a model for me and that the old man was my father. I had to take care to point out that it could just as well have been about my grandfather or my great-grandfather.

WACHTEL You grew up in similar social circumstances to your father's.

BANKS My father was born in Canada. Three of my grandparents are Canadian. My father's a Nova Scotian who came to the States when he was in his teens. A working-class family: my grandfather was a plumber; my father's a plumber; I was briefly a plumber. I was raised in New Hampshire, and went to high school in Massachusetts.

WACHTEL A recurrent theme in your work—although not so much in this new novel—is male violence. Your characters experience disappointment, frustration, even desperation. There is a chain of violence—from father to son. In your own family there are several generations of unhappy, violent men.

BANKS My country—I'm speaking of the United States in particular, but I think it's true for most of North America—is infected with it. Male violence is a disease that poisons our society from the domestic level all the way up to the international sphere. The December 1989 shootings at the University of Montreal, for instance, were pointedly aimed at women. There is something out there that is frightening, and it's gender specific.

WACHTEL But you're a guy, and you were beaten as a child.

BANKS I wasn't abused throughout my entire childhood, but my relationship with my father was shaped by fear. I think that's not particularly uncommon.

WACHTEL How were you able to break the chain of violence?

BANKS With great good luck, the care and love and tolerance and abiding patience of other people, and circumstances—I guess that's luck, isn't it? I got out from the family, early on. I ran away when I was eighteen, and began to build a life for myself, and a consciousness based on information I could never get from my family and the small town and class-bound world I had been raised in.

WACHTEL You went back, then left again in your twenties, then you went back again. You kept going back to small-town New Hampshire. Why?

BANKS Yes, although I've been away now since 1982. But now I live in small-town upstate New York, which is not all that different. When I was in my early twenties I could rationalize it every time. It was because I belonged to the union up there and I could go back to that local and always get work as a pipe-fitter or whatever. Later it was that real estate was cheap. You can always justify it. I had a job then, teaching or something. Now I think it had everything to do with reinvestigating, compulsively, my own childhood and adolescence. I don't think it was a nasty kind of compulsion—that I went back to touch the wound again and again. Rather, I had a sense that at the centre of that part of my life lay a great and terrible mystery, and if I could only somehow solve it, I could go on. I feel I have. I don't altogether joke about not having lived in New Hampshire since '82. But I left then with no desire to return—for the first time, really. I was forty-two years old.

WACHTEL What did you solve?

BANKS What mystery did I solve? I think the mystery was the way in which I was both like and unlike my father and men like him. I think I solved it in a way that didn't sentimentalize me or him, and didn't judge me or him. That took a new kind of maturity—maybe that's why I had to wait around until I was in my forties!

When I was younger, I either did one thing or the other: I was always either sentimentalizing him or judging him. Sentimentalizing myself and my noble quest, or judging myself and my failure to transcend my background. It was a kind of dialectical situation, back and forth, back and forth. In some important ways the writing of *Affliction* ended it. The process of writing the book didn't end it, but the possibility of writing it didn't really exist until after I had resolved this dilemma, this very personal and central conflict in my life.

I think it's a conflict that exists for a lot of men. In the United States, certainly, the whole men's movement—as associated with Robert Bly and *Iron John*—is, I think, a dopey fixation on fatherhood and finding the good father. That's the sentimentalization part. It's an indicator, interesting as a symptom, rather than as a cure—I see it as just another sophisticated invention of the same disease—but it's a very interesting symptom because it is so widespread. There are so many men out there who, at bottom, regard themselves as afflicted. The men's movement is a response to that, although it's not even a bandaid cure; more than anything else, it's a denial.

Some people sense that my perspective on men's lives and the male psyche, if you will, is similar to the movement's, in that it starts from a similar assumption—that is, that there's something radically wrong with the male psyche in our time, and that has been true for a long, long time. But the cure will not be found by running around in the woods, jumping on each other's backs and beating drums. That's playing boy scouts.

WACHTEL Alice Munro writes about how trying to move out of

your own class, out of a working-class background, is seen as a betrayal—"Who do you think you are?" She eventually used this as a title for one of her books. Who do you think you are, that you think you can leave? Reading books, speaking with that city accent. Was it like that for you?

BANKS It wasn't as hard for me as it is for some people because I got out early. But I did feel that conflict certainly, that sense of being judged, and of being a threatening person, within the context of family. I think the old paradigmatic North American immigrant experience—of one generation sacrificing itself so that the next generation can go to college and learn a profession, so that the third generation can enter the arts (as John Adams, I think, first described it)—doesn't describe the experience of those of us who have been on this continent for ten, twelve or fourteen generations and are still asked to sacrifice ourselves for the next generation. I see a kind of deep, bleak pessimism in African-Americans and white Americans—the "poor white trash," let's say— who have been here for so long that they don't believe in that American dream any more. They're not willing to sacrifice themselves for it, because they know what'll happen: the next generation will get beaten up on and they'll have to sacrifice, and so on down the line. They understand themselves as a kind of economic cannon fodder. As a result, if anybody does try to move up and out of that situation it's not seen as a point of pride, or as a betrayal, but rather as a kind of exposure—revealing the hidden reality that we live inside the most hypocritical myth in the world: if you work real hard, and you're good, you will end up owning a block of apartment buildings or something like that. Americans are taught to believe this so that they will work real hard and be good. And they do. And they still don't get to own the apartment buildings.

WACHTEL You do that. You work real hard, and you're good. And you're doing okay. I'm not talking morally but creatively.

BANKS I still don't own a block of apartment buildings. And I'm this radical exception, the anomaly, not the rule. I've got where I am through happenstance. I did everything wrong. I ran away to

Florida at eighteen instead of going to college. I was married a whole lot of times. I jumped around and didn't do anything solid. It's not that I've managed to steadily improve myself in the predictable ways. I've been more or less struck by lightning.

WACHTEL You've been described as a literary realist, giving voice to neglected lives. How did you discover that what we might call blue-collar fiction, rather than pipe-fitting, was your turf? And what do you think of the term "blue-collar" fiction?

BANKS It's not so bad. At least it points to what we think of as class; it's class-conscious fiction in that sense. But that's only one factor of my writing—I hope it's only one factor. I think it's only one factor of the writers I admire, like Raymond Carver or Richard Ford, who are normally gathered under that umbrella, sometimes rather uncomfortably, as if we all ended up there waiting for a bus. I think it's an interesting observation, a generalization, and like all generalizations it doesn't really describe the circumstances or the thing it's supposed to be describing.

There are many writers—North American fiction writers in particular—who are now in their late forties, early fifties and coming to maturity and visibility at much the same time, whose shared sense of the world—a history that they share—is rooted in the sixties. It was a politically self-conscious time, a time of social awareness, and it was for them the first world outside their families and their schools. Our writing is informed by the events and historical circumstances of our youth. That's something I share with Joyce Carol Oates, Raymond Carver, Richard Ford and who knows how many others. We were all formed in the crucible of the sixties.

I believe this is the mature work of that generation of writers. Think of the so-called Lost Generation of the twenties and thirties: Fitzgerald, Hemingway, Stein and so forth. We find it very easy to say, "They were all struck numb by the experience of World War I," but, in fact, during that war they were all late adolescents—around eighteen, nineteen, twenty, twenty-one. That was their first experience of the larger world outside their family in Oak Park, Illinois, or wherever, and their work reflects it later. I think the core, the crucial experience for the writer occurs in that late-adolescence, early-twenties period.

When I began to write I floundered around for quite a while, like most young writers, although maybe more than most; it took me a while to learn my trade. It seemed as though I was starting from the very beginning and didn't have many models available to me. It was difficult mapping out my own territory. By the time I was in my late twenties or so, it was pretty clear that I was going to have to work with what I had, and it was a matter of finding methods for doing that. I gradually began to attach myself to the work of writers who had had similar material to work with, to see what their approaches were to that material. It turned out, more often than not, that the realists, in the American tradition of Stephen Crane, Theodore Dreiser, Sherwood Anderson, Nelson Algren and Richard Wright, were of more interest and use to me than the so-called high modernists.

WACHTEL Many of your characters aren't initially very likeable, but you win us over, you get our sympathy. Wade Whitehouse is not a guy I think I'm going to like, or even want to spend much time with. He's a rough, hard-drinking, violent man, but then you made me care. You make the reader care. Is this a deliberate strategy? To take a pretty repugnant guy and make him matter?

BANKS No. I must myself be drawn to these kinds of guys. After the recent mass killing in Texas, where twenty-two people were shot in a cafeteria, a psychologist provided a profile of the type of person who drives a pickup truck through a glass window of a cafeteria and shoots everybody. He's a loner. He's been bitterly disappointed in life; he seems to be unable to sustain any relationships—with parents, women or friends. He drinks too much. He's been recently fired. It was like reading a profile of Wade Whitehouse.

I guess I'm drawn to them because I feel that they aren't that different from me or a lot of people—maybe one step or one fork in the road different and there might I be. I don't know. I'm thinking aloud here. I have this sense of how perilous my own journey has been and so I'm very conscious of how it might have gone another way. I might have ended up sitting too late in a bar, in rural New Hampshire or someplace, drinking beers and growing ugly, and ended up shooting somebody.

WACHTEL One of the impressive things about your books is the way you get inside these kinds of characters to the extent that even a resistant, reluctant reader like me gets hooked.

BANKS I think that's one of the great pleasures of being a human being—that you can extend yourself, get outside yourself and identify with somebody who appears to have nothing whatsoever to do with you. I take what you've just said not so much as a compliment to me but as a compliment to the species.

WACHTEL Male violence also features in your novel *The Sweet Hereafter*, although it occurs before the book begins. We discover that a father has been sexually abusing his daughter. This is a subject many women are writing about now, but I was surprised that you chose to tackle it, and that you wrote from the girl's point of view.

BANKS I don't know why I wouldn't want to write about it any more than anything else that happens to people and causes them great pain. I have four grown daughters. I've raised them and watched them and thought a great deal about them and my life with them.

I let the girl speak for herself. I don't know what she thought, or what she really experienced. But I do believe that I could be a witness and she could tell me, and anyone else who cared to read the book, what had happened to her. The form of the book is depositions by the four characters. So she's speaking in the first person. I felt quite comfortable doing that. As long as I could let her speak, and it was plausible to a female reader, then I had no misgivings whatsoever.

WACHTEL Your novels usually take us through the conflicts and turbulence of the male psyche. You once quoted James Baldwin on how the most vivid portrayal of racist America would have to be written through the mind of a white supremacist.

BANKS I tell you, I think it's a lot easier for me to imagine what a child, a fourteen-year-old girl, would say about having been sexually abused than it is for me to imagine what her father might say. There's where I had the problem, in the section of the novel dealing with the father. As it turns out, I didn't let him speak. Maybe the true novel about sexual abuse will have to be written from the point of view of the abuser. But that's not a novel I think I can write.

WACHTEL The framework of *The Sweet Hereafter* is a terrible accident: a school bus goes off the road in a small town and fourteen children are killed. Why did you decide to use this kind of disaster as your starting point?

BANKS My other books have ended with disaster. So let's get this one out of the way and get on with it! What I really wanted to do was to track the aftermath and monitor how people dealt with a calamity. Also I think I wanted to write a moral fable, in a way, to explore the entry of death into the world. Sometimes the best way you can do these large things is on a small scale. It's a small town in upstate New York, a small group of people.

The school-bus accident is a common, almost a generic event. You read about it in the newspaper, and you don't think about it any more. This story was generated by an account of such an accident in a small town in south Texas in 1989. The article was really more of a follow-up piece, six months later, dealing with the long-term effects on the town. The community had come apart: people were suing and countersuing each other; alcoholism and drug abuse and domestic violence had increased; more people were getting divorced. It was a Hispanic community. I didn't know anything about south Texas or Hispanic communities, but I knew a lot about the northeast and Anglo communities in small towns. I decided to set the story there and explore the ramifications. That's how a novelist works: what if? and what happened? What if there was a school-bus accident one winter morning in your town, and you knew the people, the families of the town? What would happen to those people? That's what engaged my imagination.

I had four narrators. It seemed that four would give me a sense of community in a way that three wouldn't, and that a fifth would be redundant. The bus driver, one of those trusted, competent, down-to-earth middle-aged women who do so much of this kind of work, is the witness closest to the event. Then a father of two small children killed in the accident gives his perspective. A negligence lawyer provides an outside point of view. He also turns out to be the engine that drives the plot and provides much of the drama. Finally, a child survivor, a fourteen-year-old girl who is a paraplegic as a result of the accident.

WACHTEL This seems to be a story about blame: who's responsible, who's at fault, which is a perfectly natural response to tragedy, right after "Why me?" But you reject that. You reject the impulse to find out who's responsible.

BANKS It's so difficult for us to accept causeless events in a secular age. Something in us refuses to accept that events could occur without there being a material cause. We don't have the religious or philosophical apparatus that would allow us to integrate these experiences in those terms, so we try to impose causes on events. The question of blame is paramount in that. There are many events for which there are no material causes. As a result of our difficulty in accepting such events, we tend either to misread them entirely or to describe them to ourselves unrealistically, which is another way of saying we deny their existence or meaning entirely. I think this is a crucial struggle for survivors of terrible accidents or catastrophes. In our time we're almost forbidden to grieve or to deal with these experiences in any realistic and healing way.

WACHTEL Although looking for responsibility does seem like such a natural impulse, you want somehow to resolve something. If you could just figure out why this happened.

BANKS There's God's will. In a sense, that allows us to go on; if you can accept that into your bones, then you can go on, you can heal. But if in order to do that you're forced to operate on a level of sentimentalism—which is true of a lot of people's relation to religion—then that's another form of denial.

Finally, it comes down to the difficulty we have in accepting

the frightening fact of death in our lives. Most of us have no apparatus with which to make sense of it. The novel tries to dramatize
that absence and people's struggles to find an alternative way of
making sense of the presence of death. The death of children, of
course, throws that into high relief. That's what the negligence
suits are all about. The reaction of the father of the two dead children—his depression, alcoholism and withdrawal—are also a
denial of reality. Finally, the female characters seem to be both
more courageous and better equipped to handle the tragedy than
the male characters in the book.

WACHTEL You use "Nothing is the force that renovates the world"
from Emily Dickinson as an epigraph. Somehow we're to be content with Nothing as the answer.

BANKS Or to understand it as the force that energizes and renovates the world, to accept and welcome it, in a philosophical sense.

WACHTEL Like Job, are you proposing some sort of redemption
through acceptance of our fate?

BANKS Yes, I think perhaps I am. I suppose it's an old-fashioned,
Old Testament point of view, without that particular vocabulary. I
think most novelists are inherently, deeply and radically conservative.

WACHTEL Small-town life in your fictional town in *The Sweet
Hereafter* is bleak and hopeless even before the accident, even
before the children die. That's partly why it's so devastating,
because the role of children here seems to be to keep you from the
black hole—I think one of your characters says that.

BANKS The children are incredibly important. I wouldn't say they
were all unhappy, or that their lives are stunted or particularly
thwarted. After the accident they're obviously suffering and in
pain, and grappling with very large issues, but there are also families and relationships and connections to a community that is
strengthening to them. That's very important. Even though it's
hard and unflinching sometimes, small-town life is often a source
of great strength and comfort as well. I think you see that in the
novel. I want it to be seen.

WACHTEL Initially, the small town responds to the tragedy in what one of the characters calls "the best way a small town could respond," and is very supportive. Then everything starts to unravel. The novel ends with a demolition derby at the county fair, a display of mock violence and revenge that provides a kind of communal catharsis.

BANKS I wanted it to work that way, to dramatize the community's acceptance of the void in their lives and their ability to go on through coming together in the kind of comic ritual of a demolition derby.

I believe very strongly in community—family and the next-largest circle out and the next, all the way out. We so glibly attribute human virtues to our communities, like a just society, a kinder and gentler society, but we don't accept responsibility for infusing our community with these virtues. We're willing to do it up to a point, in our own family, and say, "If I have a kind family it's because I've been kind." But as the circles get larger, as we start talking about our block, or our town, or our city, we start to lose contact with our responsibility. We start to feel less and less attached, less responsible for the moral quality of that society. Yet it does depend entirely for its moral quality on our ability to take responsibility until we come to the largest circle of all—I mean the nation state. And the moral qualities of the nation state depend upon how much we, its citizens, are willing to take responsibility for them. Otherwise it's a fantasy, a dream, a hypocritical lie. It's a slogan, which ends up manipulating and putting to terrible use people's lives. Witness my own country's kinder and gentler incursions in the Middle East, the terrible hypocrisy of that.

WACHTEL It's interesting that at the centre of these ever-widening circles is the family that you still believe in, despite your own early experience.

BANKS We don't have much else to work with. You have to start somewhere. That's where almost all human beings develop the capacity to connect with other human beings in a crucial and important way, building, through the family, or something like the family, an immediate circle of interdependency. That's where your moral values are enacted, in the most immediate way. I guess you have to start with the family, don't you?

WACHTEL So you really did work through all that.

BANKS I don't know. Maybe I have this morning.

October 1991

Spalding Gray

I first became aware of Spalding Gray about five years ago when his one-man show *Swimming to Cambodia* was made into a movie. It was an unusual movie—as Gray describes it, eighty-seven minutes of "a raving talking head—mine." Gray calls these performances monologues and sometimes calls himself a monologist or "sit-down comic." He comes out on stage, wearing an open-necked shirt, sits behind a table, rolls up his sleeves, and tells stories. His props are a notebook and glass of water. In *Swimming to Cambodia*, Spalding Gray uses the experience of his small role in the movie *The Killing Fields* to talk about genocide in Cambodia, American foreign policy and prostitution in Thailand, but mostly to talk about his own life, and what it's like to be Spalding Gray—an off-off Broadway stage actor, apparently free associating.

Spalding Gray is persuasive and entertaining. His stories are carefully crafted for dramatic effect. He has written thirteen monologues, which he has performed in the United States, Canada, Europe and Australia. *Monster in a Box*, also released as a movie and a book, is about a novel that Gray worked on for years. He brings it on stage as a prop—a 1,900-page manuscript. A monster in a box. And he talks about writing and not writing.

That monstrous manuscript—shaved down to a couple

of hundred pages—was finally published as *Impossible Vacation* (1992). It is a coming of age story about growing up in New England, where the protagonist tries to extricate himself from his increasingly crazy mother, and then sets off around the world in search of meaning.

When I saw Spalding Gray one morning in Toronto, he'd been up late, dancing, and seemed to fall into a semi-doze while waiting for the interview to begin. He said he likes to go to bed listening to audio tapes—especially Raymond Carver's "Cathedral"—because the human voice puts him to sleep. I said I'd try to keep my questions short.

———————————

WACHTEL You've described your performance monologues as "autobiographical journals"—whether they're about trying to buy a house in the country, or about the experience of acting in a movie. How autobiographical is your first novel, *Impossible Vacation*?

GRAY Very. I like to call it "auto-fiction," whatever that means. I guess I mean that it comes from stories in my life, but that I took on a persona very close to me, although he's more lost. He hasn't found anything yet. I didn't want him to be a successful actor or monologist, so he's one of those people who can't find his passion. At the end of the book he realizes that all he can do is write it down, that that's what he's going to do; he starts chanting: "Write! Write! I'm going to write, yes, because I have nothing else I can do but to tell the story." He sees telling the story as redemptive. So it ends where it begins. The book is a lot about the search for paradise and perfect moments and the mistaken idea of paradise as being a place outside of the mind.

WACHTEL Why "auto-fiction"? Why retain even the veneer of fiction? Why call your character Brewster North, rather than Spalding Gray as in some of your monologues?

GRAY I was hoping to move in a new direction by playing with the idea of fiction and a persona, and to save myself a little bit from myself. I would free up my imagination some, which in fact I did. There's more fiction in the book (in my monologues, I do hyperbole), and I had more fun with it than I could have, had I stuck to Spalding Gray. It gave me permission to play with what didn't happen, to stay with a certain amount of truth but to recycle my life, go around the same stories and themes in a fresh way, from a different perspective. It was like putting on a different pair of glasses.

WACHTEL So much of your work has been devoted to telling your own story. In your movie monologue *Monster in a Box*, you even say, "I can't make it up! I don't know how to make it up! I can't invent."

GRAY I wanted to address that problem. My closest male friend was very bothered by the fact that I used a persona. He said it just didn't work for him. It's like Bob Dylan playing electric guitar at the '69 Newport Folk Festival. People had a really strong reaction to it.

I want to develop Brewster North as an ongoing character. I want to write a series of novels about him. I don't say this is a classic novel, because it doesn't have a lot of character development in it; it's seen through the first person, very much like *Catcher in the Rye*.

I now have a separation in my life, which I think I needed. I can dump things that would belong to the Brewster story, and then sort out things that are my own story. I feel a little less exhausted now, a little less like I have to *live* everything that happens. I can have a little slower old age and not feel like, "Oh my God, what am I going to write about? Nothing's happened!" I can begin to move Brewster around in my imagination, like on a chess-board. I see him going to Australia and Bali next.

WACHTEL You've talked about being drawn to Thomas Wolfe and those autobiographical mega-novels. Clearly, writing *Impossible Vacation* was a difficult thing for you to do. At 1,900 pages, the manuscript was huge. What was the pull of fiction for you? Why did you feel so driven?

GRAY I'm not sure that I've done that much fiction. I'm on the doorstep of it. I think the pull of it is the dialectic between fact and imagination, the way that personal history is always fiction to start with. Memory is always the memory of a memory, never a true memory, because you're re-remembering a memory, and so it goes. Down that hall of memories you can allow imagination to enter in and begin to play. I have been ruthless—although my monologues are entertaining and fun—in sticking to what I call the truth. Now I'd like to free up a little bit and dance it. I think fiction is a kind of dancing and playfulness in which, like a child, you make up a story.

I'm not real keen on fantasy, but I like "hard" fiction. I like Raymond Carver, John Updike, people who are hard into real life. Not like the South American writers who are writing more dream-like pieces. Carver, even in his last poetry, said, "Why not tell what really happened." I've been telling what really happened for so long, I may be asking the opposite question now: "Why not make something up?" I was always a fan of Robert Lowell rather than, say, Wallace Stevens. I always felt the need for that diary form of poetry.

WACHTEL Do you find it harder to write than to perform because you have to do it alone, without witnesses?

GRAY Yes. It's about making choices. The audience helps me make a choice about the right phrase or story by the way they react, through their concentration, laughter or silence, their presence. The reason why the book was so big was that I overwrote, hoping that I would find the right phrase. I compared it recently to playing tennis against a brick wall or playing with a partner. Playing with a partner, like playing to an audience, means getting immediate feedback; writing off the white page is a "brick wall" for me. The ball would come back, but with the same force I had hit it with. It was solipsistic. There was no intermediary. Then I began to read it into a tape-recorder, for transcription, and that did help.

WACHTEL When I read your novel, I can hear your voice. I can almost hear you talking to me. It's a very persuasive, compelling voice, whether in print or in person. Do you want to grab the reader by the ear, so to speak?

GRAY Not consciously. That was the only way I knew how to write, and it grew out of having worked in front of a live audience, working in the first person, saying, relentlessly, "I'm going to tell you this story, this is what happened to me."

WACHTEL Brewster North needs witnesses to feel alive, to feel that he exists. Do you feel that too? Is that part of performing for you?

GRAY Yes. I tend to disappear when I'm alone. It's hard to explain. It feels like I'm not there, like I'm psychically disappearing, that I don't exist. A kind of panic takes over me, particularly when I'm in a foreign land. I went to Bali in 1986. I was walking up and down the streets. Seeing the place wasn't enough for me; I had to be seen. I think it had to do with the fact that I'd been touring Australia for two months; I'd been in front of audiences of 150, 200, 300 people—that's 600 eyes. I think the eyes actually inflate you, make you larger than you are through their energy. When you lose that, it's almost like withdrawal. No one's seeing you, so you're not seeing the things around you. At one point I thought that in order to write my book I'd have to have my therapist in Los Angeles come over and sit in a corner of the room, so he could witness me, as a writer. He would give me definition. I proposed to get married in front of my therapist; I needed a witness for the proposal.

For whatever reasons, it seems to me that nothing is real until it's witnessed. That's part of why I work in front of audiences. So when I was audience-deprived in Bali, I was a wreck. I was walking up and down, my red shorts pulled up to my chest, groaning, moaning, talking to myself, thinking, "What am I doing here when I could be in Australia, in the desert, with a beautiful twenty-three-year-old, riding camels." I didn't know what I was doing there until I was recognized by a fan (who had seen me perform in Boston). "Aren't you Spalding Gray?" Oh yes, I am now

Spalding Gray. He had defined me. He said, "You look like you're in trouble, you've got to go see this Balinese healer." So I went every day at cocktail hour, to try to cut down on my drinking—I'd been drinking a lot in Australia. My cocktail-hour ritual was to visit this healer every day at dusk. He spoke very little English but we'd hang out together. He wanted to know what was wrong. I said, "What's wrong is that every time I come to a place, I think I should be in the place I left. I really want to be in Australia with this woman, on camel-back, and not in Bali. What can I do?"

"I've never heard of this disease," he said with great laughter. "I think you should go to an apothecary and get a shot."

Just before I left, he took out a bunch of magical drawings, and asked me to find one I could relate to. I found a little man with no head but eyes in his chest. I framed it and put it on the wall. He said, "You have to talk with this and ground yourself." So began my relationship with this little man, this icon.

Just in telling you the story I realize that the little man also became my witness, with the eyes in the chest, hanging on the wall. I still have this icon. I work with it occasionally.

WACHTEL Have you traced this to an experience of invisibility in your childhood? You've talked about growing up in a very repressive environment.

GRAY I haven't been able to analyse that one. A terrific need for witness, and when it's not there, I have the witness within me, which is the writer, the writer's eye that watches. Sometimes that's not strong enough to carry me, particularly in a foreign country. Certainly Brewster North is obsessed with all levels of being seen.

When I first started to think of doing solo work I had an image. I was about to leave the Wooster Group, an experimental theatre group in New York that I had co-founded, to go solo. It was 1979. I kept having a vision of myself running down 42nd Street in a red jockstrap. I knew I wasn't going to do that as an art piece. I was barefoot, and I would never want to go barefoot down 42nd Street. God! I didn't try to analyse the vision, but I realized it had to do with exposing myself, not physically, but psychically, by going solo. I don't know what the red jockstrap represented.

WACHTEL It surfaces again in *Impossible Vacation*.

GRAY Brewster becomes a life-model for drawing classes, as I was. When I first came to New York City, I discovered that one thing I liked was spacing out and meditating, but being witnessed doing that. So I would model for forty-five minutes, stand still, go into a trance. At the same time I was always aware that I was in the eyes of the art students, that they were keeping my body on this earth while my head was elsewhere.

WACHTEL When Brewster North is modelling he has to wear a jockstrap. He doesn't like them, finds them ugly, and he dyes it red.

GRAY He finds white too clinical.

WACHTEL This novel starts with your childhood. You've talked about it before, describing it as a doubly repressive environment—New England and Christian Science.

GRAY Right. Great denial of the body. I think that has a lot to do with it, right there. Certainly in Christian Science, we were taught that whenever the body was ill there was an error, a mistake—it didn't exist. If it was a beautiful day, and my Grandmother Horton was out sailing in my grandfather's sailboat, everything was beautiful. The boat was wonderful. But any kind of disease was an error in thinking. It was a strange way of looking at life, a kind of schizy way—that when everything was good, it was good; when it was bad, it didn't exist! It was hard to find the shadow there.

It also applied to the body. I talked about that in my monologue *Sex and Death to the Age 14*, about how I used to use my mother's stand-up mirror to look at myself and masturbate in front of. Growing up as a Christian Scientist, it took so long for me to realize I had a body. I had to use a mirror to prove I had a body.

WACHTEL A mirror is yet another way of witnessing.

GRAY Yes, the mirror is a witness. You become a lover of yourself. Certainly I have very strong narcissistic tendencies, which are echoed in that book.

WACHTEL You describe a dialectic between your parents—your mother spiritual and non-drinking, and your father a beef-and-bourbon materialist. How did that dialectic resolve itself in you?
GRAY I don't think it has resolved itself. I go between the two—probably drinking too much at night and then doing penance in the day, when I eat very pure food and do my yoga and take a hot bath and prepare myself for the night.

It's also there in the way I *think*, in that I go from a very practical, cynical, hard-core view of life and then am drawn towards flighty, more spiritual things. One aspect of that dialectic emerged recently in a new monologue I've been testing out called *Gray's Anatomy*, in which I have an eye operation. Before I have the operation, and give in to the doctor and modern medicine, I explore alternative healings. The monologue is about finally capitulating, but it's also about going to a Christian Scientist practitioner, to a sweat lodge, to a Brazilian shaman, to an Indian healer—I even go to a psychic surgeon but am afraid to let him reach into my eye and we have to do a magnetic healing. In a way it's an ingenuous search, because somewhere I always think that finally I'll come back to the doctor.

That monologue I think clearly points to a dialectic within my mother, who had healings—I saw her have healings—but in the end was not able to heal herself from a nervous breakdown, because in Christian Science it takes a mind to heal a mind. You must be split in your mind; you must have a mind that says, "This is a mistake, and I am God's perfect child." If you can't do that, then you're completely mad. You've lost all ability to pull yourself up by your bootstraps.

It's funny, because I often saw my mother and father in competition over who would live the longest. If you looked at them early on you'd think, "My God, my father's drinking, he's smoking Camel cigarettes, he doesn't exercise. My mother is always walking, she doesn't smoke, doesn't drink." She went crazy and killed herself. He's eighty years old and still drinks bourbon every night!
WACHTEL I see that split in you. You talk about yourself as a

Freudian existentialist, and at the same time you're interested in Eastern mysticism. You interviewed the Dalai Lama. There's obviously something you want from that non-rational side.

GRAY Because I believe in it, I believe the non-rational side is operating in me, and if I don't recognize it I'm going to suffer for it. I am a doubter, and I haven't doubted my doubt yet. But I am curious about ways of thinking, ways of coping. I'm most interested in how someone deals with the fact that at any moment they could disappear forever. Most people live their lives as though they're going to live forever. How do they fool themselves into that? I think it's by keeping busy. When I interview the audience, I often ask, "When you got up this morning, how did you avoid thinking about death?" I ask detailed questions about coping and getting through and being happy.

I turned thirty-five in the Himalayan mountains, very close to the Tibetan border. I remember it being a terrific shock to me. Maybe because I was in a foreign land. But it occurred to me, at age thirty-five, that I was going to die, forever. Up until then this had just been an intellectual idea, but then it was something I intuited. I think it had to do with being up there, in the Himalayas, having an odd birthday.

WACHTEL One of the things I like about the way your mind works is that, for instance, you will discuss the subject of reincarnation with the Dalai Lama, but then the wry part of you will use it in a monologue, and say things like, "I never fly on an airline where the pilot believes in reincarnation."

GRAY The Dalai Lama had such a great sense of humour. When I said that line to him, he laughed immediately, he didn't even have to think about it. My idea with the Dalai Lama was that I would only ask prosaic questions, and I went off the track and asked him about meditation. We got a little lost. I was just going to ask him what it was like to stay in Fess Parker's Red Lion Inn, in Santa Barbara. I wanted to talk about what it was like to stay in American motels. We were going to just talk about that, and we got off the track. I messed up.

WACHTEL There's a remarkable amount of sadness in *Impossible Vacation*: the mother's breakdown, then the kind of breakdown of her son (who is more or less you); he's depressed, scared of his own life. The mood is very different from your monologues. Is this book a glimpse of the darker side of Spalding Gray?

GRAY I think it is. I really think that my bottom line is sadness. I don't laugh a lot. There's a deep sadness in me that, sometimes, is connected to the world. There's a German word for it. I can't tell the difference between the world sadness and my own. But I was never able to be sad in a monologue. I wouldn't allow it. I also felt that I had a talent to entertain and make people laugh, and that that was a gift. At the same time, I was getting very tired of doing that. I felt like I was avoiding the sad side of myself, the shadow side. I was determined to write that into the book but also to include humour. Renée Shafransky, my wife, said just after we married, "I'm now ready to read the book. Do you want me to read it as an outsider or as your friend?" I said, "Read it as an outsider and tell me what you think."

First of all she found it needed more editing, which she worked on, but she also said, "I thought I knew you well through your stories, but to read this in print is very hard for me. It's *very* difficult. This is a very sad book. It's a book I don't think should be published." She was trying to persuade me not to publish it. She thought it would alienate a lot of my audience. I think she's wrong.

When I finished it I looked at it and got very frightened. I had a very rough bout then. I saw it as a mirror and I saw that things hadn't changed as much as I had fantasized they had, that the way I was in 1976 was, psychically, very much the way I am now, only I'm more successful so the success was a bit of a buffer. But it was a mirror.

I also got very frightened because I had just turned fifty. It was summer, and that was the time that my mother started to go mad—at fifty years old, in the summer. I thought I was going to repeat it, that I'd introjected it and was starting to act it out. I had a lot of struggles in therapy, being reminded that I was *not* my mother, that I *was* someone else. One of my therapists—at one point I had two, an east coast and a west coast one—my Los Angeles therapist said, "You've got to understand, when your mother was having that nervous breakdown, and you were nine years old, a nine-year-old boy doesn't push things away. They take it all in. They don't have that boundary, that protection of saying, 'This is not something I want a part of. I'm getting out of here.' You take it in."

To some extent, I had introjected and would act like her, in that summer when I turned fifty: I was pulling at my hair, being very nervous, crying out, talking to myself. I think I'm past that now, but I'm still working with it a lot. I feel I'm in that area of danger, needing to act out that breakdown and suicide. Writing the book helped me think about it as story, as narrative. Again, changing the persona to Brewster North helped a bit, protected me and gave me that necessary distance.

Some of the book is still too painful for me to read out loud; I start to cry from it; it affects me very deeply. It's as though that event is still there when you re-create it. My younger brother— who suffered a lot, I think, from the suicide because he was there for it, sleeping above the garage—doesn't have any memory. He does not remember any of the events. I've talked to him about it, and he reads my book as though it's a fiction. Strange.

WACHTEL You talk about the loss of boundaries both in *Monster in a Box* and in the novel, how during the summer when you were nineteen your mother was having a breakdown and you just couldn't get away. Every day you'd pack up the car to go away, yet you just couldn't leave.

GRAY That's right. But no, when I'm nineteen she's not having a nervous breakdown. Then she's courting me, we're lying in the sun. I was twenty-six during the second nervous breakdown. But when I was nineteen I desperately wanted to get away to Provincetown, and I couldn't. It was too comfortable just having her as a swimming companion. She would infantilize me and make it too sweet to get away. There was no edge there. We'd talk about every-thing. She was really open. I'd be reading the existentialists, and she'd be reading her Christian Science. We'd compare the two. We'd talk about my girlfriends, sex—I didn't *have* any girlfriends at the time, probably because of her, so it was about her relation-ship with my father—films we'd seen, a lot of things. It was like we were best friends. It was very odd.

It was also very comfortable. Leaving would mean taking a risk, going out and being alone and hopefully finding a woman, which I didn't until very late, not until college. Not really until after my mother's suicide was I able to have a relationship that was ongoing.

WACHTEL In *Monster in a Box* you're seeing a therapist. Things are going well, and part of why they're going well is because you can talk to him without performing. Is that rare for you?

GRAY Yes. With the therapist I would come in and simply enter-tain him with my stories, all the latest weekly stories. They wouldn't be going anywhere; they'd be stories, but they wouldn't be getting to a point. He would never stop me. I would make him laugh.

I want to say something about this story business, where it's a problem for me. I turn things into a story so quickly that I don't feel them. A good therapist has got to stop me from that and warn me about it, so that I talk with him or her the way I'm talking with you now. I'm not leaping into anecdote very quickly. But I could do that so quickly—something happens to me, it's a story before it's felt. Often, if someone asks me how I feel I tell them an anec-dote rather than the feeling, because I'm so fast, I'm so good at it. I think that's something in my life I'm trying to stop. I am working with a new therapist (but I'm not, because I'm on the road). When I'm in New York, I see him.

One of the most difficult things for me would be to risk taking time off from public narrative and acting. When I'm not in front of an audience, I tend to need one so badly that I get in situations where I just begin to perform on the dance floor, in public situations; I become very flamboyant and exhibitionistic. I just have that terrific need in me. I'm a showman.

WACHTEL You've been described as a WASP Woody Allen. I guess that's because you come across as a somewhat neurotic, verbal agonizer. In *Impossible Vacation* sometimes it's more like Woody Allen meets Henry Miller, because there's a lot of sexual searching in the book, as well as searching for a way to live. Does that come with the territory, writing about the sixties and seventies?

GRAY I suppose it does, although one never thinks that one has had enough sex. There was so much free love, sexuality, in the air in the sixties, but in reality not enough of it for me. So I think the book is that way too: Brewster's never quite getting it; he's looking for it. I don't know if you read the *Kirkus Review*, but the review there said, "The best writing about sex since Henry Miller, and the best writing about breakdowns since Sylvia Plath." I thought, what a combo! My first image was of Henry Miller and Sylvia Plath in a motel room. She has her head in the oven, and he's lifting her skirt from the rear.

WACHTEL Oh, God!

GRAY And I thought somehow that typifies this book. That's the kind of extreme imagery that's in the book. The sexual revolution was very strong for me—I grew up in the fifties, and I was *so* repressed sexually. I was a virgin until I was twenty, in college. The sad thing is that, finally, when the liberation came, it was very difficult. I was living with a woman and trying to be monogamous, and finding that impossible because of all this liberation going on around me, and me wanting to try out this, that and the other. Now, because of AIDS, we're right back in the fifties, only it's not a puritan consciousness, it's a virus. It's almost a puritanical virus, like the Puritans mixed this virus, bred it and let it loose. It's odd and discouraging how it's all gone full circle. I feel I'm right back in the fifties, only I'm fifty—fifty-one.

WACHTEL But you just got married, so it's okay.

GRAY Sure, that's supposed to cure everything.

WACHTEL Why did you get married at fifty?

GRAY I got married because I had an eye operation, and Renée found it difficult to get to me in my room, as the girlfriend. She said, "Spald, you're probably going to be in the hospital a lot more from now on, because you're getting older. I think we should get married." So I proposed to her, in therapy actually. I said, "Do you still want to get married?" She pulled her sweater over her nose and started giggling. She took that question as a proposal, and we got married.

WACHTEL The novel ends at a point where Brewster wants to start writing, to tell his story. *Monster in a Box*, which is about writing and not writing *Impossible Vacation*, ends at the opposite pole. At the very end of the performance monologue, you say, "Enough story. No more story. I'm going on vacation." Is that a joke?

GRAY No. It's interesting that you should pick that out. It's one of the only sections that Renée wrote. It had actually ended with a section from Thorton Wilder's *Our Town*, where the stage manager (who I'd played on Broadway) looks up at the stars and gives the sign-off speech. It's a very beautiful speech, meditating on the stars, but we couldn't use it because we didn't have the rights. Instead, Renée wrote a beautiful speech that encapsulated the same mood. It ends with me saying, "After three months' run of *Our Town*, I went upstairs to pack up my monster. I'd finished the book at last. The character's made it to Bali and he's lying there in a hammock, looking up at the stars, remembering that first vacation he tried to take in Mexico and how, when he came home, all he found left of his mother was ashes in an urn, in a box by his father's bed. Now, looking up at the stars, he suddenly feels such a sense of peace, such a sense of presence, he thinks maybe he should forget about the story and try to take a vacation instead."

And this is a contrivance, written by someone else. I find it very difficult to say those lines, yet very pleasing at the same time, but I know they're a fake, I know they're a fiction. The reality is me wishing I could forget about the story and take a vacation, but I wouldn't know what that was anymore. I'm not interested in going to museums, or lying on a beach. I like observing people.

Renée used to organize the vacations in the old days. I've taken them, but only after I've been working in a place. Then they tend to be very frantic, not relaxing.

WACHTEL So a vacation is impossible.

GRAY Yes. It's a contrivance, and why would one want to take a vacation anyway. I don't understand it. I'll be working for as long as I live, because I enjoy my work. I would prefer to work two or three hours a day, seven days a week than to work eight hours a day and take weekends off, and obsessively try to relax, throwing everything into the weekend.

WACHTEL So you're not going to set the story aside. You're just going to keep living it and writing it.

GRAY The story is ongoing, but right now I have to say that I'm rather emptied out. I don't have any story I need to tell. I have the new monologue, about my eye operation, but I find I'm not real interested in telling it. It has to do with a physical condition, and I'm more interested in mental conditions, in how my psychology is operating and how it's changing, or if it's changing at all. I don't want to go over the same neurotic patterns in a monologue again. I'd like to objectify my neurosis into the culture, and tell a story about how I feel America is neurotic in some way, to take a theme like Star Wars and look at that in a personal way, but I don't know how to do that.

WACHTEL You did it in *Swimming to Cambodia*.

GRAY Yes, but that was integrated for me, in the sense that it was an integrated experience. It was a perfect structure already, because it was while I was working on a film, *The Killing Fields*, about the Cambodian genocide. I see Star Wars as an American psychosis—$90 billion spent in the next fifteen years to build a sky-dome, to protect us from what? A jihad? Who is going to smuggle in a bomb, in a fishing-boat, from Cuba, into New York harbour? It's not going to happen. How does one, in a personal way, approach Star Wars?

My idea is I'll get a nice short haircut, put on a Palm Beach suit, go to the Pentagon and try to find the front door. Then I'll go in and say, "Can someone please help me? I'm a proud American. I've been paying an *enormous* amount of taxes, and I see on the pie here that twenty-three percent of it is going to defence. A large part of it, I'm told, is to build a Star Wars shield over us, a dome that's supposed to protect us against rockets. Can I please speak to someone about that, because I just want to know *why* you're doing it?" See where it goes. It won't go far, but at least it will be personal. It has to be personal for me. It can't be about going into a library and researching Star Wars and the atom bomb. That's one story, but it's not my story.

I need to tell my story, and I don't know what the next one will be, or whether there will be one. I expect there will be, but I want to be courageous enough to be ready to give up the monologue, just like Rimbaud gave up poetry at nineteen and started running guns. I don't think I'll become a gun-runner, but maybe. I can't see it. I've never seen the future. I'm not a futurist. I'm a past man and sometimes a present man. I refer to myself as a be-here-then kind of guy.

June 1992

interview prepared in collaboration
with Greg Kelly

Michael Ondaatje

I found it particularly gratifying when Michael Ondaatje became the first Canadian to win Britain's leading fiction award, the Booker Prize—or rather to share it with the English writer Barry Unsworth—because Michael Ondaatje is a writer of such grace and accomplishment that he does us proud in the world. Ondaatje doesn't write stereotypically Canadian fiction—of social, pastoral or psychological realism. He is a poet, of course, but more than that, he's a painter—with words. It's hard to think of another writer who creates such visually evocative images: a choreography of movement and sensuality. Recently I was asked to describe Ondaatje's work in a sentence—ten words or less. "He's a sensual poet, unafraid of violence or the bizarre," I said.

Michael Ondaatje was born in Ceylon (now Sri Lanka) in 1943. When he was eleven, his parents separated and he went to England to attend school and be with his mother. He never saw his father again. As an adult he returned to Sri Lanka and wrote not exactly a family memoir but what he calls "a gesture," *Running in the Family* (1982). In a way it is Ondaatje's easiest and most seductive work.

Ondaatje was nineteen when he came to Canada from England to continue his studies. He wrote poetry; he won prizes. He was twenty-six when his collage of poetry and prose about the nineteenth-century American outlaw Billy the Kid won him his first Governor General's Award. His second came for a poetry collection called *There's a Trick with a Knife I'm Learning to Do* (1979).

In 1987 Ondaatje published *In the Skin of a Lion,* a dramatic and romantic novel about the building of Toronto that transforms the city into an exotic, almost mythological place. Set in the twenties and thirties, it's full of unforgettable images: a nun falling through the air off a bridge, caught in the arms of a Macedonian labourer; a thief drenched in blue paint in order to camouflage his escape across blue roofs.

With *The English Patient* (1992), Ondaatje moves abroad again, this time to Italy at the end of the Second World War, and to Libya and Egypt, where he plunges us into a desert romance with all the resonance of *Lawrence of Arabia* and *Casablanca.*

I talked with Michael Ondaatje in Toronto about a week before he won the Booker Prize. He had already been fêted in England, where the launch of his novel coincided with the announcement of the Booker shortlist, but he wouldn't speculate on how a win might change his life.

WACHTEL *The English Patient* takes place mostly at the end of the Second World War, in Italy, in a hilltop villa in Tuscany. It's a kind of bombed-out Garden of Eden for the quartet of characters who find refuge there.

ONDAATJE I'm not quite sure how that developed. It probably grew out of a version of wartime Italy that I'd had in my mind for a long time—essentially a combination of high culture and art with a military presence.

WACHTEL At one point, some Oxford mediaeval scholars of Italian culture come to brief the soldiers on where the fortress towns are. In this way you superimpose the mediaeval history of Italy onto the modern war-torn country.

ONDAATJE Originally, I thought *The English Patient* was going to be a contemporary book, set entirely in that one period of the Second World War. But once I got into the desert stuff, and through that, to Herodotus, I began picking up a sense of the layers of history. I was going back deeper and deeper in time. There are churches in Rome that stand on the remains of two or three earlier churches, all built on the same spot. That sense of history, of building overlaid with building, was central in my mind—*unconsciously*, I think. Looking back now, it seems to have to do with unearthing, baring history.

WACHTEL The villa is very evocative. You create such extraordinary visual images around it.

ONDAATJE When I began the novel, the villa was in my mind as a very limited space. It was almost like being inside a lyric poem. There was the nurse, the patient, darkness all around them, and a few yards of hallway. But I needed more. It was something like when I was working on *Billy the Kid*, I needed to move out of the lyric form and into prose.

I'd been working on *The English Patient* for about a year when I went to Italy. I started to look for the right place, and I found a nunnery—it had been a nunnery before the war, then it was taken over by the Germans, and later by the Allies. It was a wonderful place—a long driveway, all those cypress trees. That gave me a *real* landscape.

WACHTEL Did you bomb it out in your mind? In the book there are walls missing, roofs missing...

ONDAATJE I had to remove some of the furniture and displace some of the walls. By that point I was seeing everything in terms of Italy, 1945 (the way I saw Toronto in 1932, living here while writing *In the Skin of a Lion*). So the villa was complete in my mind, absolutely, even if I only used three or four rooms, everything was there. That is very important to me as a writer, to have that very tactile landscape for my choreography, for moving people around a room. I remember there were some things I couldn't put into the book. I wanted us to see Hana running along the hall where there was a rope, and she was swinging off the end of it into an open area...but I didn't know how to write that.

WACHTEL That's Hana, the nurse. You still use a lot of acrobatics, though—people tumbling down staircases, doing handsprings across rooms...It's curious that even though it's set near the end of a most terrible war, there's still a sense—in *this* place—of Eden before the Fall. Is it an Eden only in relation to what's to come?

ONDAATJE One of the things I discovered in the book was that I thought that this *was* an Eden, an escape, a little cul-de-sac during the war, and this was where healing began. Then, with the news of other bombs, suddenly this became, perhaps, the last Eden.

WACHTEL The nuclear bombs dropped on Japan become the Fall, which is followed by the expulsion from the Garden—

ONDAATJE Right, right. I sound quite sure of all this now, but at the time I don't think I was very conscious that this was going to happen, or even that this was a kind of Eden before a Fall.

WACHTEL You said somewhere that you are usually about three pages ahead of your reader, as you write.

ONDAATJE I think I am. One of the things that surprised me with this book was the arrival of Kirpal Singh. I suppose, subconsciously, it was just waiting to happen, but it came as a complete surprise. Kirpal Singh is a Sikh soldier with the Royal Engineers, who's been travelling through Italy defusing the bombs left by the Germans. There's a pivotal scene in the book in which Hana is at her lowest, almost suicidal though it is just hinted at. She starts playing the piano in the villa, and at that point two soldiers walk into the room. It was such a surprise to me, as a writer. I thought, Wait a minute! What's happening here?

No one believes that I wasn't expecting them. But it was a *moment.* I thought, okay, I've got these two other people in the room, and then I had to wait to see what would happen. I started to investigate Kirpal Singh, trying to find out who this person was, what his job was. And that became, in a way, a new part of the book, a new character whose presence fills one-quarter of the novel.

WACHTEL Each of the quartet of characters who take refuge in the villa are, in one way or another, maimed. Is it their wounds that bring them together?

ONDAATJE I think everyone thinks they're healing everybody else, in some way, but they're all wounded. Caravaggio wants to coax Hana out of a mental state she can't get out of, and doesn't want to get out of.

Caravaggio, an old friend of Hana's father, is a character from *In the Skin of a Lion*. In Toronto he was brash and wild and on top of things. In this book he discovers a high level of mortality around him. He sees that Hana, who is more like a niece, has withdrawn utterly from the world. I was interested in his relationship with her, how he had to be very tentative and careful about how he approached her. He would bully her at one moment, then pull back and say nothing; it's the most difficult kind of dealing with family. Although he is maimed as a result of the war, he's more interested in her. Perhaps his trying to discover the true identity of the Patient is also for Hana's sake.

WACHTEL But Hana thinks *she's* taking care of Caravaggio.

ONDAATJE And she also thinks she's taking care of the Patient, and the Patient later says, "Well I got her to read to me because she wouldn't talk." Everyone's the little hero in their own minds.

WACHTEL Most striking, I think, is the English Patient himself. A man who fell out of the sky, who burned up in an airplane. There's very little left of him other than his mind and his memories. Why did you want to write about a burned-out man, someone whose body is destroyed that way?

ONDAATJE I'm not sure. Certainly, he was the character who began the book for me. Almost the first image I had was of this man who was a complete mystery to me. I had to find out who he was. And then a lot of the landscapes and situations that had been in my mind for a long time, that had to do with the desert and with exploration, entered the book.

I'd been to parts of the desert in North Africa, which had always fascinated me, but I hadn't really thought about its staying with me. Once I started writing this book, though, I realized that this guy had crashed in the desert, and had been involved with the Bedouin. So where in the desert was he? Which desert? Libyan? Egyptian? I had to do some research at the Royal Geographical Society in London—a wonderful place. My first day there, a Mr. Trout came down the stairs. He said, "What can I do for you?" I said, "I want the desert in 1935," and he took me to a room, which was *covered* with newspapers, just scattered on the floor for about the last hundred years. I started to read about explorers from that period.

The English Patient is a totally anonymous figure. Everything about him has moved into the brain, there's nothing sexual or athletic left. Meanwhile everyone else in the villa is doing handstands all over the place. Yet he is one of the main sexual forces in the story. *That* kind of tragedy interested me: the fact that he had been completely altered by the accident into another kind of person, perhaps a more interesting, better person, in some way. I'm sure that his relationship with Katharine, the wife of a colleague with whom he had had an affair, is much more tender in memory than it was in reality. Theirs was a tough romance; he doesn't understand what happened—what he did to her or what she did to him—until now. He could only understand it later.

All these things grew out of this one image of a burned man. And the research at the Geographical Society put me in touch with certain stories that were half fiction, half fact.

WACHTEL This may sound like an odd question, but did he have to go to such an extreme, did he have to be so burned, did he have to lose so much of his physical self to gain that sensitivity?

ONDAATJE I'm not saying that he gained the sensitivity *only* because of what had happened to him. People seem to read him as more burned than *I* read him.

WACHTEL I think he's described as an eggplant at one point.

ONDAATJE His skin is the colour of aubergine, eggplant, yes. But worrying about how much you describe a burned man was, finally, a technical question. I think if I'd described him in any more detail, there would have been an impossible, Gothic element to the whole thing, so that we couldn't get into the character and spirit of the man. Reviewers have described him using words like "charred." But I just wanted someone who was static, who had almost become that statue I write about of a dead knight in Ravenna. It's a very beautiful, liquid-looking piece of stone. That was the image I had of the Patient, lying there, almost like a fresco. And that maybe echoes the cave-painting in the desert, or Katharine lying in the cave in the desert; there was a kind of echo.

WACHTEL Your fascination with the desert taps into what I think of as a peculiarly British mythology—the exoticism of Lawrence of Arabia, the desert as an unmapped place, a place of absolutes. Is that part of what draws you there?

ONDAATJE What I was tapping into was not my take on the desert, but the English take on the desert, the mental state of those Englishmen who were happier in the desert than they were in Putney. That was very central.

WACHTEL Going back to Kip, the bomb-defusing expert, who comes on the scene as a surprise to you, why did you want to know so much about how to defuse a bomb? You describe in remarkable and vivid detail how to go about it.

ONDAATJE I didn't know very much about these things, and I've totally forgotten it all now. If you brought a bomb in here right now, that would be it—I'd be out the door! What I wanted to do with those scenes was to get into *his* mental state so that he could talk about a collet head without explaining what it was. I didn't want to step outside and describe this man defusing a bomb, which is the way we always see it, in a movie, say. So I completely eradicated background and time. All he's doing is listening to music over his earphones and becoming involved with the geography of this thing, a bomb, that's about eight inches wide, and he's theorizing about it. Almost like writing a poem. It was not so much the technical stuff but his thoughts while he was doing this that interested me most.

WACHTEL *The English Patient* is a beautifully written book. I noticed in some of the reviews from England that the fact that you're a poet is sometimes held in your favour and sometimes held against you; the poet as novelist spells trouble or the poet as novelist spells beauty—depending on the viewpoint of the reviewer. As a poet, as a sensual poet, you don't seem interested in writing a conventional, psychological novel. How would you answer a question like, What is *The English Patient* about?

ONDAATJE It is a book about very tentative healing among a group of people. I think it is that most of all. It's also two or three or four versions of a love story. There's the love of Caravaggio towards Hana, and Katharine towards the Patient, and Kip towards Hana. Even Kip towards the Patient. For me, it primarily concerns *situation*, as opposed to theme. That's how I imagined the book, and how I see the book. They're barely spoken relationships. For instance, I worked a lot on the association between Kirpal Singh and the English Patient, erasing the background, erasing oversaid things.

WACHTEL Do books come to you in a mysterious way?

ONDAATJE They come mysteriously and very gradually. It's really a case of lugging something around for about five years, and leaving things behind in somebody's house and having to go back and pick them up again, building an arc situation. My books begin with very small things—overheard conversations, or personal and historical details. You build the pieces over a period of time. Then you have to try to knit them all together in some way, and it becomes something very different from what you thought you were writing while you were writing it. When I began I had no idea this was going to be the book. I usually go towards a certain tone; but in this book the tone of the English Patient's story, once I found it, opened up all kinds of things. And running against that was the thing about acrobatics; for instance, the relationship between Hana and Kip is more like that of lion cubs than adults. They're retreating into a past.

WACHTEL Is there a struggle in you between the poet and the novelist? Earlier you were saying that sometimes you write something that starts off as a poem, and then you have to break into prose.

ONDAATJE That need to move out of poetry into prose happened only with *Billy the Kid*; I needed to build that corral, that landscape and so forth, with prose. Since then I know when I'm writing poetry and when I'm writing prose. With the last two books I've been so intensely focused on them that the idea of writing poetry was diverted, or contained within the prose. David Malouf told me recently: "Every novel has about a thousand lost poems in it." I think that's true. My novels don't have that *Ben Hur* sense of looking down and encompassing the full scope. My book may have that kind of scope, but it's pieced together with little bits of mosaic. Each scene tends to be written from the point of view of that private, poetic voice—not so much in terms of language but in how one sees things.

WACHTEL Are you still writing poetry?

ONDAATJE Now and then I write it, but not very much. It's all gone into this wretched book.

WACHTEL Do you miss it?

ONDAATJE Poetry? Yes, I miss it. I think I would miss it more if I couldn't write the books the way I do. If I stopped writing poetry I would feel a very personal, private, intimate whisper was lost. I suppose the book has enough of that, in small scenes, where nothing much happens, just someone sitting by a dry fountain, waiting for the water to come down.

WACHTEL Whether it's Billy the Kid, or a New Orleans jazz musician, or your own father, you often start with historical individuals in your fiction. In *The English Patient* you started with an image in your mind of a man crashing a plane in the desert. But then during your research you found an historical figure on whom to base that dream. Why do you turn to fact for your fiction?

ONDAATJE I find the world around me much more interesting than what I can come up with inside my own head. If you write just what you know or what you have experienced, you've got about a book and a half. Writing links up one's own life with the history of our time, which may go back to the fourth century. You place yourself against the cave wall, where hundreds of years of art have been inscribed, then you link yourself to it in some way. For me, that's the relationship between history and writing, all contemporary writing. I'm always more fascinated by minor characters in history, people who don't usually get written about. In that sense *Billy the Kid* was an aberration; he was too famous. *Coming Through Slaughter* was different. Buddy Bolden was famous but no one really knew him very well. In *The English Patient* I drew on Count Almásy the spy, but mostly on the explorer, a really respected explorer. I used the first part of his life and then moved on into fiction.

The strangest thing I have discovered as a writer in the last few years is the intimacy of fiction. The first books I wrote as novels were based on historical figures: Billy the Kid, Buddy Bolden, and then in *Running in the Family* I focused on my father. Writing these books was essentially like living with these people for about five years, and I started to discover I was being more honest when I was inventing, more truthful when dreaming. Anyone who has listened to a politician or businessman knows you can make facts and figures say anything. When I wrote *In the Skin of a Lion*, even though the book had historical sources, as did some of the characters, they were pretty much invented by the time I finished the book. And then I found that I missed these characters terribly. I realized I was more intimate with them than the people I had written about before, even members of my own family. This was not about someone else but rather inventions of the self, sides of the self. This is the intimacy of fiction, what Vargas Llosa calls "truth by lying." Much the same thing happened with *The English Patient*, even though these four people may seem very different from who I am.

WACHTEL There's a consciousness in your books of the way that stories are told. The epigraph to your last novel, *In the Skin of a Lion*, is from John Berger: "Never again will a single story be told as though it were the only one." There are a number of allusions in *The English Patient*, as well, to the way books are written. You write, "Many books open with an author's assurance of order…. But novels commenced with hesitation or chaos. Readers were never fully in balance." What does all this mean to you?

ONDAATJE I really wasn't expecting all this writing stuff to come out in this book.

WACHTEL "This writing stuff?"

ONDAATJE The comments about writing, about Kipling, about how novels begin. Perhaps I was getting into the mind of this last humanist.

WACHTEL Your burnt-out man.

ONDAATJE My burnt-out man. Who's been trouble all his life, and now is trying to see how the world and his life fit together. He's a man of very few words who talks like crazy, and who's read all the books and is coaching his young nurse in literature. He makes all these grand statements about literature that I'm not sure are true, but suddenly the books became major characters—the spines of books, writing in books, and libraries. Books were an important presence in the novel, like the court or the chorus, standing and watching what was going on. Again there's the sense of history behind these characters.

WACHTEL But also an awareness that narratives are not necessarily linear anymore, that stories get told in—your own word—a mosaic. That is a good image.

ONDAATJE I don't believe stories are told from A to Z anymore, or if they are, they become very ponderous. I'm used to commercial breaks. We discover stories in a different way. I discover something about you after knowing you X number of years, and then after thirty years I will find out some other changes that occurred five years earlier. That sense of discovery, of memory, and how we reveal ourselves to each other—none of that is chronological. Hana will read twenty pages of a book to the poor Patient, and then she'll read on to herself, then carry on aloud twenty pages later, and he's utterly lost the plot. I like that.

WACHTEL You've written about another "lost Eden" in your memoir, *Running in the Family*, set in your childhood home of Ceylon, or what's now Sri Lanka. What was life like for you there?

ONDAATJE When I think about it now, I think what was most important was a sense of an extended family, as opposed to the usual nuclear family. There were my mother and father, but also, after the break-up of their marriage, all the uncles and aunts who took one step forward. I felt supported; I had no real sense of a rift. I glommed onto everybody else. It's odd that I should talk about that first, but in terms even of a book like *The English Patient*, or *In the Skin of a Lion*, the nuclear family is replaced by a kind of extended family. Hana talks about Patrick as her father. Patrick is not her real father, but by now, in her mind, he's become her father, through that kind of support and affection which has very much to do with family, but nothing to do with blood. That's something that has come out of my childhood. The landscape, politics and religion affected me also, on a subconscious level. These are things I want to discover now. I don't think *Running in the Family* said everything—not that I would try to write that book again. It was an attempt to clarify some things when I was of a certain age. Certainly the religion would interest me more now than it did then.

WACHTEL You left Ceylon for England when you were eleven, and then you came to Canada when you were nineteen. The question of home, national and emotional identity, seems to occupy both you and your characters. In *Running in the Family*, there's a line: "I am the foreigner, I am the prodigal who hates the foreigner." What have these moves meant for you?

ONDAATJE They were all traumatic moves for me, but I don't think I showed it very much. They were traumatic in retrospect. They weren't *bad* traumatic; it was suddenly, okay, now you've got to grow up, now you've got to wear long trousers and a tie. It was a physical change more than a mental one. There was something in me that was able to click into having to become an 'Englishman.' That was probably the most traumatic. I really did wear shorts until then. I'd never seen long trousers on anybody, except a priest perhaps. Or socks. It was very odd. I remember taking an exam, when I was in Sri Lanka, to go to school in England, and half the questions were mathematical questions, to do with pounds and shillings. I didn't know what a pound was. I was guessing wildly. Then there'd be basic, central questions about culture, such as, How many members are there in the Oxford rowing team? What was the Oxford rowing team?

WACHTEL If you describe Sri Lanka as a place of extended family, when you went to England, it was not only a dramatic climatic change, but you were primarily with your mother, or you were sent to school or you were cut off from all that.

ONDAATJE I was at school, but for some reason our family has always managed to maintain that extended family. My mother was there, my brother, my sister, and there was a group of friends they had of all ages; it was very much a community. I stepped into that. It was just getting used to different manners. But I did lose friends, and I lost uncles and aunts I was very close to.

WACHTEL You don't write much about Canada, except for your last novel and some of your poetry. Does that say something about your sense of self here?

ONDAATJE I think I write quite a lot about Canada. I don't write essays or portraits of Canada, but a lot of what I felt about the country went into *In the Skin of a Lion*, and most of my poetry is about the landscape around me, the people and emotions around me. I don't sense that I'm avoiding it.

WACHTEL Do you feel Canadian?

ONDAATJE I feel Canadian. As a writer I feel very Canadian. I became a writer here.

WACHTEL You once said you were interested in people who are tentative about where they belong, and I was thinking the desert certainly is a place of shifting borders and uncertainty.

ONDAATJE The characters in *The English Patient*, especially the

Patient and Kirpal Singh, are displaced or, as one of them says, "international bastards." There are a lot of international bastards roaming around the world today. That's one of the book's main stories. Those migrants don't belong here but want to belong here and find a new home. That element is also in *In the Skin of a Lion*, in which everyone's trying to get home. Even Caravaggio escapes in order to go home, which is the first place the police would look for him. In *The English Patient* everyone is fearful of going home. Hana's fearful, and the Patient hates the idea of home and nations, and Kirpal Singh has been befriended and is enamoured of certain English things for a while. They don't want to go back to where they were from.

WACHTEL But they do, in the end.

ONDAATJE Most of them do, yes. We don't know what happens to a couple of them.

WACHTEL You choose romantic subjects to write about—the exoticism and romance of the desert, for instance. Your books, your poetry especially, are filled with love and romance. You yourself, I think, cut a romantic figure. Have you *ever* seen your life in romantic terms?

ONDAATJE I don't see *my* life in romantic terms, but I want to see life in romantic terms. There is a difference between art and life, and this is the difficulty when one talks about the romantic or the exotic. Obviously my version of Toronto is an exotic version on some level. By writing a book, by creating a piece of art, you are altering, synthesizing, compressing reality—thirty years into ten pages—and the minute you start doing that you are simplifying reality, and that's a problem. So you try to be complicated in that romanticism, I suppose.

I don't think the Patient is a romantic figure, or that he sees himself that way. But because we have five or six characters, we're not always with him. We see him only at certain crucial moments in his life. This may allow us to see him as romantic. His career as an explorer is very solitary and quite boring. You cross the desert for seventeen days, and when you get to the fourth truck, you wait another day for someone to turn up. I don't see that life as romantic. I don't see the lives of any of those characters as romantic. Because I live with those characters for five or six years, I try to find out as much as I can about them, putting them in different clothes, dressing them up daily, giving them this quirk or that joke. When you're creating a character, you make him or her as interesting as you can, and once you start doing that you move from the obvious to something very individual, and that's perhaps why people see them as romantic.

WACHTEL So from the outside, we can see *you* as romantic, but from inside, you know better.

ONDAATJE That's right. I'm the usual creature of habit.

October 1992

interview prepared in collaboration
with Anne Gibson

Amos Oz

A few years ago, Israeli writer Amos Oz described Israelis as people who want the best country in the world, the purest, with the highest moral standards—or they are totally disillusioned. Curiously, Oz says, "the outside world tends to view Israel with much the same perspective." Disillusionment is a theme that runs through Oz's fiction. The gap between an idealistic Zionist dream and the harsh realities of Israeli life leaves his characters baffled, bruised—and disillusioned.

Through his speeches and political writing, such as the collection of essays *The Slopes of Lebanon* (1989), Amos Oz is an articulate and impassioned voice of dissent. After serving in the Israeli Army during both the 1967 Six-Day War and the Yom Kippur War of 1973, he became a prominent figure in the Peace Now movement, advocating the creation of a Palestinian state. In his controversial journalism Oz explores not only disillusionment, but also moral degradation and responsibility.

Amos Oz's novels, essays and short stories have been translated into eighteen languages and published in twenty-five countries. Born in Jerusalem in 1939, Oz lived on Kibbutz Hulda, where he taught literature and sociology, for most of his life. Now he makes his home in the desert town of Arad, near the Dead Sea. He spoke to me

64

from the CBC studio in New York. Not long before our conversation, his novel about a retired Israeli secret service agent, *To Know a Woman* (1991), was published in English.

WACHTEL Your work has explored many of the complex divisions within Israeli society and the tensions within the Israeli psyche. The choices you have made in your own life reflect some of these conflicts. You transformed yourself—your life and even your name—when you were a teenager.

OZ Like many Israelis, I am a man who shaped his life through a series of decisions. When I was about fourteen I rebelled against my father's world. He was a militant right-wing Zionist, a scholar, a very middle-class person. I grew up in a house full of scholarly footnotes, where all debates and discussions were comments about comments on literature, things like that. I decided to live on my own on a kibbutz and become a simple, uncomplicated farmer, a tractor-driver, a kibbutznik.

I suppose I had had enough of the heavily intellectual, ideological atmosphere at home, where people were endlessly talking about universal redemption, about revolutionizing Jewish life, about changing their own lives, about being born anew. They were chatting about it day and night, but that was about it. I decided I wanted to be the one to get down to business and *do* it. But after many years in the kibbutz, I discovered that it also was full of chatty ideologists and great talkers. I ended up dividing my time between driving a tractor and writing books. And now I am sitting in a room full of books, writing even more books—probably exactly what my father had hoped for me—which may testify that most rebellions tend to go in a semi-circle, if not a full circle.

WACHTEL As part of your rebellion you changed your family name from Klausner to Oz. Why Oz?

OZ Oz in Hebrew means courage, strength, daring, determination—more or less everything that I needed badly when I left home for the kibbutz. I don't know that I have it now but I needed it then, so I made it my name.

WACHTEL Had you read *The Wizard of Oz?* Did it have any reverberation?

OZ At that time I had no idea. Now of course I'm aware that he must have been my great-uncle or something.

WACHTEL The kibbutz is an image that many people still associate with Israel, although quite a small percentage of the population actually lives collectively. You spent a lot of your life on a kibbutz that has been described as idealistic and left-wing. Kibbutz society has provided you with material for your fiction. Tell me about kibbutz life. What attracted you to it as an individual and as a writer?

OZ Before I came to live there, the kibbutz was the personification of Jewish, Zionist, socialist idealism. In my teen years I was heavily inspired by Tolstoyan ideals: going back to the land, living a simple and idealistic life, working hard. I found all that in a kibbutz, to be sure, but I found a lot more than that. I found every component of human complexity. I found ironies, contradictions, ambivalence and ambiguities—for which I am very grateful. For a storyteller it was a gold mine.

It is a microcosm of the human experience. If you live for thirty years in a small village with 400 human beings, you get to watch the genetics at work, how the genes travel from one generation to the next. Now, if I had lived in New York City, I would never have had such an intimate acquaintance with 400 different—very different—people. From an historical point of view it was good fortune, it was a privilege. I knew those people very intimately, I knew them inside out. Of course, the penalty I paid was that those people knew about *my* life—a hell of a lot more than I'd really like them to know. But that's only fair.

WACHTEL Did the fact that the people on the kibbutz knew you were a writer create any self-consciousness? I read that one fellow on the kibbutz would comb his hair every time he passed your window, in case you wrote about him. Was there a self-consciousness in that environment?

OZ That hair-combing neighbour is a somewhat humorous illustration, but I had to be very, very careful *not* to be eccentric. For example, each time I did my turn as a waiter in the kibbutz dining-hall, I had to be the quickest waiter. I couldn't afford to be, by a hair's breadth, slower than the next waiter, otherwise they would not say, "Amos is tired today" or, "Amos is distracted." They would say, "Here goes the celebrity, the world celebrity." I had to be aware of the necessity—the duty, really, the inner duty—not to make the entire kibbutz aware of the fact that there was a celebrity living amongst them.

WACHTEL And they weren't self-conscious about becoming your subjects?

OZ No. I've never used real-life models in a direct way. If I had done that I couldn't have lived there. But I've always been fascinated by looking closely into the lives of so many people who are so very different from each other in age and background. You have to bear in mind that the people on this little kibbutz had no less than seventeen different countries of origin. This is probably as cosmopolitan as any middle-sized town in Canada.

WACHTEL At least. The image of the hardy kibbutznik, the rugged soldier, driving a tractor, picking oranges, courageous, resilient, the pioneer—this has become the stereotypical image of the Israeli. But there is another side of Israel, darker, often tormented, that you explore in your fiction. It is a nocturnal Israel, a refugee camp with more nightmares per square mile than any other place in the world. Tell me about that night world of Israel.

OZ More than half of all Israelis were not born in that country. They are immigrants, many of them not just ordinary immigrants but refugees. Most people came to Israel not to improve their standard of living or to find streets paved with gold; they came because they were chased by the devil, they were victims of anti-Semitism, of racial hatred and discrimination, of misunderstanding and stereotyping. So many people who have, so to speak, seen the devil with their own eyes are now concentrated in this small country and are in the process of forming a new nation, bringing all their former love-hate relationships with the old countries. Each and every one of those immigrants is at the same time attracted and repelled by his or her old country, as in a disappointed love affair. This is pretty much the case with my own parents. They came from Eastern Europe, from Russia, and for the rest of their lives they loved-hated Russia in particular and Europe in general. They were very European people who were rejected by Europe for being Jewish.

WACHTEL Yet from your writing one gets the sense that, because there's such a complex tangle of histories in this new Israel, they have re-created some of the racial hatred, the discrimination, the misunderstandings that they fled from.

OZ Yes, it is ironic that the only way these people—who were victimized by very crude nationalism in many countries—could escape this persecution and oppression was by forming their own kind of nationalism, which at times becomes as xenophobic, as ethnocentric and as insensitive to the sufferings of others as the nationalisms that victimized those refugees. This is very ironic, very sad and very tragic.

WACHTEL You write out of an awareness of that mixed heritage; you have called yourself a tribal storyteller. How did you become the storyteller, the witness of all this?

OZ I have been writing stories almost since I learned the alphabet. Since early boyhood I have been dispersing my solitude as an only child—and as an oversensitive child—by carefully watching other people and playing all kinds of imaginative, fantasy games. If I was him; if I was her. Where does he come from? Suppose this man was married to that woman; suppose that kid was the son of those parents rather than his real parents. Things like that have been part of my inner life, my conscious life, for as long as I can remember. So I can't identify a particular point at which I became what I am—a witness. That *is* a good definition. I try to be an involved, passionate and active witness, but nonetheless a witness.

WACHTEL For whom? Who are these stories for?

OZ If the case is Israel, then I am the witness for the prosecution. But at the same time, I am also a witness for the defence. And I am also the family of the accused, and the brother of the victim. And I am on the bench. I am everywhere in this trial, in this process. It is immensely important for me to look reality straight in the eye, try to capture it and interpret it. If you ask for whom I stand, I would say for my time and place. The fact that some of the things I write have significance in faraway countries may only testify to the strange fact that literature, at its best, tends to be most universal precisely when it is most provincial, local and parochial.

WACHTEL How do you encompass the roles of prosecutor, defence, judge and jury, all at the same time?

OZ D.H. Lawrence once said that to be a novelist you have to be capable of identifying yourself intellectually and emotionally with half a dozen differing, conflicting and contradicting points of view with an equal degree of inner conviction. This is what the game is all about. I can play tennis singlehandedly, running from one side of the court to the other quickly enough to catch and respond. This is what the art of writing novels and stories is all about: being able to put yourself in the shoes and under the skin of different people.

As a political being, I believe I am still capable of understanding what makes my opponents or my enemies tick, how they feel. In fact, part of my sense of political mission is to explain, for example, to the Israelis what it means to be a Palestinian under Israeli occupation. Or even to explain to Israeli liberal doves like myself the rationale behind the position of the angry, frustrated and untrusting Israeli hawks. As a political being I take sides. I am not detached or neutral, as I try to be when I write a novel or a story.

WACHTEL Why is it important that these stories be shared, that they be recorded and put out into the world?

OZ When I write, I am not thinking about the whole world reading my stories eventually. I do think it is important that what I have seen, experienced and witnessed becomes part of the collective memory of my people, and possibly of other people, because the richer and more complex our collective memory is, the more sensitive we may become as human beings.

WACHTEL You are considered one of the most important Israeli writers, one of the first to be known internationally. You're identified as an Israeli writer who is engaged, who goes out into society and documents and challenges or, as someone in your book *In the Land of Israel* says, "who rats on us to the world." You've therefore taken on a public role, articulating the experience of Israeli Jews. How does this influence your choices as a writer of fiction?

OZ I drew a line there. I tried to make it a very straight line. I have my monastic study where I write my stories. I don't much like the term fiction; a testimony which sounds like fiction is probably a false testimony. I write my novels and my stories, trying to watch, to listen, to decode, to decipher. I've never written a story or a novel in order to convey a political message. I have never turned my storytelling into a vehicle for propaganda purposes. But at the same time, I do have a role outside my study, as a vigilant of the language. This is very political.

Each time my ear catches a false note, a degenerated note, a dehumanized idiom or expression in the language, I write an angry essay or an article. I crusade politically against what I regard as corruption, as evil or as dehumanization. I focus on those particular expressions which can entail dangerous consequences. For instance, wherever human beings are referred to as parasites, then, logically, extermination of human beings might follow sooner or later, because you exterminate parasites. Wherever human beings are referred to as elements—positive elements, negative elements, educated elements—then the society is on its way to becoming dehumanized. People are not elements; they are not building blocks; they are people. Wherever territories are referred to as liberated territories, there is something dehumanized about that. Territories cannot be liberated. The term liberation can only apply to human beings. I'm trying to be vigilant towards those kinds of distortions of the language.

WACHTEL Turning to your novel *To Know a Woman*, I know we're not supposed to identify the author with his central character, *but...* You've made the central character an ex-secret agent. He uses some of the same expressions you use, and you've even said that a secret agent is the perfect metaphor for the storyteller because he *has* to get under other people's skin and see different points of view.

OZ Which means that up to a point I identify with this character. Of course, if I were really him I wouldn't be able to write the novel; I wouldn't be able to distance myself to the extent that is necessary and crucial in order to write such a novel. But yes, I do to some extent identify myself with Yoel, the protagonist in this novel. And indeed there is a certain similarity between what a secret agent does for a living and what I do for a living: identifying with other people, empathising with different and sometimes faraway points of view, being very attentive to details, trying to piece together the seemingly unrelated. There are certain striking similarities there. But I would not press the comparison all the way. I would not turn every secret agent into a potential novelist or every novelist into a potential secret agent.

Yoel is a man in the middle of changing his priorities. To some extent this is a novel about middle age, when things that were crucially important to you become less important, and things that were marginal in your life suddenly assume new importance and centrality. Your self-image changes.

It's also a novel about a man who has been busy all his life collecting information and piecing together facts and who now realizes that facts may sometimes be the worst enemies of truth. He becomes obsessed with truth, searching for domestic truth, family truth, the truth about his own life—through the women in his life—but also with metaphysical truths, the simplest secrets of the world, such as the migration of birds or the turning of the leaves or the change of seasons.

WACHTEL But he is frustrated. These truths are unfathomable. He keeps thinking he will come to understand things and then finds that he can't. He concludes that there's an order, but you can't decipher it. *Nothing* can be understood; everything holds a secret.

OZ In this respect, this is not a spy novel. It is an anti-spy novel, because at the end the reader has less certified information than he or she thought there was at the beginning. Many things that looked certain end up being ambivalent and double-edged and misinterpreted. *But* Yoel discovers a certain kind of knowledge about himself. He learns to come to terms not just with the women around him but, first and foremost, with the woman inside him, the feminine component of his own personality, something that for an active, macho man (embroiled in some of the most romantic exploits of espionage and secrecy) is very difficult to accept. I personally believe that this is crucial and essential: that a man can accept and learn to coexist with the feminine components in his personality, just as a woman should enrich her life by coming to terms with the masculine components in her personality. This is one of the underlying subjects of the novel.

WACHTEL Do you also find that life is full of unfathomable secrets? And is writing a way of unravelling those secrets?

OZ Yes, I find that life is full of mysteries, yet I find myself perhaps more fascinated by presenting the questions than by finding the answers. But you know, every casual encounter in a train or an airplane, in a railway station, holds so much mystery, so much secrecy. Just another person is a mystery. Sometimes inanimate objects strike me as immensely mysterious. They have a secret life. They hide away, they disappear when you want them. If you look really hard, you don't find them, but if you decide, you don't really need them, then they humbly creep out of their hiding place and present themselves to you. So this secret life of the inanimate—the stars, the planets, the change of seasons, the trees, the light—is sweet to the eyes and it is mysterious. I'm not sure that I'm eager to decode and decipher all that. I just want to watch it.

WACHTEL At the end of *To Know a Woman*, Yoel, as you've eloquently put it, finds the female in himself. But there also seems to be a kind of existential resolution. He discovers a compassionate side in himself. He becomes a volunteer in a hospital. There's a scene where he's sorting laundry, and you write that he "yielded himself to this act of sorting laundry with silent elation. 'I am alive, therefore I take part.'" Would it be fair to read into this more than an individual story solution?

OZ I am not a preacher. What I say is, cherish what you see around you, and if you see pain which you could ease, then do it. Do it. It's something you are going to enjoy in the end; it's something that will enrich you. All this is verging on a cliché. It is not a monumental new message for humankind. I am not in that business; I am a witness.

I have a very deep respect for human beings, even for those I do not like. Paradoxically, I would say that sometimes I can, in a way, like even people whom I immensely dislike. This I can do.

WACHTEL How is that?

OZ When I was gathering the materials for my non-fiction collection *In the Land of Israel*, I deliberately talked to the extremist, fundamentalist, fanatic, zealous fringes of the Israeli political and religious spectrum. This book deals mostly not with a cross-section of Israeli society but with the most extremist views. I have discovered in me a measured, restrained amount of sympathy for what has turned them into what they are. So, in a funny way, I've almost liked even that which I could not stand, perhaps through a certain routine exercise I use: reminding myself that, with a slight twist of the genes, or a slight variation of my own biography, I could have been one of them—if I were not on my guard, if I were carried away by certain urges, if I let vindictiveness, anger and frustration overwhelm me. Then I would be one of those fanatics. I can truly put myself under the skin of a fanatic, and know what makes a person into a fanatic.

WACHTEL You do seem drawn to people holding extreme positions. Reading some of the essays in *In the Land of Israel* made me wonder if it was the writer, the storyteller in you who was drawn to the dramatic of these extremes.

oz That's not an unfair observation. I regard *In the Land of Israel* as a travel book, not as a sociological study of Israeli society. It is a travel book to the fringes. Yes, I am fascinated by fanatics. In a sense—if you promise to take this with a grain of salt—I'd say that I'm almost a world authority on fanaticism.

wachtel Is normal too boring?

oz Not at all. Look at Yoel. He is as normal as one can get. I've deliberately made the *monumental* effort of writing a whole novel about what you might call a middle-of-the-road, good man. It's immensely difficult, you know. Viciousness, fanaticism, corruption, degeneration—all those lend themselves easily to fiction. Look at Dostoevsky, at what attracted him. But the more I live, the more I am attracted by the challenge to write about a normal person, like Yoel. And in *To Know a Woman* I believe I have succeeded in describing and penetrating a good man.

wachtel So even the expert on fanaticism is intrigued by the nuances of normalcy.

oz Absolutely, absolutely. Well put.

wachtel I want to turn to Middle East politics for a moment. You surprised and, in some instances, angered a lot of people in the peace movement by supporting the Gulf War. You have argued that you can be a peacenik without being a pacifist. When the war began, you said that Saddam Hussein's defeat *might* bring about a more realistic attitude on both sides of the Arab-Israeli conflict. How do you feel about that now?

oz I still think there is an opening for realism. I'll be careful. I would not give you a prediction accompanied by a timetable. I think the worst part of the Israeli-Palestinian conflict is behind us—the worst part being the time when both sides had a kind of cognitive block about each other. Those were the days when the Palestinians believed that if they only rubbed their eyes hard enough, Israel would go away like a nightmare or a mobile exhibition. And, at the same time, very many Israelis believed that there was no Palestinian issue, that there were no Palestinian people. The whole thing was nothing but a vicious invention of the pan-Arabic propaganda machine aimed at eroding the moral basis of Israel. Now, like waking from anaesthesia, people on both sides are opening their eyes to realize, sometimes with horror, that the other is just not going to go away, and there ought to be a solution that considers that fact.

WACHTEL I'm surprised by your optimism. In your recording of Israeli life and the Israeli psyche over the last twenty or twenty-five years, disillusionment is the common theme that runs through your work.

OZ I was cautious enough not to give you a timetable to accompany my optimism. I never belittle the stupidity of politicians, their lack of imagination or the apprehensions, fears and suspicions of the people. So I don't know whether this realization is going to materialize in a solution in the next month or year. But I insist that the worst is behind us. We may see a lot more violence, we probably will see a lot more turbulence, but the worst *is* behind us. If you asked every single individual between the ocean and the desert in the land of Israel-Palestine what the solution will be in the end, I suppose eight out of ten people—Jews and Arabs, Israelis and Palestinians—would say (sometimes with a deep sigh of despair or high screaming about injustice) that in the end there is going to be some kind of partition and a two-state solution. It's dawning on everybody in the most painful way, but it *is* dawning on everybody. Hence my—what is the politicians' cliché?—"cautious optimism."

WACHTEL There is also something cautiously optimistic about the end of *To Know a Woman*. Your books often deal with different configurations of families—families torn apart, families reconstructed or reinvented families. In this book you introduce the phrase "urban kibbutz." Yoel wants different people to have the opportunity to live together.

OZ I don't know if the ending of *To Know a Woman* is an optimistic one. It is assertive of life itself. Yoel renounces his job, loses his wife and, in a very different way, "loses" his daughter by realizing that she must lead her own life, that she can't be a substitute for his wife, she can't be his mate for the rest of his life. By realizing all that he is also realizing that he is confined to a *deep* solitude. Yet he is enthusiastic about life. As it says in Ecclesiastes, "The light is sweet to the eyes." This is a great realization.

If you are also lucky enough to have a friend of sorts, or maybe two friends, a next-door neighbour who is occasionally making love to you, a little garden of your own and a nice house, a couple of skills at your fingertips and a voluntary occupation—part-time, as a volunteer in a hospital—then you are a very privileged human being. It's a hell of a lot. That's what the novel is about.

Now, if you call this optimism, it is optimism. I know that some people would call it a "living death" and would scream with despair at the thought that this was what life boiled down to after all the sound and fury of our teenage dreams. But I regard this as a novel which ultimately relates to life in the most humbly assertive way—and enjoys it. Yoel learns, perhaps for the first time in his life, to enjoy living. In his professional life he was thrilled, he was fascinated, he had a very, very alert inner life. He was on tiptoe for years, full of adrenalin, but very little joy. Now the adrenalin is fading, life takes on a different rhythm.

March 1991

interview prepared in collaboration
with Sandra Rabinovitch

A.S. Byatt

A.S. Byatt was born in Sheffield in 1936. When she took the part of Antonio in a school production of "The Tempest," her teacher declared, "I don't like your name," which was Susan. "I shall call you Antonia." The name stuck, and when Byatt started publishing she decided to use the two initials in her writing name, "because it was nothing to do with the family and it sounded rather like T.S. Eliot."

A.S. Byatt published her first novel, *The Shadow of a Sun*, in 1964. Other novels include *The Virgin in the Garden* (1978) and *Still Life* (1985). But her career appears to divide in two: before and after *Possession*, the 1990 novel which took the Booker Prize and won Britain's richest literary prize, the Irish Times–Aer Lingus International Fiction Prize, as well as enormous popular success in North America as well as England.

I first met A.S. Byatt when she came to Toronto in October 1988. She had recently published *Sugar and Other Stories*, but she still wasn't well known outside a limited circle of admirers. Critics accused Byatt of being too literary and academic; in one novel, a character thinks of T.S. Eliot while making love. I asked Byatt about these complaints. "It's absolutely true," she said, "my books are thick with the presence of other books, but I feel that out there in the world there must be other people who read as passionately as I do and actually know that books constantly interweave themselves with other books and the world."

At that time Byatt was just finishing *Possession,* a novel that took her much less time than usual—only two years—to write. And the rest is history. *Possession* is a rich satisfying book that operates on a number of levels: the Victorian love story between two poets; a modern, tentative love story between two scholars researching the Victorians; and a literary detective story, using mock Victorian documents, such as journals, poems, letters, and fairy-tales. Two years after *Possession,* Byatt published a pair of novellas, *Angels and Insects* (1992), also set in mid-Victorian England.

This interview with A.S. Byatt took place just before she won the Booker. She spoke to me from the CBC London studio.

———————————

WACHTEL In *Possession,* a young academic is examining a dusty manuscript in the Reading Room of the London Library. He's researching the work of a Victorian poet named Randolph Henry Ash, and he teams up with a woman who's studying another poet, someone Ash may have had an affair with—namely, Christabel LaMotte. What attracted you to this idea of creating a mystery and a romance out of academic research?

BYATT It came to me, in fact, with the word, which was the title, *Possession.* It really comes out of my passion for that great Toronto scholar Kathleen Coburn, who was working on Coleridge in the British Library when I was working there. I looked at her one day, walking around, making notes on Coleridge's notebooks, and I thought, she can't have thought a thought for the last thirty years that isn't in some sense *his* thought, and then I thought, everything I know about his thought has been put together for me by her. And I thought, you could write a wonderful novel called *Possession* about the relationship between a dead poet and a living scholar, who really, as it were, was in possession or was possessed.

The word slowly began to develop all sorts of other resonances. I thought of all this in 1972—the book was a long time in the gestation. There was a sense of economic possession, because there was a slight argument when Kathleen Coburn took the Coleridge manuscripts—somewhat secretively—across the Atlantic, so I thought one could have a sort of transatlantic scholar trying to get possession of these letters in a purely physical and also financial sense.

There's also the sense of demonic possession. I started thinking about how obsessed the Victorians were with séances and spiritualism and the voices of the dead speaking through the living medium. The poet Robert Browning, who is one of the people I most admire and love, wrote poems about many, many periods with many, many voices, all of which—from primitive Caliban in the mud and St. John the Evangelist dying in the desert through to the seventeenth century—he felt were somehow speaking quite distinctively through him. And I thought that you could compare the spiritualist séance with Browning's poems as a way in which the voices of the dead speak through the living.

Much later I had the idea that there's also a sexual aspect to the word *possession*. So I thought if I had not just one poet, but two, male and female, in love with each other, there would be that sense, too, in which they came to possess each other. After that I got the idea of having two scholars who came to possess both the poets and finally each other. And then I saw that it should be called a romance, because this was essentially a romantic plot. I dithered with the idea of actually using the love of the two Brownings, and then I decided (a) this would be inhibiting to my writing and (b) I would be in for lots of libel actions from Browning scholars, so I gave that one up.

WACHTEL So is Ash loosely based on Browning? And Christabel LaMotte, the woman poet, on Christina Rosetti?

BYATT   In fact, I couldn't use Christina Rosetti because Christina has a kind of Christian piety which I'm quite unable to reproduce, not being a Christian. And I wanted something tougher and harder and clearer and cleaner and stranger than that pre-Raphaelite thing, so I turned to someone who I think is the greatest woman poet of all, Emily Dickinson. I read and reread her poems and her very strange letters and picked up hints from her style, out of which I made an English version of her. Then I realized that my Christabel had a kind of sexual frankness which almost no English women, except George Eliot, had in those days, so I made her part French, and that brought with it all the Breton mythology which comes into her poetry. So she's a kind of Emily Dickinson, who was a disciple of Keats and loved reading sixteenth-century poetry.

WACHTEL   You're no stranger to erudition—your earlier books are full of references to Eliot, Milton, Lawrence, Spenser—but here you seem to be having more fun with it. You invent more than seventeen hundred lines of mock Victorian poetry in the different styles of the different characters, plus journals and letters, Gothic fairy-tales, biography and autobiography—it's a marvellous mixture of the apparently real and the fabricated, although of course the whole thing is your own fabrication. Do you feel more relaxed with this literary or academic material now?

BYATT   Yes, I do. It's partly because I've given up teaching. I mean, there are very simple reasons for it. I stopped being a university teacher and decided to be a writer, and in some curious way this made me feel much freer with what I was doing. I wanted to write a comedy and I wanted to keep it light—although in fact quite a lot of the Victorian plot is, seen from one angle, tragic—but I wanted it to have a kind of Shakespearean warmth to it. And I think one should acknowledge one's debts: I was inspired by Umberto Eco's *The Name of the Rose*. I saw that one could be at once both very serious and quite funny, and write a detective story into the bargain. I suddenly felt a terrible need to have a complicated plot, which I'd never had.

WACHTEL As one of your characters says, literary critics make natural detectives, so you're able to merge those two styles together.
BYATT That's what I thought.

The two researchers in fact *are* detectives: they are constantly
searching for clues, and they get quite excited when they discover
a line of poetry which gives them a clue to a whole set of ideas, or
indeed to the entire behaviour of their hero. I felt I could write a
literary detective story that needn't be quite so papery, because
once I'd written the poetry the scholars were actually doing the
kind of detection that one really does with poems, which is finding out their meaning, the real feeling behind them, what the poet
was really concentrating on. The poems I wrote contain various
clues to the detective-story plot, but they're also, in my opinion,
where you encounter the two poets most nakedly, at their fullest
flow.

WACHTEL You've written scholarly works on Wordsworth and
Coleridge and edited some of George Eliot, and I'm told you have
a border collie named William, after Wordsworth. How did your
immersion as a scholar in this material come into play when you
came to write about it fictionally, to recreate that world fictionally?

BYATT It was very useful, first because I knew the whole scholarly
world in the way any good detective-story writer has to know the
world in which they've set their work. At some much deeper level
it goes back to long before my teaching really, when as a girl I read
a great deal of Wordsworth's poetry, Coleridge, Browning, Tennyson. I learn things by heart very easily, and my mind is possessed by very long quotations, which sing about when I'm sitting
in taxis. And here I was suddenly able to write a book in which the
rhythms of the way I actually think were useful. So it's more primitive, I think, than being able to use my scholarly knowledge,
though my desire to be a scholar in English literature also grew out
of being possessed by the rhythms of the English language in this
way.

WACHTEL When you say you were reading these poets when you

were a girl, were they just part of what was included at school or did you seek them out?

BYATT It began with my mother really. She herself read English at Cambridge. When I was a little girl during the war she was teaching English to sixth-form boys. And the first books I remember her giving us were three children's paint books—Tennyson's "The Lady of Shalott," Browning's "The Pied Piper" and Tennyson's "Morte d'Arthur." The poetry went down the left-hand side of the page and there were these rather pre-Raphaelite pictures, which we filled in with colour, on the right-hand side—of King Arthur getting the sword out of the lake or Sir Bevidere throwing the sword into the lake. I used to chant these poems to myself in bed—I didn't understand half of them—which I think is a very good way to encounter great poetry. In fact, in every novel I write, in some curious way the rhythms of that very early exposure to those poems come out.

WACHTEL You talk about being possessed as a young girl by the rhythms of poetry, by the language. You do show a kind of tenacity about the past. Reading *Possession*, one has the sense that the Victorian poets are perhaps more engaged with life than are the modern scholars, who seem a little anaemic at times. Do you favour the Victorians?

BYATT Oh, yes. This is part of the whole joke of the novel: the dead are actually much more alive and vital than the living. One reason for this is that the living are possessed by a particularly modern literary theory, which means that they have to explore the sexuality of the people they are researching. They have to work out the sexual implications of the language they use, especially the feminist who is researching the work of Christabel LaMotte. Like all good feminists she is totally obsessed by sex—you have to be— and obsessed by the language in which you describe sex and gender and sexual relationships. This has caused her to feel a faint disgust and a faint unreality about her own body and life.

The Victorians, on the other hand, were quite sure that they were real people. They didn't have modern theories of there being no concrete personality, of everybody being just a kind of mixture of moments in time and voices of the language speaking through them; they really believed that they were important people and that what they did mattered in the eyes of God and in their own lives.

When my two Victorians either wrote something or fell in love, these were, to them, large and important acts. The poor moderns are always asking themselves so many questions about whether their actions are real and whether what they say can be thought to be true, given that language always tells lies, that they become rather papery and are miserably aware of this, and this is part of the comedy. Of course, they then become possessed by the passion of the Victorians.

WACHTEL It seems odd that they enjoy the vicarious passion of the Victorians, since we tend to think of the Victorians as being repressed.

BYATT If you are repressed, your passions run very deep and very powerful, if they get out at all. I think we're deeply repressed by thinking so hard and so much about how we ought not to be repressed, and we're very insecure about whether what we do has any real importance. Anybody who really reads Victorian literature will discover that the Victorians were not unaware of powerful passions of all kinds—sex, greed, hunger, ambition, the desire for money. They weren't all painful prudes; they had a strong sense of decorum, which ruled that certain things couldn't be said. But my father always used to say to me, if you read the novels of Anthony Trollope, you could actually decode where the characters have sexual experience that the author is not allowed to describe, and I know that my father could do this. I think we've lost that skill now.

WACHTEL I thought one of the reasons you might be partial to the Victorians is that you're pro-creator rather than pro-critic—that is, you favour the *creators* of poetry rather than those who dissect it afterwards.

BYATT Absolutely. Of course, I spent a lot of my life as a critic and

I've derived a lot of knowledge and satisfaction, and indeed pleasure, out of really getting hold of a piece of writing and trying to sort out how it works and how it came about. But I do feel that recent academic styles and theories have made the writer feel at risk. Roland Barthes, for instance, talks about how the author is dead. Modern theories of reading propose that the reader actually constructs the text *while reading*, that every reader constructs a different text and that therefore the author has no authority within the text. Whereas I know exactly the feeling of the reader making up his or her own story as he or she reads it, I really do think that writing it is quite different. Nobody could argue that somebody who looks at a painting is actually painting it; they're only seeing it and putting it together as a secondary activity. There's a huge arrogance among literary critics who claim that critical activity is as great and as important as the first act of making the work of art. I think it simply isn't, and writers have got to stand up for themselves and say, What I do is actually something which requires long training and considerable skill, and it should be respected at that level of technique and skill; my material is my own and unrepeatedly my own.

WACHTEL You do seem to be having fun in *Possession* with the various notions of modern literary criticism or critical theory. At one point you talk about the cut-throat ideological battles of structuralism, post-structuralism, Marxism, deconstruction and feminism. What do you make of all these fashions?

BYATT I find them partly very exciting. I actually quite like reading the books; I enjoy reading Derrida and thinking about deconstruction, because I like thinking very hard. What I am quite frightened of is the kind of empire-building that's going on in universities. I feel that universities just at the moment—at least in England—when it's least desirable, have turned in on themselves, and that university English has become a discussion of and about university English. This is actually very bad for the relationship of what I prefer to call "writing" rather than "literature" to the outside world and the general reader.

Universities have always been accused of being ivory towers. In our country they're under threat because they're inadequately funded and they seem to have lost a lot of respect. And just at that moment they start discussing power simply in terms of university departments and theories of reading. To read English at university now is to get very excited about theories of language, but not to go through that primary process of reading patiently and listening to the thought of somebody who has written down what they have written. I feel that something has been lost. To be truthful, when I was teaching university—I stopped in 1984—I felt it was impossible to go on teaching the kind of thing that was really exciting my students and to write novels. It was one or the other—either I immersed myself in theory or I went out and read some theory and wrote novels. I decided to get out. It's not that I'm hostile to theory; it's just that they're somehow incompatible activities.

WACHTEL When you started writing fiction more than twenty-five years ago, you said that one of the things you wanted to do was to record modern life and the inner life of women. That has changed in your writing, but *Possession* does look at women's roles in the academic world. For instance, the Victorian poet Ash is revered, but his female contemporary, La Motte, is largely neglected except by feminists. Is this part of the campus comedy or is it your experience that literary scholarship treats women unfairly?

BYATT Literary scholarship has treated women unfairly for many generations. But some of the attempts by feminist critics to put this right have caused two things to happen that I don't like: one is that a lot of women students read nothing but writing by women—and I think one should always read writing by both sexes—and another is that they are discovering not very good writers and saying these are our forebears, we must say they were very good writers. It is no good, I think, trying to claim that Elizabeth Barrett Browning is anywhere near as good a poet as Robert. It distorts our literary judgment to be driven into a corner and to have to do that.

I think my picture of Christabel LaMotte as a woman who wanted to be a great writer and wanted to have her writing at the centre of her life, and the precariousness of her sense of this, as opposed to Randolph Henry Ash's assurance that he could simply go on writing and that people would read it with respect, is accurate as a depiction of the Victorian period.

WACHTEL The modern scholars share a fantasy of being in a clean, empty, white bed, in a clean, empty room, having nothing and wanting nothing. Is this a response to Victorian clutter? Is this a twentieth-century vision? And did you ever have that fantasy of the clean white room?

BYATT It's a very twentieth-century vision. I think it's a response to post-Freudian sexual clutter, really, and to the intense market pressures of modern academic life. It's also a response to sixties sexual liberation, which in fact meant for many women that they were pressured into having a very active sex life, whether or not that was what they wanted, because the current ideology said that that was what you should want, that you should want continuous, joyous sex. This couple are slightly older than that—this is the generation that was at university in the seventies. I think both these people just want to be left alone to work out who they are, with all these theories of what they are besieging them, like wasps.

And yes, I quite often had that fantasy. Christabel had it because she wanted to write, she wanted to be alone. I had it all the way through boarding school, where I shared a bedroom with eight other girls and my one ideal in life was to have a room of my own, as Virginia Woolf said, and to be in it, quietly. And then, during all my years of very happy married life, and having had four children, I've also had this coexisting fantasy of being able to be alone in a white room, with a white bed, and just think things out. I think it's something that you absolutely need if you're then going to be able to move back into the world and live in it.

What I'm partly saying is that I'm in no way a creature of the sixties or early seventies who feels that life should be lived in communes or groups; they frighten me. And I suppose I've made both

Roland and Maud temperamentally rather like me. Of course, Roland has also got himself into a hopeless love affair with somebody for whom he feels responsible and to whom he is deeply attached, but with whom he no longer wants to go on living. He would just like not to have this situation but can't get out because he's a nice man.

I thought, what am I going to do with her? Because she had become rather abrasively and mockingly angry and a failure, and she was hanging around his neck like a dead weight, and yet I rather liked and admired her. I decided that one could take a purely Shakespearean-comedy way out—something Iris Murdoch has been doing for some years—and just suddenly change things overnight by bringing somebody into her life who, quite unexpectedly, it turns out she prefers. Shakespeare would have done that without blushing. So I thought, well, if he can and Iris Murdoch can, I can—so I did.

WACHTEL Near the end of *Possession*, you observe that coherence and closure are deep human desires that are currently unfashionable. Clearly you're not afraid of being unfashionable, because you give us coherence and closure. There is even a self-conscious observation by the characters at the end—an analogy to a Shakespearean comedy or to the conventions of the mystery story, where everyone is finally brought together. Does this licence reflect the luxury of your being better recognized or of getting older?

BYATT It's partly that, and partly a sense I have of the changing requirements of modern fiction. There has been a very long period when the one thing everybody abused was the well-made plot. We were taught by the delicate novels of, say, Rosamond Lehmann in the thirties that you had to have an open ending— the hero went through various tribulations and at the end was looking out on the world not knowing what was going to happen to her. And then writers like Robbe-Grillet in the sixties said even more strongly that plot and character are the real enemies of the novel, that we must get rid of them at all costs. I think there was bound to be a reaction, and that is why books like *The Name of the*

Rose, which exploits the formal structure of the detective plot even while doing something quite different with it, have given recent readers such delight. I think there is a genuine narrative hunger. People, having said plot is trivial, have now come back to being technically interested in it, so one can actually exploit it quite coolly.

I haven't used the plot naïvely: I have pointed out that I am actually going back to writing novels with plots as a technical experiment. But it has given me intense pleasure. I love those Victorian novels in which, when you come to the end, you're told the whole history of every character from the end of the story until their dying day. I love that kind of thing, it makes me very happy. I don't see why we shouldn't have it: it's not wicked, as we were told in the sixties, it's just pleasant. Everybody knows it's fiction, but then everybody knows the whole thing is fiction.

WACHTEL You have in the past made use of autobiography in your writing, though you seem perhaps most self-effacing in *Possession*. Maybe that's because you're so busy being all the voices and all the poets and scholars. In an earlier book, however, a collection of stories called *Sugar*, the title story was very autobiographical.

BYATT And it was probably the only thing I shall ever write in the first person. It was an account, as truthful as I could make it, of the death of my father, who collapsed in Amsterdam and was brought back home to England and died. The story had great formal coherence, because it was about the nature of truth and about the nature of lies, and thus about the nature of fiction. It opens with a description of my mother, who loved telling stories, and told a great many lies—some of them conscious, some of them unconscious—and my father, who was a rigorously truthful person, a judge and a judge of evidence.

When my father was dying I suddenly realized that all I knew about my grandfather—his father, whom he had never talked about—was what my mother had made up. The whole of that story is based around this contrast between my parents—the lying, fictive one and the totally truthful one, who was dying, and with him all the truth about what my family history had been. It's a story which both tries to be accurate, though it leaves out a great deal, and questions how accurate human memory can be and how much fiction goes into our recounting, even of what we try most desperately to tell truthfully.

WACHTEL Do you see yourself as, in a sense, your father's daughter, because you have to find and weigh the truth, but also your mother's because of the importance of invention and the fiction writer's imagination?

BYATT Yes, that is very much what I do. In a sense, "Sugar" was written by the daughter of my father, trying desperately to be accurate. It's about my grandfather who had a sugar factory here and made boiled sweets out of different-coloured sugar. My parents meet in the middle, and I say, or the main character says, of my mother, "I suddenly saw that my whole life, my whole past, might be her confection." And the word "confection" brings together the idea of sugar and fiction, truth and lies and making things up, and I was pleased with having found that word, which just came to me as I was writing a sentence—I didn't start with it as one of the central ideas. But it is like that, yes. And although I loved my mother much less simply and much less straightforwardly than my father, in some curious way she's become the heroine of that story, with all her desperate attempts to retell everybody's life in the way most favourable to her. She is the ground of the fiction.

October 1991

interview prepared in collaboration
with Sandra Rabinovitch

Jane Dunn
on Virginia Woolf
and Vanessa Bell

Virginia Woolf and her sister, Vanessa Bell, were at the centre of the Bloomsbury set—a dazzling literary, artistic and intellectual circle that flourished in London early in this century. In fact, the two women created it. They gave Bloomsbury its name, after the neighbourhood—then inexpensive and unfashionable—where they lived in London as young, independent women.

In the last twenty years, there has been a remarkable revival of interest in Bloomsbury, and especially in Virginia Woolf. She was an assiduous and brilliant writer—of novels, memoirs, criticism, journals and letters. And her own life was so tantalizing and tragic, marked by madness, sexual abuse and suicide, that Virginia Woolf makes a fascinating, and well-documented, subject. Less is known about her older sister, the painter Vanessa Bell, although there was a biography in 1983, and later a memoir by her daughter, Angelica Garnett.

What is original about Jane Dunn's *A Very Close Conspiracy* (1990) is that it's not a double biography but a study of the relationship between two sisters, a sibling relationship of extraordinary intensity and ambiguity. Virginia knew Vanessa from the day she was born in 1882 until the day Virginia died, the day she drowned herself fifty-nine years later. Jane Dunn feels that Vanessa was the love of Virginia's life. Of *A Very Close Conspiracy* Angelica Garnett wrote: "By presenting us with a double portrait, its two subjects seen in relation to each other rather than in isolation, we come so much nearer the living reality, in all its complexity, its doublesidedness, its light and shadow. This is one of the few books which allows me to believe that the author actually knew both my mother and my aunt, and [it deepens] my understanding of both of them and their relation to Bloomsbury."

Jane Dunn was born in South Africa and grew up in England. She is the eldest of six sisters and two brothers. Her biography of Mary Shelley, *Moon in Eclipse* (1978), won a Yorkshire Post Award.

WACHTEL You posed a question to yourself that I would like to put again to you. Why were you so foolhardy as to walk into the hornets' nest of Bloomsbury? There were already so many books by and about Virginia Woolf. There's even a fine biography of Vanessa Bell. Why enter the ring?

DUNN You may well ask. I think I'm still asking myself that question, in some respects. It's very daunting to go into an area that is so overexposed, and I was extremely loath to do so, for many reasons. But I could not forget the idea that had been put to me, which was that a study of the two sisters would make a fascinating book. Eventually I decided, blow it, I'll forget about all the criticism I'm going to get for writing *another* book on Bloomsbury, and I'll just wing it.

WACHTEL What was it about the sisters that really drew you in?

DUNN Sisterhood is a fascinating relationship—extraordinarily important. It lasts a lifetime for most of us, if we're lucky. A sister begins and ends life, roughly, with us, whereas parents usually die before us, and children and lovers and husbands enter our lives at a much later stage. Sometimes husbands and lovers leave; sisters don't, even if they fall out, as in a way these two did at a certain point. There was an emotional alienation of sorts, yet thirty years later they were able to make reparation. Between friends thirty years is too great a divide. So there's something terribly moving about the permanence and continuity of a sisterly relationship.

But Virginia Woolf and Vanessa Bell are particularly intriguing as sisters, as they are in many respects *equally* interesting. You can often have a famous or gifted sister and a more low-profile, ordinary sister. That is interesting in itself, but it doesn't allow for an equally weighted portrait of a relationship. With these two, although they were so different, they had equal power, albeit of a very different sort, which was beautifully chronicled—largely by Virginia. This is an absolute gift to anybody who is writing about her, since any quote you want to use from her illuminates and uplifts one's own thesis.

In common with a lot of writers, I was interested in but wary of Bloomsbury. I had just done a biography of Mary Shelley. I have always found that relating to women is something I can do well. I'm the eldest of six sisters and two brothers, and I could probably be accused of being elder-sisterly with an awful lot of my friends and family! Women intrigue me. I feel at least I can *know* something of women; I don't think I know much about men at all. I've realized, in my approaching middle age, that they're not *like* us, and it's a huge mistake to think they are! They're wonderful but completely alien.

WACHTEL The relationship between Virginia Woolf and Vanessa Bell was creative as well. Early on, the two of them divided up the artistic turf: Virginia was to be the writer and Vanessa the painter. But I understand Virginia always considered writing a superior art to painting. Didn't that undermine this partnership?

DUNN This was a big problem for Vanessa, until she met fellow-souls who were interested in art. She grew up in a literary family, where the written word was sacrosanct and where the visual arts were considered of no consequence whatsoever. Certainly there were many times when Virginia would dismiss painters as a load of madmen. During the First World War, she commented that, when the whole of Europe was up in flames, all they could be concerned about was whether they'd used the right shade of yellow. Vanessa was notorious for being totally uninterested in the outside world. She'd look at newspapers just for the pictures, so would buy the *Daily Mirror* largely because it was a big, pictorial tabloid and she liked looking at the pictures.

There's a wonderful, perhaps apocryphal story of her sitting next to Asquith—when he was our Prime Minister—at a dinner, and trying desperately to make conversation. She was very shy and socially inept. As an opening gambit she turned to this elderly, distinguished man and asked him politely whether he was interested in politics! One can absolutely believe this was true. Poor Vanessa was ill-educated, her art was considered deeply inferior to the literary art, in this literary family. Virginia had already claimed the superior art.

WACHTEL Their compact was formed early in childhood: them against the world. You quote Virginia as saying, "It thus came about that Vanessa and I formed a very close conspiracy." Why conspiracy? It's a word that suggests something a bit sinister.

DUNN It's a wonderful word. If you go right back to its root, it means a breathing together. It does also have these rather exciting, sinister connotations—we're rebels, we're terrorists, we're going to make a life that is different from the rest. This is exactly what Bloomsbury was. What Bloomsbury was so often accused of was a terrific exclusivity. But what it was, was born out of insecurity, out of the fact that they themselves felt outsiders in the strictly hierarchical society into which they were expected to move effortlessly. So when they had a chance to make their own society, they made it even more exclusive than the world that they had tried and failed to enter—as young women being launched into London society.

WACHTEL You quote the biographer and essayist Lytton Strachey, who was of their circle, describing Virginia and Vanessa as the two most beautiful and witty women in England. That may be somewhat hyperbolic but they *were* a very attractive pair, and you point out that men would fall in love with both of them as if they were a single person. This was certainly true of Leonard Woolf, who ended up marrying Virginia, once Vanessa got snapped up by Clive Bell. But it was also true of Clive Bell, who married Vanessa but was attracted to Virginia. Why did Clive Bell choose to marry Vanessa?

DUNN It's very interesting. Clive was part of Vanessa's revelation that there was a world where art mattered. When Virginia and Vanessa went abroad after their father's death they met Clive Bell in Paris. He introduced them to a bohemian artistic life, which centred on painters, not writers. This was an ecstatic time for Vanessa, who took to this continental trip with enormous gusto. Clive proposed to Vanessa quite soon after that. Why he chose Vanessa no one can tell. She was certainly more voluptuous and Clive was an *extremely* libidinous young man. It may be that there was more of a sexual *frisson*. With Virginia, you did not get any sense of sexuality flowing towards you, whereas I think Vanessa was ripe and ready to discover sexuality, and Clive was the right person to show her.

But she kept on turning him down, very firmly. She said, "I want to live with my family." They'd just got their freedom from their father and had moved into these huge, cold, vast-windowed houses in Bloomsbury, which she adored. So she did *not* want to go off with Clive. But the moment Thoby, their beloved brother—the one they fought over, who came between the sisters—died of typhoid after a trip to Greece, Vanessa, within four days, accepted Clive's proposal. It was very much against her deepest instincts, but she could not face another terrific grief in the family: their mother had died; Stella, their half-sister, who had stepped into their mother's shoes, died very rapidly. I think they felt that any bit of happiness was going to be very quickly stamped on, that the cat of fate, as Virginia characterized it, would pounce the moment they relaxed and enjoyed themselves.

So Vanessa accepted Clive and, as recorded in the most extraordinary letter, transmuted her grief into ecstatic happiness. She refused to allow herself to grieve for Thoby. All this would come up much later in her life and really hit her hard.

WACHTEL You delineate the two sisters as complementary rather than alike. If anything, you set up oppositions: motherhood versus creativity; life versus art; Vanessa as the great, fecund goddess and Virginia as the chaste intellectual. Did this kind of division of the psychic turf keep things more in balance between them?

DUNN The centre of the whole thesis of my exploration of their relationship was that they *needed* to divide up the world, their work and their emotional life in order to moderate their competitiveness as much as possible. They polarized each other. Their abilities were actually not so clear cut. Vanessa is actually a very good writer, but she felt terribly inhibited doing *anything* with words when Virginia was there. She ran away from the intellectual further than she might have done if she hadn't had Virginia as a sister. Virginia also had a painterly eye; all her novels have very painterly aspects to them. And she was envious of the painter's life, the painter's collaboration, the fact that painters (I'm thinking of Duncan and Vanessa particularly) could sit together, or stand together, at their easels in terrific harmony, painting from the same model. Virginia envied this. Being a writer is so solitary.

Dividing up the world was necessary for them in order to save their relationship, but it polarized them, and narrowed and stultified them at times, too.

WACHTEL It seems to me it could also exacerbate the sense of rivalry.

DUNN Exactly. The moment one stepped out of her prescribed area and tried to enter the other, such as when Vanessa became famous as a painter in the thirties. Virginia was very discomposed by this. She flung up these classic words: "You have the children, the fame by rights belongs to me!" This is what was so wonderful about Virginia: she was so candid!

WACHTEL What did Vanessa think when Virginia said that?

DUNN I think she probably half agreed. She once wrote laughingly—I think to Roger Fry—"Virginia suggested that I should be a writer. She suggests everybody should be a writer who actually can never threaten her." But when Julian, Vanessa's first-born son, wanted to be a writer and a poet Virginia was extremely miffed. Virginia was jealous of Julian anyway. She always considered herself to be Vanessa's first-born—an odd sibling rivalry here. When Vanessa was talking to Virginia about Julian's wanting to be a poet—this was when Julian was going off to Cambridge, and he was a big, sort of loutish, attractive, energetic boy—Virginia said, "I think he'd probably make a better lawyer." Vanessa was extremely angry about this. She felt once again this terrible, jealous sister was keeping it all for herself.

WACHTEL Vanessa was the older sister, the maternal one, and Virginia turned to her all the more forcefully after their own mother, and then their mother-surrogates, died. Certainly Virginia was important in Vanessa's life and came to her aid at crucial times. But one does get the feeling that this is one significant source of imbalance between them—that Vanessa was the love of Virginia's life. You quote Virginia writing to Vanessa, "With you I am passionately, unrequitedly in love." How significant was that imbalance?

DUNN I think this very demanding side of Virginia was quite an embarrassment, at times, to Vanessa. When Virginia would arrive at Charleston Farmhouse—Vanessa's house in the country, in Sussex—she would come in and demand what she called her rights. She would kiss Vanessa on the inside of her arm, or *demand* some sort of physical affection from her. Vanessa was an enormously constrained, inhibited person and she would, I think, almost recoil from her incorrigible younger sister's demands. Once those "rights" had been supplied, the two sisters would settle down into the most easy, gossipy relationship. But I think that that side was very difficult for Vanessa. She once said, "It is a part of me that, when people desperately want something from me, I become even more frozen and less able to give it to them, so that I appear much more cold than I mean to appear." I think this is something we can all recognize, something we deplore in ourselves, but when you have this terrific, clinging demand on you, you sometimes can't meet it.

WACHTEL Do you think it has to do with an emotional imbalance in the relationship or does it go back to the expression of it and the physicality of it, of Virginia's being more drawn to women and Vanessa's being more drawn to men?

DUNN I do believe that Vanessa was the love of Virginia's life. By its remaining, to some extent, in an idealized and fantasized form she retained the romance of it. That's why she can write, even in her fifties, extremely loving and flowery sentiments to Vanessa. I think, sadly, Duncan Grant was the love of Vanessa's life. It's interesting that she chose him, when she knew very well the limitations of the love he could offer her.

WACHTEL Vanessa was married to Clive Bell. She then had an affair with Roger Fry, but afterwards she fixed on a declared homosexual painter, Duncan Grant—the man she spent the rest of her life with—fifty years.

DUNN "Fixed on" is a very good phrase. It is a great puzzle. This was a woman, a sexual woman, awoken to sexuality by Clive Bell, who was a great lover of women and was certainly experienced by the time he came to marry Vanessa. The early part of their marriage is documented—with amazement, really—by Virginia, who watched her sister blossom and become like a "tawny god," as she describes her. It was quite frightening to Virginia, too. She thought, "What is this thing that happens between a man and a woman that can so change a woman?" This is what frightened her about getting married herself—that somehow some part of herself would be breached and she'd be changed forever. She watched with amazement this transformation of her sister into this outgoing, confident, beautiful woman.

WACHTEL But Vanessa later chose Duncan. Do you have an interpretation of why she would choose Duncan, in relation to Virginia?

DUNN I'm afraid Vanessa's patterns of feeling were so set up in her childhood that she had to be the mother, the giver. Virginia accuses her of being a selfish woman who can only give and never take. Vanessa chose Duncan, who she thought was a genius. She had grown up with a genius, she had grown up with Virginia, she had always been secondary to Virginia. She now chose a man to whom she put herself secondary. She thought he was a far finer painter than she was. And he was an exceptionally charming person. In loving Duncan she diminished herself and her art. She gave up her sexuality in her early thirties, although it was the most difficult thing for her to do. Her letters to him make the most painful reading. They are desolate. When he is off with his boyfriends she is terrified of losing him. She sacrificed herself, as in some ways she had done for Virginia.

WACHTEL What about Vanessa's presence, or influence, in Virginia Woolf's writing? Do you think that Virginia wrote about women like Vanessa as a way of trying to understand her?

DUNN Yes, I think that's a very important point. Virginia actually states on a couple of occasions, that it is an enormously exciting intellectual—and emotional—exercise for her to unravel this enigmatic character. There's no doubt Vanessa had a most intriguing and hidden character. In *Night and Day* Virginia set out to explore her. She said, "You're going to be wonderfully mysterious, like steam coming up from between paving stones. You crack the paving stones and there you find it all." There is the sense of this hard, impenetrable carapace that is Vanessa, with volcanoes under her skin, as Virginia once said of her.

In *Night and Day* Vanessa is pictured as a woman who controls everything. Virginia makes her a mathematician, but she is an outsider in her own family, as Vanessa was as an artist in a family of writers. She is a woman whom people are attracted to but cannot understand, and they fall by the wayside. It's not a complete picture. In Mrs. Ramsay, in *To the Lighthouse*, Virginia further rounded out the character. Mrs. Ramsay is not only Vanessa; she's also their mother, Julia Stephen.

To the Lighthouse is a magnificent book, and the autobiographical interest in it is wonderful. Virginia said she set out to exorcise herself of her parents' influence, that until she wrote that book she thought of her mother every day. Reading it, Vanessa was moved to tears, which was quite something for Vanessa. She said that it was quite extraordinary how, although they felt they had hardly known their mother, Virginia had managed to bring her so vividly to life. Virginia says she's certain that Vanessa's character helped her realize their mother's character in Mrs. Ramsay. She is very critical, too, of Mrs. Ramsay. She recognizes the seductiveness of her character but also the vanity of her need to control. There's a wonderful quote: "All this need of hers to give was vanity." This is what she also accuses Vanessa of.

WACHTEL You suggest that Vanessa became so accustomed to being at the centre of Virginia's writing that she was jealous of Vita Sackville-West, Virginia's lover for a time, more for usurping her role as literary subject in *Orlando* than for usurping her role in life.

DUNN Yes. Also her letters, the love letters. Virginia wrote wonderful letters to Vanessa—probably amongst her best. Vanessa valued these, and needed them, particularly at certain times in her life, such as early on, when she was married to Clive and missing Virginia enormously. She pleaded for letters, and Virginia wrote her beautiful ones. When Virginia started writing to Vita, Vanessa wrote to her, "I don't want you being unfaithful with your pen." These letters are wonderfully candid; and they do fit into my theory. You may well argue it's too neatly stereotypical, but they slip in there neatly time and time again.

WACHTEL When Virginia was almost sixty, not long before her suicide, she wrote to Vanessa, "Do you think we have the same pair of eyes, only different spectacles? I rather think that I am more nearly attached to you than sisters ought to be." Did Vanessa feel guilty or responsible when Virginia killed herself?

DUNN It's a question people always ask. Julian's death—in 1937, while driving an ambulance in the Spanish Civil War—was a blow that destroyed something in Vanessa. Virginia's suicide letter to her in a way explains why Vanessa did not collapse again after Virginia's death.

Virginia's suicide letter to Leonard is the most moving and noble letter I think anybody could write. She is utterly concerned for him. She tells him that he's been wonderful to her, has done everything for her, and that they have been the happiest couple there could be. But she cannot again face going into the madness alone. It's a most extraordinary letter. To Vanessa she writes much more intimately. I think the letter shows how far they have travelled together and how much they understand each other. For she says something like, "I wish I could tell you how much you mean to me, but I think you know." And that is all she says. Here is the proof of the intimacy of their relationship. With Leonard she had to go to such trouble to say, "You have been wonderful, it's not your fault." With Vanessa, all she needed to say was, "You know, you understand." And perhaps Vanessa did.

October 1991

Alice Munro

Alice Munro has been called a writer's writer—and many writers, both in Canada and internationally, do love and admire her work. But Alice Munro is also a reader's writer. She writes with intelligence and compassion, carrying the reader with her in her explorations of character, in search of some kind of understanding—no neat resolutions, just trying to figure things out in an elegant, moving way.

When Alice Munro began writing she described herself as a "shy, uncertain housewife" living on the west coast. She sent her stories to CBC Radio, where they were first broadcast, and she had work published in small magazines. Today, *The New Yorker* has first refusal on her work. This unmistakably Canadian writer writes and rewrites and meticulously crafts her stories, producing three or four a year, and a collection about every four years.

In 1990 Alice Munro won the $50,000 Molson Prize in honour of her work and the Trillium Award for *Friend of My Youth*, judged the best book published in Ontario. She'd already won three Governor-General's awards, the first in 1968 for her very first book, *Dance of the Happy Shades*.

Friend of My Youth is her seventh collection of short stories. A new book is a useful occasion to try to winkle out an interview from Alice Munro, who prefers to stay out of public view. She lives in Western Ontario, near the town where she grew up, and spends winters on Vancouver Island. She'd agreed to the interview at the last minute, informally, when we met at a friend's reading. Once she'd said yes, she was relaxed and candid. In the studio I asked her to read from the title story, about her mother and their uneasy relationship, and when she came to the phrase "the bitter lump of love I have carried all this time," her voice caught ever so slightly. Just a beat and she recovered; you couldn't hear it on the tape. Afterwards she expressed surprise at how it could affect her still.

————————

WACHTEL I'd like to go right back to the beginning. What is your earliest memory?

MUNRO It's such a rural memory, you'll think I'm making it up. I was too small to look over the wall of the pigpen, but I had climbed up on the boards and I was peering over, watching my uncle feed the pigs.

WACHTEL You grew up on a turkey and fox farm.

MUNRO It was a fox farm when I was a very small child. Then it became a fox and mink farm. After World War II, people didn't wear fox furs any more. Nobody minded the idea of wearing fur, but fox furs had become unfashionable. So we went out of business, and my father became a poultry farmer—chickens and turkeys.

WACHTEL When did you know you wanted to be a writer?

MUNRO I really can't remember. I think when I was about ten or eleven. Before that, I would tell myself stories a lot, and I would make up endings for stories that didn't satisfy me. *The Little Mermaid* is the one I chiefly remember because it has a *horribly* unhappy ending. She changes into foam on the sea, she doesn't get a soul; she doesn't get the prince or a soul. I thought that was just very hard luck.

WACHTEL What did you give her?

MUNRO I think I gave her the prince. I don't think I worried about the soul!

Then I used to think about being a movie star. I used to make up a lot of movie stories that I would be in. Somehow, from the movie-star bit, I slid into the writing-things-down bit. I started writing poetry and then stories. I was into it quite thoroughly by the time I was twelve.

WACHTEL You have told me that you come from an environment that is inhospitable to writers, that doesn't honour writers.

MUNRO I'm a descendant of a pioneer family. There are quite sensible ideas in such families—that it's very important for people to know how to do physical work. So I was trained to do domestic jobs, as the most important thing that I would ever have to do. Also I lived in an environment where there were no labour-saving devices; we didn't have running water or anything like that. I had to learn to work hard. We all read in our house, but it was seen as a luxury, something you did when everything else was done. There were stories in the community about women who had become readers, in the way that they might take up drinking, and how the men would come in from the fields and there would be cold grease in the frying-pan and no dinner ready, and under the bed there would be fluff-balls as big as your head, and it would all be because the women read! I've no doubt this happened. That kind of reading was probably a total escape. They probably read romances and things about royalty and stuff like that, the sort of stuff I like to read sometimes myself.

WACHTEL So it was very iconoclastic to think you could be a writer, in that environment.

MUNRO I very early on got the notion that my real life had to be hidden, had to be protected. I didn't think you could go to your teacher or your parents and tell them what you really thought about anything. I knew that was a bad idea. So I got used to this early. I didn't need encouragement or reassurance. I suppose I lived a very deceptive life, but it didn't bother me.

WACHTEL You said once that there's a betrayal involved in leaving home, especially if you're from a working-class family, because you begin to talk differently, and that you feel guilty about that.

MUNRO Certainly it isn't one of my major guilts, but it does create a gap. Class divisions used to be a little more definite than they are now. There is still a different way of talking, though it's not so pronounced. In some places in Britain, for instance, if you left home and got a BBC accent and then went back, people would not care for that. But you did become a different person in a lot of superficial ways to make yourself acceptable in the world away from home, and you were apt to feel a bit of a phony, I suppose, when you went back home. Usually I take on protective colouration very readily, without having to think about it. So there isn't a big conflict. I generally do what is expected.

WACHTEL The title of one of your books is *Who Do You Think You Are?*, a reprimand that alludes to the inescapability of your background.

MUNRO I find this very interesting and complicated. In the story, the first time someone says "Who do you think you are?" it's a teacher reprimanding a student in class for trying to shine, to show off. I was brought up to believe that that is absolutely the worst thing you could do. I don't know if this has a Scottish or a Presbyterian origin—it seems to me it's rather Canadian. It wasn't confined to my background. "Who do you think you are?" comes the minute you begin to let out a little bit of who you would like to be, as soon as you start constructing somebody that is yourself. Of course, we all construct ourselves, so there's always a little worry about this. Are you trying to shine? I think most of us would rather undergo severe punishment than ridicule. It's so difficult to think that you may be acting foolishly. I think that keeps a lot of people from trying this self-construction business.

WACHTEL You had a lot of different jobs on the way to becoming a writer. There are several that surprised me—one was picking tobacco?

MUNRO Yes, I picked tobacco when I was at university, one of the summers. I also waitressed one summer. Everybody's waitressed. One summer before that, when I was a high-school girl, I worked as a servant for a family in Toronto. At that time it was thought that country girls made good servants, which they did. I knew how to do a lot of things that most sixteen-year-old girls didn't know how to do. So I was fetched down from the country. I didn't like it.

WACHTEL It sounds like a Victorian novel: pluck the country girl and plop her into this upper-class home. Did it sharpen your writing antennae?

MUNRO Oh, certainly. It was probably a very important experience that way, because I saw all sorts of class things that totally surprised me. I thought I knew a lot, because I had read a lot, but I really had hardly any experience. I was a very naïve person in some ways. Being a servant in a household, you see things about your employers that they don't show to people who are their equals, because the ideal servant has no eyes or ears. But I had them. I wrote a story about that, in *Dance of the Happy Shades.* I think the story's called "Sunday Afternoon." It's a very early story, it's not that great, but it came out of that experience.

WACHTEL You're the eldest of three children. Did that give you a sense of extra responsibility? How do you think that affected you?

MUNRO It gave me a certain amount of bossiness, which I conceal some of the time. I was five years older than my brother and six years older than my sister. I thought I was bringing them up in the right way. They have a different idea about this, I think. I enjoyed it, and I had a sense of power. I had to do a lot of housework because my mother became ill when I was eleven or twelve, so I was doing fairly heavy work in my teens, but that gave me a great sense of achievement and responsibility. Bossing people around, saying, "Don't track dirt over that floor, I've just scrubbed it," and all those things. It was much easier than being a teenager who was expected to do chores under someone's supervision. I got to be the boss.

WACHTEL The first real story you ever wrote was about the death of your mother; it's called "The Peace of Utrecht." The title story in your most recent book, *Friend of My Youth*, is about a woman who's thinking about her mother, who died young—the "bitter lump of love" she has held in relation to her mother. *Friend of My Youth* is dedicated to the memory of your mother. Can you tell me about that relationship?

MUNRO It was a very difficult relationship. Mothers and daughters generally have fairly complex relationships, and ours was made much more so by my mother's illness. She had Parkinson's disease, which was not diagnosed for a long time. Parkinson's has very peculiar symptoms so that it can seem in the beginning like a neurotic, self-chosen affliction. And it was seen as such by some in the family. It also has some rather bizarre effects later on. The voice becomes thickened and eating becomes difficult. There's no control over saliva. There are lots of things that are very difficult for a teenager to face in a parent.

All that made me very self-protective, because for one thing I didn't want to get trapped. In families like ours it is the oldest daughter's job to stay home and look after people when they're in that situation, until they die. Instead, I got a scholarship and went to university. There is enormous guilt about doing that, but at the time you're so busy protecting yourself that you simply push it under, and then you suffer from it later. But I think if you're realistic at all you also look at what you had to do. There were all these fairly hard problems to solve when I was seventeen, eighteen.

WACHTEL Do you feel regret now?

MUNRO That I didn't take the chance of relating in a different way? Yes, I feel terrible regret, but I also feel that it's practically impossible at that age to do so, so I don't think I feel an unreasonable guilt about that. I wish I could meet my mother as I feel now, but—and I think this is true between all mothers and daughters—by the time the daughter gets enough confidence that she doesn't feel threatened by her mother, that she knows her mother is not going to change her into somebody that her mother wants her to be, then, quite often, the mother is dead. Because to get to be this kind of person, you're probably forty-five or fifty years old.

I don't think that much about my relationship with my mother and what it did to me. I sometimes feel terrible regret about her, what her life must have been like. Often, when I'm enjoying something, I think of how meagre her rewards were and how much courage, in a way, she needed to go on living. I appreciate all that, but I also feel so sad that it had to be that way. Now I think there is more care available for people in her situation. They aren't quite as isolated as she was. There's more recognition altogether of illness and that the people afflicted are human.

WACHTEL The title story in *Friend of My Youth* is about a woman and her mother, but then it takes off and it allows the mother to tell her own story. It's about a love triangle, about two sisters and a farm worker, whom the mother knew when she was young. I got the sense, in the way the story circles around, that you were trying to figure something out when you were writing it.

MUNRO I was trying to figure out why I needed to write this story! The germ of it was given to me in the story about the two sisters and the farm worker. I thought about them and I thought about their self-dramatization, with the aid of their religion, and what happened to them. Then suddenly, without my making a decision, my mother's story began to weave around it. When I started I was going to write about Flora and Ellie. Then I wrote about my mother, circling around the Flora and Ellie story. Then I began to write about writing a story, which is where I finally end up. Then I come back to the mother.

I knew I was struggling with the subject matter of my mother. I hadn't thought I'd tackle that part of my life ever again. In fact, when I wrote that story I really thought I had moved on from autobiographical or personal stories. What interested me in the story was this idea that, after a while, we don't want the stories changed, even in a better way. The dream business...I did have dreams like this for years. The mother appears in the dream and things aren't so bad. Well okay, be happy about it. But you've constructed your whole personality, and your feelings have their roots in something different and you can't quite give that up. So I thought, this is a really interesting layeredness of feeling and I want to write about it. That ties in with how I would have seen the story of Flora, at first in that very classic way—the teenage girl imagines the story as she would write the novel, the classic tragedy. Then it's all turned around by the idea that Flora might be working in a department store and going out with a man or something, which stirs the ingredients around and you've got a whole new world to deal with.

WACHTEL Is that part of writing stories? To try to figure something out? Do you ever write stories where you already know everything at the beginning and you just put them together?

MUNRO I don't usually bother to write that kind of story any more because it doesn't interest me enough. It works, but it doesn't give me enough pleasure. Now when I write a story I'm always trying to figure out what the story is all about—not how it will work, but what it's really about. This to me is the pleasure of writing.

WACHTEL Many traditional stories lead to a moment of insight, an epiphany, that sort of thing. Your stories have moments of insight —

MUNRO Yes, and then they're proved wrong!

WACHTEL Or there's something that in one instance happens, a moment of accidental clarity, then it evaporates; they're that ephemeral.

MUNRO The moment evaporates, or the insight leads to something else. That's what I meant when I said flippantly that they're wrong. I want the stories to keep going on. I want the story to exist somewhere so that, in a way, it's still happening, or happening over and over again. I don't want it to be shut up in the book and put away.

WACHTEL That kind of open-endedness also implies that things don't necessarily improve or get better, that there isn't really—as in the title of one of your books—a progress of love.

MUNRO I haven't lived a whole life yet, so I can't tell you. We'll do an interview sometime later! But that doesn't depress me, the idea that things don't "improve." If you ask me what I believe as a person, I'd say that life gets better, or one's ability to put up with it gets better. But things change. One of the things that interests me so much in writing and in observing people is that things keep changing. Cherished beliefs change. Ways of dealing with life change. The importance of certain things in life changes. All this seems to me endlessly interesting—that is the thing that doesn't change or that I certainly hope doesn't change. If you find life interesting, it just goes on being so.

WACHTEL Some critics have found *Friend of My Youth* sad, elegiac, that sort of thing. Is it misguided to expect happiness in modern fiction?

MUNRO I'd like to think that there are lots of periods of happiness in the stories. It's all muddled up: happiness, sadness, depression, elation. As I said, the constant happiness is curiosity. I wouldn't set out to write a story that I thought was depressing, because that would depress me. But I notice that sometimes other people's stories that I like very much are criticized as being depressing. And I feel very puzzled about the person who's making this judgment and what they like to read or what their lives are like. Maybe a lot of people are happy all the time.

WACHTEL I want to try out a theory on you. One of the ways you exhibit your craft as a writer is that you give us in these stories a profound sense of absence. There are absences everywhere: deaths, vanished worlds, missing spouses, broken marriages, one character even has a missing eye. What do you think?

MUNRO I can't deal with theories very well. But yes, absences certainly interest me. Loss, which everyone experiences all the time. We keep losing ourselves and the worlds we used to live in. Whether this is more a factor in modern life, I don't know. I think maybe it is. Nowadays people do go from one sort of life to another. It's not uncommon now to go from one marriage to another or from being one sort of person to being an entirely different kind of person. So you've got all these rooms in your head that you've shut off but that you can remember. I think some people don't really bother much with remembering; it seems a useless activity. But most writers are addicted to it. I suppose I am, too.

WACHTEL Your stories are getting very, very complex. It's a bit like a three-dimensional chess game sometimes. There are so many layers of things going on and crosscutting in time and memory. Or it's like a pile of snapshots that are all shuffled up. Why do you do that?

MUNRO I just like to. I can't get a grasp on what I'm trying to talk about unless I do that. I don't do it to make things difficult. You might think it's the challenge of writing this way, but I don't think that's true. It's that I see things now in this way, and there is absolutely no other way I can deal with the material of fiction. You'll have something that is awkward, that is difficult to work in, and you think, I can cut this, I can streamline this, and it doesn't work. It's got to go in somehow.

WACHTEL At the beginning of one of your stories a character taking a creative writing course is told not to try to put in too many things at once, so she makes this long list of all the things she wants to make sure she gets in there, and hands it in as an appendix to her story.

MUNRO Of course I haven't done that and don't know of anybody who has, but it seems to me that if you wrote the sort of story she is advised to write, you'd be very worried afterwards, thinking, But I didn't mention that and that was also part of what was going on at the time, and I didn't say that afterwards, and so on. To me, what you have when you pull all these things out is not the story. I suppose this is a kind of anti-minimalist way of writing. I can enjoy minimalist stories. They seem to me to have a singular force, but I couldn't enjoy writing one.

WACHTEL That's because yours have a multiple force. In a story in *Friend of My Youth* called "Hold Me Fast, Don't Let Me Pass" the narrator ponders questions like: What makes a man happy? What makes a woman happy? Do you know what makes you happy? Are you happy?

MUNRO Yes. It's as I said, it's being interested. This is the thing I hope will never leave me—a very high level of interest most of the time. When that vanishes, which it sometimes does temporarily, I think it would be awful to live like this, going through the motions of life. But we all experience times like that. It's also very important to me to love certain human beings and be loved by them—then what happens in their lives is very important. But underneath, the thing that would help me survive anything, I think, is this interestedness.

WACHTEL In your fiction there is often sex without guilt. In fact, given the complexity and the attentiveness of all the characters, I am surprised at how little guilt there is generally.

MUNRO That's part of being interested. If you find something interesting—really interesting—it's very hard to regret it. You may think, Oh, that was frivolous behaviour, that was selfish behaviour, that was perhaps damaging behaviour—but wasn't it interesting. Why would a person who feels this way now about something have felt that way then? Regret fades away in the face of interest.

WACHTEL Why are you so interested in adultery?

MUNRO Adultery is like modern theatre in the adventure it offers in ordinary people's lives. I suppose it always did, but much more in men's lives than in women's in days gone by, and more in rich, idle people's lives than in ordinary people's lives. The opportunities have become much greater. The guilt about it may be less, but it's still there. It's a way of expressing themselves, perhaps, for people who have no other way, because people get boxed in and there's this role it's possible to play, very briefly, which gives people a sense of still existing. Then, of course, it leads into all kinds of other things. It's a drama in people's lives that I think a writer is naturally attracted to.

WACHTEL Like your earlier books, *Friend of My Youth* has been enormously successful. Do you allow yourself to enjoy this success or do you still cling to feelings of insecurity?

MUNRO I do both: I enjoy it and I'm insecure at the same time.

September 1990

interview prepared in collaboration
with Richard Handler
and Sandra Rabinovitch

Jonathan Raban

Jonathan Raban was born in Norfolk, England, in 1942. He was so fascinated at age seven by *The Adventures of Huckleberry Finn* that when he grew up he decided to pilot a sixteen-foot aluminum skiff down the Mississippi. He wrote about the adventure in *Old Glory: An American Voyage* (1981). His first travel book, *Arabia Through the Looking Glass* (1979), was prompted by curiosity about his Arab neighbours in London. In the mid-1980s Raban determined that the best way to rediscover his home country would be to sail a thirty-foot ketch, the *Gosfield Maid*, around the British Isles. The result was *Coasting* (1986)—a book set during the Falklands War that is part reportage and part autobiography. In it Raban tries to get some perspective on what he calls "the home I'd always been running away from."

A decade after Raban's journey down the Mississippi, he undertook a second voyage to America, retracing the immigrant experience in the New World. He began on a cargo ship, stopped in New York, travelled to the South, to Seattle and finally to the Florida Keys. His account of the trip, *Hunting Mister Heartbreak*, was published in 1991. In a curious twist, Raban himself ended up as an immigrant to America, and now lives in Seattle, where he keeps a boat and recently edited *The Oxford Book of the Sea*. He has also written one novel—*Foreign Land* (1985)—about an elderly Englishman who returns to Britain after spending his life abroad.

I met Jonathan Raban in Vancouver, when he attended the International Writers' Festival there. In a worn leather jacket and felt hat, he flashed charm and wit, betraying how he deftly manages to negotiate the world in his travels.

WACHTEL You've described yourself as a timid traveller, but you once took a sixteen-foot aluminium boat 2,000 miles down the Mississippi. And without any seafaring experience—with just, I think, a three-week crash course, you sailed around the British Isles on your own in a thirty-foot ketch. For a timid man, you put yourself through some pretty adventurous experiences.

RABAN Modify timid to stupid. You never know what you're taking on at the beginning. These things always have the grand clarity of simple ideas. You wake up at three o'clock in the morning and you think how nice it would be to try to revisit home by sailing around it, coming by sea to every place you've ever known in your life. Or, what a way to string the United States together: to drift down the Mississippi. You have a simple picture in your head of a small rowboat, gently adrift on a purling stream. You can do these things precisely because you don't know what's in store for you. By the time you've got a boat and you're at the top of the river, or you're beginning to set sail around the British Isles, you're in too deep to draw back. But I *am* a timid traveller and certainly a timid sailor. I'm the kind of person who begins to sweat slightly when the wind blows more than fifteen miles an hour and begins to gibber when it reaches twenty-five miles an hour. But I like it.

WACHTEL Do you like what it does to you—the kind of concentration these intense travelling experiences require of you?

RABAN I think that's an exact description of what happens. It *does* intensify the mind no end, and you do concentrate. So much travel through landscape is done in a purely voyeuristic way by people who have no purpose there. The moment you're navigating, for instance, you have a job, and that job is real; it's a life-and-death job simply to stay alive and orient yourself within the world in which you're travelling. I also discovered that travelling down the Mississippi in a small boat suddenly gave me a great deal in common with the people I was meeting in the towns along the way. They were river people, they had boats, we were able to gossip about our engines and the tricks of the river, about shoots and wing dams and slews and all the rest of the river talk. During the course of travelling down that river I became an accredited riverman. I had a real job and I learned the language.

What I hate is travelling *across* the landscape, in a car or a train, where you feel completely disconnected from the world in which you're travelling, where you're a mere spectator of it.

WACHTEL You manage to strike up marvellous conversations with people. How do you get people to accept you so quickly?

RABAN You have to remember that the books I write are very highly shaped versions of real experience. They're not the log of the trip, they're not a literal record. I don't carry a tape-recorder; I use my memory rather than a notebook when I'm writing. What I like to do is to try to distil the whole experience in memory and then write out of the memory rather than trying to write a piece of literal reportage about the journey.

It's curious. I've written both fiction and these books that people insist on calling travel books, which is a term I hate. The two processes are quite different. Writing a novel, I sit down and sort of dream myself into the situation that my characters are currently undergoing, until it seems to me that it's really happened and what I'm doing is remembering it, then I write from that memory. Almost the reverse process takes place in writing about a journey. I let the whole thing settle to the point where all the inessentials have been forgotten and the thing begins to sit in one's mind, like something one has imagined. Once the journey has become a sufficiently *imaginary* memory, then it begins to be possible to start recreating it on the page, in a fictive and gainful way. So when you talk about striking up conversations, I don't know that I really do strike up conversations. Those conversations in the book are pieces of dialogue that have been distilled out of memory and experience that happened rather a long time ago.

WACHTEL   That's a beautifully symmetrical image—the parallels between the two kinds of writing.

RABAN   I don't think they are two kinds of writing; I think they're one. I don't think that one changes hats.

WACHTEL   You have a witty and self-mocking style. When you write that you wanted to run away to sea you observe that you were almost forty instead of the standard thirteen. Why did an almost-forty-year-old want to run away to sea?

RABAN   That's a very hard question to answer, apart from admitting that there's probably an element of juvenility in my makeup that I'm never going to escape, and better now—at the age of forty-eight—to simply admit to it. But no, there must be some less glib answer than that. At the time—this was in 1981—my life was in something of a mess in London. It was a standard, midlife thing; at forty, you want to come to terms with where you stand. That meant making a reckoning with England, my own past and the nation's political past. This was just after Mrs. Thatcher came to power. In fact, while I was writing *Coasting* the Falklands War was taking place. It was England at a very, very interesting period of its modern history. And to come to terms both with one's own personal past and with the national past and the national present, I needed to get away. In order to come home you do sometimes have to run away.

WACHTEL   As you say, home is the hardest place to get into sharp focus.

RABAN   I believe that absolutely, and this is something these books that are called travel books deal with terribly directly. If you think of Bruce Chatwin's *In Patagonia*, Paul Theroux's *Great Railway*

Bazaar, Colin Thubron's *Behind the Wall,* they are not about their ostensible subjects. You're not really reading them because you want to find out about Patagonia or what India looks like from the windows of a train or to really meet the Chinese. Some readers may, but I think the majority go to these books because they identify with that solitary person in the centre who is trying to make sense of a strange world. And it's his alienation, or her alienation, within that world, the attempt to try to reconcile his or her own presence with the complexities of the world as it presents itself, that people identify with. What people are responding to in this current fashion for travel books is a sense of how un-at-home they find themselves at home.

Bruce Chatwin, in the middle of the Australian bush, is a perfect emblem for the way in which one might find oneself, sitting in a commuter train coming into Toronto or New York or wherever and trying to work out why one is here. I think it's that question—what am I doing here?, the title of Chatwin's posthumous collection of essays—which these books attempt to answer. It's that question readers most identify with. All these landscapes are really symbolic. They are inner landscapes. They're not the real landscape of China or of Patagonia. They're much more like landscapes of the mind.

WACHTEL In *Coasting,* the book about sailing around Britain, you've chosen a title that evokes that. You acknowledge it, alluding to lazy schooldays, but you also say that the coaster is someone who "uses the minimum of effort to go down a slippery slope on the margin of things." I already know that the minimum of effort is just a pose. You want to make the reader feel comfortable, but you're sweating. I'm interested in that life on the margin.

RABAN I've always been very interested in the margins, partly because I grew up on the margins. My father is a priest in the Church of England, so I grew up in a succession of clergy houses of one kind or another, on the outside of any community that we were in. We're talking class-stratified societies here; we weren't the gentry, but we had affiliations to the gentry; we weren't the village working class, but our income was very much more like a village working-class income than a gentry income. The vicarage was this awkward middle ground between the two which had access to both worlds but was rejected by both worlds. One felt an outsider in both.

There was no place in that society, as I grew up, in which I could say, yes, I belong there. The only place I belonged was this strange house called the vicarage, and the vicarage was an island. It seems to me that in some funny way I've stayed on that island ever since. I haven't been able to get off.

WACHTEL That's so curious to someone from this perspective. The vicarage plays such a central part in our picture of England, as in the works of Barbara Pym.

RABAN I do think Barbara Pym sentimentalizes her clergymen. She very clearly sees clerical life from outside. The mere use of the phrase "clerical life" conjures up George Eliot. Go to George Eliot and then you see the real outsiderdom of the priest even in nineteenth-century society. I grew up in the vicarage at the very time when secularism was on the rise—this was the post-World War II, 1950s sudden decline in church-going. My father represented a whole series of beliefs which were being rejected out-of-hand by practically everybody in the community except those who paid old-fashioned lip-service to them. And this was a curious position to be in. I also became an atheist at the age of twelve, which didn't make life in the vicarage any easier.

WACHTEL Travel books and novels obviously share a common history.

RABAN The journey is, of course, the oldest story form in the world.

WACHTEL And novels such as Defoe's *Robinson Crusoe* or Sterne's *A Sentimental Journey*, or even Swift's *Gulliver's Travels*, are modelled on this kind of travel motif. But when you sit down to write a novel you get outside the persona you create when you write the travel stories.

RABAN The persona varies. I'm glad you used the word "persona," because you have indicated a major truth, which is that that first person, that "I" who resides at the centre of nearly everybody's travel book, is not actually quite the same as the author. He is a character. The character in my books changes a lot, I think, from book to book. The "I" in *Hunting Mister Heartbreak* is very definitely different both from me and from the "I" in previous books. I have to say that he is altogether nicer than I am. You'd much sooner meet him than meet me. He is earnestly in quest of a place to live. He comes to the United States with all those innocent immigrant assumptions about it and tries to find a place for himself in this strange world. He's not a quarter as vain and prickly as I am. I quite like him.

WACHTEL Why is the "I" of *Hunting Mister Heartbreak* different from the "I" of *Coasting* or the "I" who went down the Mississippi?

RABAN *Coasting*, my English autobiography, is about growing up within a class system and taking stock of it. *Hunting Mister Heartbreak* is about the hopeful immigrant.

There's an evolution of these personae. It started for me with a book called *Arabia Through the Looking Glass*, which came out a long time ago. That book was probably the nearest I've ever come to writing a straight travel book. It took off from the tradition of English travel writing, which is comic writing really. It's the Englishman abroad, and the Englishman never quite gets things. He's quite sure of his own values. He's rather like Alice in Wonderland. Alice is terribly certain of herself. She's such a prig! For that first first person, I borrowed—that's why it's called *Arabia Through the Looking Glass*—that Alice-like attitude towards foreigners. In successive books that self began to mutate.

WACHTEL When you filter the experience of a journey, you shape it and give it some sort of plot. Do you also have to find a character to suit the shape of each journey?

RABAN Exactly. You're saying it better than I could.

WACHTEL A few years ago, when you finally came out and wrote a novel—*Foreign Land*—you were quoted as saying that one of your motivations in writing fiction was that you had come to loathe that "rabbity innocence of the wide-eyed traveller."

RABAN Oh yes, I did. I do now. The next book is going to be a novel. I've had enough of writing in the first person and badly want to get out of it. Changing personal pronouns in writing is terribly important. You have to see how the world looks through other people's eyes. You can do that to an extent, within the first person, but sometimes—particularly writing a long book like the one I have just finished—you ache from the constriction of living within that tall, narrow capital letter, which strikes its way down. I've been reading a lot of proofs lately, and opening the proofs and seeing that I, I, I, I—those vertical strokes on the page...

WACHTEL But you are a tall, lean man. You must identify with that?

RABAN Not so lean, alas!

WACHTEL There is an apparent autobiographical quality about these travel books, these records of a journey, because of the I. Some critics say that you're too coy, you don't tell enough. Others say *Coasting* is clearly autobiographical, because it's your England. How do you decide how much of yourself to reveal?

RABAN I don't think you make that decision; the book, in a way, makes that decision for you. All writers are in some sense secretaries to their own books, which emerge by a process of dictation. You start the thing off and on the first few pages you're in control, but if the book has any real life of its own, *it* begins to take control, *it* begins to demand certain things of you, which you may or may not live up to, and it imposes shapes and patterns on you; it calls forth the quality of experience it needs. Or that's what you hope happens. I don't just sit, making conscious decisions externally about how much of my experience I am going to use. I look at the page, and I see what the page needs; the page needs that, so that goes there.

WACHTEL You've said that when you actually set off on a journey you try not to make specific plans or to have too much structure, that "the true and sincere traveller"—quoting Thoreau—casts oneself adrift in the world to, as you put it, "dog-paddle with the stream."

RABAN *Hunting Mister Heartbreak* represents for me an interesting development in this line of thinking. I *don't* like making arrangements. What I wanted to do, writing *Hunting Mister Heartbreak*, was to write about America in seven chapters. I had my immigrant figure, I had the notion of America and I gave myself seven chapters, but I would not know where I was going from chapter's end to chapter's end. That was the essential point of it.

I'd grown tired of the approach in which you make the journey, you take notes and then you come back and try to turn the whole thing into a story, even though the story might want to lead somewhere else. I thought, this time I'll let the book take control and dictate to me where I go next. So I would go to the United States, spend two months living there, playing at my immigrant life, then I would go back to London and write it. Once I was getting near the end of each chapter, I'd ask myself where the book wanted to go next and I'd go back to whatever point in the United States the book seemed to demand, which eventually got me to Seattle and the Florida Keys.

WACHTEL Seven chapters. That's a biblical number. Why did you want to do America in seven chapters?

RABAN Seven is a magical number, and it's the number that means quite a lot but not very many. Five is too short, and thirteen would be impossible. But seven is the number of diversity and is also the number of containment.

WACHTEL Why did you decide to embark on this immigrant journey into what you call the New World?

RABAN First of all because—you've quoted Thoreau, and I love this passage—"true and sincere travelling is no pastime but is as serious as the grave, or any other part of the human journey." It seems to me that the truest and most sincere traveller is the immigrant. In this travelling century the immigrant is the person who really travels, and he travels with a heartfeltness that no tourist, no traveller moving through the world for the hell of it, because he has the dollars, can possibly imitate. I wanted to catch some of that immigrant seriousness. Also, my Ph.D. thesis—which I started in 1964 and still haven't finished, and I don't suppose now I ever will—is about immigration in the Jewish-American novel from 1874 to the present day. It really sprang out of the fact that I was enjoying reading Philip Roth and Saul Bellow. But you have to dress that up and present it in some way, so I did an awful lot of research into all those novels and autobiographies of immigrants—Jewish and otherwise—to the United States. I've always been interested in the figure of the immigrant and know something, academically, about that. I wanted, in the pursuit of true and sincere travelling, to plant myself in the shoes of an immigrant. Finally I found I was actually wearing those shoes.

WACHTEL Your life is now imitating art because you're living in Seattle as an immigrant. How did that happen?

RABAN I came to Seattle because I wanted to explore what it might be like to be a Korean experiencing America in the late part of the twentieth century. I'd written about my own and European attitudes towards America. I wanted to get a slant from a much more representative immigrant today, somebody coming from Cambodia or Korea or China. I also wanted to get the Pacific side of the United States into the book, and I wanted to get a Pacific Rim immigrant's view of the United States. So I came to Seattle to talk to Koreans, go to Korean churches, mingle with Koreans and see how far the Korean experience of America corresponded with my experience of America. I fell in love with the city, and then I fell in love with a person in the city. Now I'm living in the city.

WACHTEL En route to Seattle, how did you decide at the end of each chapter where to go next?

RABAN It usually became clear about halfway through the chapter—an answering chord coming from another place. Sometimes it was social, sometimes geographical, sometimes it was simply where I wanted to go next. I knew roughly where the book would end up. I knew it would end with the decay of everything meant by the American Dream, somewhere down on the Florida Keys. I knew the first chapter would be set on that mythic transatlantic crossing and the second chapter would be set in New York. At the point at which I began the book, I had no idea where the middle would be. But my own exhaustion and fury with living in New York for nearly three months propelled me in search of some small, self-contained centre of life—a small town in Alabama. Equally, my experience in Alabama began to lead me very securely towards Seattle. The chapters would start making suggestions about halfway through, saying, "It looks like you're bound there."

WACHTEL It struck me that, whether in New York or in Alabama, often you were staying in someone else's house, or you were mistaken for someone else. What happens to your identity when you're adrift this way?

RABAN I'm very glad you picked that up because the plot of the book is about precisely that—finding a new and a borrowed skin, in every chapter another person to become. In each chapter my name changes. You know how in America people never get your name right—you're Rabin, Rayburn, Raybone, Rainbird, everything except what you were christened. Each chapter hinges on these identity changes. In each new place I try to see what kind of a person I'm expected to be, and with that person comes another name. There's a long and, I hope, quite complicated and subtle identity game going on throughout the book.

WACHTEL Is this something that happens whenever you travel? Is it a function of being a traveller—not so much lost as adrift?

RABAN I don't think you have to be a traveller to experience this, except in the sense that we are travellers all the time. Moving from the hotel down to your studio this morning was, I suppose, a journey of a sort. As is trying to establish relations with strangers—which we in the twentieth century do more and more of the time. We no longer live in communities where for most of the day we are among our familiars—people we grew up with, were at school with, people we know intimately. We are dealing constantly with strangers. Even if we never stir from the confines of one particular twentieth-century city, most of our encounters during the day will be with strangers.

So travelling, it seems to me, becomes the central metaphor for that kind of twentieth-century, urban relationship. We have to find our feet very fast, decide who we are, decide who other people are expecting us to be, decide who they want to be in our eyes, and make a series of delicate negotiations with these strangers. Just as we're doing now, as we talk to each other between two microphones, you and I, who met about twenty minutes ago and are carrying on what has the appearance of an intimate conversation. We're seizing on those things in each other's voice that sound as if we can make connections with them. We're having a very characteristic urban encounter right now. And it is the encounter between the traveller and the stranger.

WACHTEL Are you happy in Seattle, staying in one spot?

RABAN Absolutely. There is a boat parked about two hundred yards away from the house. The boat so far has sailed up to the top of Vancouver Island, just beyond Desolation Sound, and down again. Having that boat, and that water—the water of the Pacific Northwest has me completely hooked. Seattle is a wonderful place to be able to travel from. There's travel of the most watery kind, right on one's doorstep.

October 1990

interview prepared in collaboration
with Sandra Rabinovitch

Andre Dubus

In one of Andre Dubus's short stories, a mother tells her son, "We don't have to live great lives, we just have to understand and survive the ones we've got." Pain, vulnerability and hard-won strength are the veins that run just below the surface of Dubus's fiction, set in the blue-collar world of waitresses and bartenders, mechanics and labourers. Infused with compassion, his stories and novellas revolve around relationships between men and women, the Catholic faith and the loss of permanence.

After eight books of fiction, including *Adultery and Other Choices* (1977), *Voices from the Moon* (1984) and *The Last Worthless Evening* (1986), Andre Dubus published his first work of non-fiction, *Broken Vessels* (1991), a collection of personal essays which is in part about the tragedy that devastated his own life. In the early hours of July 23, 1986, he stopped on the highway to help a stranded motorist, and while flagging down an oncoming car he was hit. Dubus lost one leg and the use of the other, and underwent twelve operations and years of pain and therapy. Then his third wife left him, taking with her their two small daughters.

For a while Dubus couldn't write at all. Finally, he began to write about what had happened, and this became the title piece in *Broken Vessels*. Here is a man determined to be honest, even when overcome with confusion and despair.

Andre Dubus became a MacArthur Fellow (the "genius" award—more than $300,000 over five years, no strings attached) in 1988. He is much admired by other writers and critics. Ellen Lesser, in *The Village Voice*, wrote that Dubus's stories "cut deep enough to leave you weeping or gasping for air." Short-story aficionados always include Dubus in their ten best American writers lists.

Dubus was born in Louisiana in 1936 and still has a slight Cajun accent underneath his New England speech. I spoke to him from his home in Haverhill, Massachusetts, just north of Boston.

WACHTEL The American writer Tobias Wolff, in his introduction to your book *Broken Vessels*, writes that the real possibility of the personal essay is to catch oneself in the act of being human. What does that mean for you?

DUBUS In a personal essay you are writing about yourself and trying to find, not the whole truth, but a truth. Then you learn that truth is something that was happening in your own life. Certainly, in some of these things I wrote, I actually caught myself, as he says, in the act of being human.

WACHTEL Being human seems to me to mean admitting to all sorts of doubts and weaknesses and needs, and not hiding behind the authorial mask of fiction.

DUBUS That's true. A book of essays, for me, is a very different experience from a book of fiction, because in fiction I've always been able to say, "Oh well, that's what she said in the story, but that has nothing to do with me." In an essay I can't say that because there I am.

WACHTEL The personal essay by its very nature makes us feel that we know you, that we know about your life and who you are, but of course even the confessional form is a kind of construct. Were you conscious as you were writing of the kind of persona you wanted to create in this book?

DUBUS No, I wasn't. Writing is a very strange process: everything you're talking about is happening while the act of writing is going on. While I'm writing—that's when I face the exposure, that's when the right word comes, or the temptation to use the wrong word and duck out, the temptation to skip something. That's when I always have to bear down and try to write as closely to what is the truth as I can feel with my senses and with my heart. After that's done and typed up and sent off it begins to feel less like me and more like something I wrote. Does that make sense?

WACHTEL Yes. You often write about what it means to be a man, about masculine values and image. You grew up in the South, in a small town in southern Louisiana, and you spent more than five years in the Marines. What do you feel shaped your own sense of male identity?

DUBUS Oh boy! You know, I don't know the answer to that. When I was younger, I was a sissy and small—I mean, I was 105 pounds when I got my driver's licence. In the fifties a 105-pound guy with his mother's car was not really an attractive item on a young woman's agenda—they liked quarterbacks and stuff. Later, when I taught in the sixties, I was very jealous of my students because then girls started liking skinny guys with long hair. Being small and sensitive was certainly partly the reason I became a Marine. The Marine Corps is full of small men! Actually, Tobias Wolff, who was a Green Beret, told me a lot of little guys joined the Green Berets, too.

Also, I respected my father, who stressed honour. He had very high standards about that, and I certainly looked up to that, too. And you can't leave out Gary Cooper; he was a shaping influence. Gary Cooper was a good person to have around: he was kind to women and children and loyal to his friends, and nobody crossed him!

WACHTEL But he was a quiet man, wasn't he? Wasn't he the strong, silent type?

DUBUS Yes, I'm not quiet, I've never been cool and I've never been able to live up to my standards!

WACHTEL You write about your role as a man in relation to your children and also in relation to the women in your life. You describe an incident in an essay called "Running" concerning one of your sons. You're jogging with your teenage boy and suddenly he turns red, he looks sick and you tell him to stop but he doesn't. And in a remarkably compact sentence you describe your reaction to this: "I believed he should stop, hoped he would not, remembered first aid I had learned years ago." Can you tell me about these complicated feelings?

DUBUS It's a very strange thing. I think if it had been a daughter I would have said, "That's it, we're stopping." You know, we *are* animals and men feel differently about their sons. There's something about being the father of a son that makes you allow him to take a risk because you know he needs to. I knew that if he actually made that run—like me, he was a small boy—it would be important to him, and I wasn't really worried that he would die. What I really wanted, of course, was for him to have the courage and the resilience to go on when he really couldn't any more, because I knew he would need that strength in whatever life he chose. Of course, a woman does too, but I'm a very tender-hearted father towards daughters, much more protective. I think had I been running with a teenage daughter, I would have said, "Honey, it's hot and, you know, this could kill you, and let's walk, you and Daddy." I'm not saying that's good or bad, I'm just saying that's the way it is.

WACHTEL In another essay you write about how you feel it's necessary for your sons to prove themselves through fighting, by being neither cowards nor bullies, and you talk about how you too had had to prove yourself to yourself. Is fighting part of being a man?

DUBUS No, I don't think so. I really think that men and women would be more fulfilled if we all lived according to the ideals of Christ, which are love and tenderness. I actually believe in turning the other cheek. What I've never understood, though, is what you do when it's somebody else's cheek. That's what that essay was about—having to prevent violence against a third party who could not defend herself. For boys in school there's always somebody who challenges you in a physical way, and unfortunately I don't think it works to tell a ten-year-old to turn the other cheek. A boy that age has to learn to swing back. My sons and I didn't learn until we were older. It's a way to prepare yourself for something much more important later on, so that when your boss or your wife or your best friend wants you to sell your soul for a better condominium you have to say, "Wait a minute, I'm being bullied here and I've got some moral integrity I have to keep intact." Does that make any sense? I'm saying it shouldn't be physical, but it turns out that at a certain age among boys there are these physical challenges and it's important for the boy to learn then to do what he is afraid to do.

It is certainly important for girls too, but generally it happens to them in a different way. You know, it's so hard to be an adult human being, and so many people sell out and live lives they don't want, that you've got to decide really early—these are my boundaries, this is where I stand, this is what I stand for. Dietrich Bonhoeffer, the German philosopher executed for trying to assassinate Hitler, had an entire page in his book *Ethics* about what you do to a human being when you slap that person's face—the deep violation of the person. It would be wonderful if human beings never felt the urge to assert themselves physically, or in any way, over other people, but that's not how the species is.

WACHTEL You also write about manliness in terms of your desire to be a provider and a protector. In one instance you write about wanting to hunt or fish, to be an old-style breadwinner, and you say quite candidly that you know you're not supposed to yearn for these male pleasures but you do anyway, and that leaves you with uncertainty.

DUBUS That was written maybe a decade after the feminist movement really got strong in the United States—I think a lot of people of both genders are paying for it now. I'm sure there was something good that came out of the sexual revolution, but there are a lot of confused people out there. Anyway, at the time I wrote that, you could not do anything for certain women without angering them; there was a whole new set of rules. The truth is in nature: Take the pheasant. The cock pheasant is the beautiful pheasant. Now, I was raised to believe that that's because he's the male, and most male birds stand out and are more beautiful. But I realize now that it's because the male's expendable; the male attracts the predator away from the nesting female, allowing her to give birth in safety and keep the species going. That's really the male function.

Men are supposed to procreate, we are highly expendable, we die sooner and things just go on without us. If you also take from the male his role as breadwinner, what is he? What is he in the world? So many jobs—I'm thinking ninety percent—are unfulfilling. At least, they're fulfilling only insofar as you know you are putting in that time and doing your best for the people you love. You'd rather be fishing or hunting in order to bring home a paycheque for your offspring and for the woman you've committed your life to. The only thing that makes most jobs meaningful is if the fruits of your labour go to something. It's not a problem I have, but I think it is a difficulty that has to be dealt with.

WACHTEL One of the moving aspects of your book is a kind of faith and optimism in relationships. You were married three times, but you still believe in marriage, even in its permanence. Why is that?

DUBUS I believe that marriage is for the good and is the essence of a society. I would like very much somehow to have stayed together with each of my wives and our children. And my not having achieved that doesn't make me like the fox in Aesop's Fable—you know, the one with the sour grapes. I know that it's worth more than most things for people to be able to stay together and love each other through all their changes, and that people without love are not fulfilled. I've never ever written what I would like to write either but I keep trying. So, I write and I date!

WACHTEL Vivian Gornick, in writing about your fiction, put you, along with Richard Ford and Raymond Carver, in a group of writers whom she called "tender-hearted men," but at the same time she suggested that there is a profound misunderstanding and distance between men and women in your books, and that this is based on a fantasy about what relationships between men and women could be like. Is this something you try to work through in your essays and in writing about your own life?

DUBUS No, not at all. She made several mistakes in that essay: the biggest one was accusing us of not understanding more than our characters do. I always do, so I thought that was a weird reading. And when she says marriage, romance, monogamy is all *passé*, that we're longing for the past, well, that's her past, too. This generation of children is going to grow up, date, fall in love, make mistakes, marry and have babies; it's not going to change.

WACHTEL What about the distance between the men and women in your fiction and their inability to really know each other?

DUBUS I do think we have a hard time knowing each other when we're sexually attracted; when we're not, there's just no problem at all. If you have a man and woman, let's say, travelling by train from the east coast of Canada to the west and they're good friends who work together, there'll probably be no trouble. If they're lovers, there's going to be a fight somewhere around Saskatchewan. I mean, I get along so well with my men friends because we're not lovers, and if one of them hurts me or I hurt him it's not really a big problem. We've never been naked in all the truth of that word, physically and spiritually. When you're really deeply involved with somebody it gives a new form to the relationship, a form I obviously have not mastered, nor did my wives in my company! I've never had trouble with a woman *because* she's a woman, but I've had a lot of trouble with women I loved and who loved me.

WACHTEL In your essays you write, both directly and indirectly, about your Catholic faith. In one essay, "Out Like a Lamb," you draw parallels between real and metaphorical sheep. What was the experience that prompted that?

DUBUS My first wife, our four children and I moved from the University of Iowa to New England. We got a really good deal on a house and seventy acres of land and a swimming pool—a two-storey colonial house, two hundred years old, the whole thing for only $105 because the landlord just wanted someone to live there and take care of the sheep and the roses. I'd always thought of sheep as these mellow, sweet little creatures, but they were really stupid beasts and they kept breaking out of their pen and then trying to get back in. We'd lead them to the entrance and they wouldn't see it and they'd run away again. We finally got very frustrated and we'd tackle 'em and punch 'em and throw 'em over the fence.

Then finally one night one of them was eating the landlady's roses. (She had terminal cancer and her husband had said, "You've got to make sure those roses are there for when we come back for a month next summer.") So I shot the sheep in the rump with some number seven birdshot, which I thought might get through the wool but probably wouldn't. That ewe just looked at me and kept chewing, and I said, I give up, you know, the roses are gone, the sheep are gone. Back in the house one of the kids said, "There's something wrong with that sheep." Her legs were straight up in the air and she was dead. I realized during that year that when Christ called us his lambs, he wasn't thinking of us as cute little things to cuddle, but as really stupid brutes who were trying to get through the gate, but once we were in front of the gate we couldn't even see it, and we just kept running away. Running to exactly where we did not want to go, which reminds me of my marital history, as a matter of fact.

WACHTEL There are Catholic writers and writers who happen to be Catholics. You've always identified yourself as a Catholic writer. What does that mean in terms of your writing?

DUBUS I see the world as a Catholic does. I didn't really know that

that was a whole lot different from other people. I didn't know that there are people who perceive physical reality as the only reality of their lives. The Catholic Church is filled with sacraments, which are physical transactions with a spiritual meaning. This really helps with my young four- and nine-year-old girls: simply peeling a banana and slicing it into a child's bowl is a spiritual act; it's an act of love between you and the child. I often tell myself that you're not just pouring Raisin Bran here, you're loving your children, and that makes me feel better about things because it's a deeper truth.

WACHTEL How do you think your beliefs affect what you write, the way you write?

DUBUS In the title essay in *Broken Vessels*, my beliefs literally led me to whatever affirmation there is in the ending, because that essay does start, I do believe, with a couple of days when I didn't want to be alive. When I'm writing fiction I'll often put a character in a situation something like one I've lived through. I'll give the character meaningless work and no religious convictions, and then give him some experience I've had—like being a divorced father. And then I put him through the same things I went through and see how he does. Or sometimes I just say, I'm going to write about a Catholic this time.

WACHTEL Five years ago something terrible happened to you that would test anyone's faith. You had a series of almost Job-like ordeals and losses. It started with an automobile accident that the title essay of *Broken Vessels* describes, along with the aftermath of that. Can you describe what happened?

DUBUS I was driving home from Boston around one in the morning, and there was a clear stretch of road on Route 93 here; no cars, it was a clear night. There are four lanes on this highway; a speed lane is the fourth one; I was in the third. I noticed a car far ahead stalled in the middle of the road and to the right a woman was at the emergency callbox off the shoulder of the road, calling the state police. I slowed down, went to the end of the speed lane to the driver's side of the car to see if she was injured. She was: she was standing beside the car crying, bleeding. So I pulled over and went to get her out of the road and I was thinking of first aid— bleeding, shock. When I got there, she said, "There's a motorcycle under my car." She pointed down and there was a black pool of liquid, which I took to be blood, so I assumed there was a motor- cycle and a crushed human being under there.

Then from around the trunk of her car, a man—her brother— came. I had not seen him. They were Puerto Ricans. He said: "*Por favor*, no speak English, please help." So we left the road and I was waving a car down because I wanted someone to go with me to look under the car. I was afraid of what I was going to see. I assumed the person was dead but I'd have to look, right? And if the person wasn't dead I don't know what I would have done; I was really afraid of the horrible body I was going to see. It turned out there was no body. The motorcycle had been crushed and that was motor oil on the highway; no one was under there. The motorcy- clist was actually unhurt; he'd abandoned his bike on the road. The woman I flagged down didn't see us. She ran into us and killed Luis Santiago—I guess he died in an hour or so—and I got very badly hurt. I was in the hospital for about seven weeks and had about twelve operations and lost my left leg above the knee. I was in physical therapy for three years and never really got back the use of my right leg, so I'm in a wheelchair.

WACHTEL You have written that living as a cripple allows you to see more clearly the crippled hearts of some people whose bodies are whole. I'll ask you a very big question, and you answer it how- ever you like, but can you tell me how the accident changed you?

DUBUS Well, you know, I'm not sure why I wrote that line now. People who knew me before and after the accident say I have changed, and changed positively. I don't know that yet—I'm still dealing with how to get to the ashtray, and longing, on a lovely day like today down in Massachusetts, to be out walking. I'm try- ing to learn to live in the present, because in a wheelchair you can- not live in the future—you get messed up because you cannot hurry and you just have to try to stay in the moment. I certainly pray more fervently and frequently than ever. And I'm afraid for people I love, ever since I got hit. I really get worried when people I know are on the road.

That perception I wrote about came to me in '88 or '89, and I assume that it must have felt like the truth at the time. Now it sounds arrogant to me, to tell you the truth, and it embarrasses me a little that I wrote it. But it also may be the truth. You see, I just don't know, and that is finally interesting. This is not a boring existence—frustrating sometimes, sad sometimes, angering sometimes and depressing sometimes, but it's never dull. I mean, I get excited over little things: finding that I can reach this or knowing where something is, and there are these little challenges and things to learn.

WACHTEL The image of a broken vessel is a compelling one. How did you come by it?

DUBUS I have this wonderful physical therapist. A woman who has been through a lot, has been a therapist for a long time and found God in, I guess, her fifties. People like that who have been around and are very worldly are just wonderful to be with. She said to me once: "You have to be flat on your back to look straight up." She was always saying things like that. One day I really just cracked up and wept during the physical therapy, which she never stopped—I mean, I was crying and walking on crutches and she and her two attendants were standing there waiting for me to fall. Then she got me up on her table to start working on my leg and she said, "It's in Jeremiah. The potter is making a vessel and he breaks it, so he has to make a new one." She said, "You can't. You can't make a new vessel out of a broken one; you have to make a new you." She said, "Now it's time to find the real you." Maybe she was just being encouraging, but the truth is, if you've been an active man for fifty years, trying to be Gary Cooper, Cary Grant and Sean Connery all at the same time, and a father too, and then you're in a wheelchair, you certainly do have to find a new you.

Now there's nowhere to go. There are no boardwalks on the beaches and no boardwalks in the woods. I mean, I can get in the car and drive and ninety percent of the places I drive by have curbs. I take pleasure in taking a drive and sometimes just stop in the parking lot watching people walk by, but it's an inaccessible world. The world is not built architecturally or spiritually for people in wheelchairs.

WACHTEL Why do you like to use the word *cripple?* There are other words to describe your condition, even neutral expressions such as "differently abled," but you reject them.

DUBUS My crippled buddies call themselves "disabled," but I don't think of *cripple* as pejorative. I think it's because I'm a writer; I don't like euphemisms; I don't like words designed to cheer me up. One of my children, my oldest son, came to visit me when I was in the hospital and he said, "Pop, you're not handicapped, you're physically challenged. It's a new phrase." I said, "*You're* physically challenged: you're breathing hard from walking the stairs. I'm crippled." I think it's a word I would have used before. I've never liked euphemisms.

WACHTEL In this book you give us an angle of observation, literally, that we rarely get in writing, in fiction, a view of the world from a man in a wheelchair. You describe a kind of fringe society that you're now part of made up of very different people, like your "crippled buddies," who got there, like you, by accident. What's that world like for you?

DUBUS Encouraging. It makes me feel so good to speak to my paraplegic friend because as soon as I speak to him I already feel better, because I *am* better off: I can feel the lower part of my body. Also, when you speak to someone in a chair you don't have to explain anything. You just get this litany of response: I hear you, I know, I know, I've been there, yes. You don't have to explain the fatigue, you don't have to explain the humiliation. A lot of bipeds do not understand what it feels like for a person in a wheelchair to be carried upstairs: you feel like a piece of meat in somebody else's hands. It's an incredible surrender of integrity, of yourself; it's also dangerous and scary; and guys get into "Hey, we can get him up, c'mon Andre!" It makes you miss your legs.

People in wheelchairs have all been through this, and instantly they know what I'm talking about, and they feel the same as I feel about it. They're the ones I turned to after meeting with a psychologist in '89, when I was really in trouble. I mean, every morning when I woke up, I woke up crying, and one morning I couldn't stop. So I called my doctor and he sent me to a therapist, and when I left the therapist I called my paraplegic buddy. And I said, you know, this is near the end of my third year, and I keep waiting every morning to wake up happy, like I've had the flu and it's over. (None of us that I know of dreams of being in a chair; you know, I always have legs in my dreams; I walk. But when you wake up, there's your wheelchair beside you and there's your crippled body. You have to dress lying down or sitting down and then make the bed under you while sitting down and all this.) And he said to me, "Every morning, the first thing I do when I wake up is cuss for about five minutes about having to get my chair into the car," which is a very difficult, intricate thing and enough to keep a sane person inside of the house for a long time.

I called him this year and I said, "You know, John, this is my fifth year and for the first time I'm starting to feel pretty good. I'm not as tired, I don't hurt as much, I feel some energy coming back." I said, "How was your sixth year?" He said, "My sixth year was my worst." So, I'm waiting to see what's going to happen in the sixth year. And no one else could tell you this.

September 1991

interview prepared in collaboration
with Lisa Godfrey

Salman Rushdie

In December 1992 the Canadian branch of the international writers group, PEN, held its third annual fundraiser in Toronto. The theme of the evening, on behalf of writers in prison, was "The Sentence is Silence." The astonishing finale was an appearance by Salman Rushdie, a writer who won't be silent, despite a multi-million-dollar bounty on his head.

On February 14th, 1989, the Ayatollah Khomeini of Iran pronounced a *fatwa* on Salman Rushdie, sentencing him—and all involved in the publication of his novel *The Satanic Verses*—to death. The Ayatollah said that the book was "against Islam, the Prophet and the Koran." A reward of $1.5 million was offered to anyone who killed Rushdie. That death sentence has since been reiterated and the bounty increased, plus expenses. In the summer of 1991, the Japanese translator of *The Satanic Verses* was murdered, and the Italian translator repeatedly stabbed and left for dead.

Salman Rushdie has been in hiding since February 1989. Despite the constraints under which he must live, he has published two books since 1989: *Haroun and the Sea of Stories*, a tale in the tradition of *The Thousand and One Nights*, written for his son, and a collection of essays and criticism, *Imaginary Homelands*. His pre-*Satanic Verses* reputation was based on two big novels: an exuberant allegory of post-

Independence India, *Midnight's Children*, which won the
Booker Prize in 1981, and *Shame* (1983), a similar mix of history, politics and myth set in a country that "is not Pakistan, or not quite." *The Satanic Verses* received the
Whitbread Prize for the best novel of 1988.

Many ambiguous phone calls, arrangements and re-
arrangements of difficult travel plans prepared the way for
our meeting. Curiously, within this cloak and dagger atmosphere Rushdie himself seemed calm and even cheerful. He
remembered that we had talked briefly four years earlier
when he had last been in Toronto and India had just
banned *The Satanic Verses*. "That's when it all started," he
said. We went into a room, alone, and talked for more than
an hour. Rushdie wants to talk; there are many things he
wants to say.

WACHTEL What is your state of mind now as we approach the end
of 1992?
RUSHDIE I'm very relieved to be here. But I'm rather tired of having to talk like a politician. I hear this political-campaigning language coming out of my mouth—which is necessary, in order to
make the points that need to be made—and I find myself thinking, *I* don't talk like this! And that's very odd. It's not the language
that comes naturally to me. I've had to learn a form of discourse
that takes place on the front page of newspapers. I remember
when this first started, Martin Amis said something to the effect
that he felt I'd vanished into the front page. He's right, to an
extent. There is no other way of dealing with this issue except to
start sounding like a politician. Ambiguities and ironies do not
work well in news reporting.

This situation needs to end—it'll never just drift away. But there are only two ways for it to end: either I will be killed, which I would wish not to happen, or the government of Iran will stop what it is doing.

Some days I feel more optimistic than others. Right at this moment, because I've managed to get here and because it seems as if there's a great deal of political interest in Canada, I feel hopeful. I used to say that hope was the fuel that all writers use. If you embark on something as long as a novel, the fuel you use is optimism. I remember saying, at the time of *Midnight's Children*, that I'd used up a lot of optimism, and that the supply is not endless, that you need it replenished from time to time. If you're unlucky, it runs out. So far I still have a supply of optimism.

WACHTEL How is it replenished?

RUSHDIE In terms of writing, you produce your books. They seem to work and people read them and seem to like them. In my case, the worst moments have been when I have felt stagnation. When I'm fighting, when other people are fighting on my behalf, when there's activity—that gives one hope.

WACHTEL Are there ways in which you accept the restraints that have been imposed on you?

RUSHDIE No. Oddly, it's harder now than it was at the beginning. I remember very clearly, on the first day that I was given protection in England, *nobody*—not the politicians, not the Special Branch, not I—thought that it would last for more than a few days. Khomeini's medieval threat was so surreal, so bizarre that I remember being told by the police, "We'll just go and find a place. We'll sit there for a few days, we'll let the politicians sort it out and then you can go back to your ordinary life." The only reason I agreed to go underground was that I thought it a short-term problem. I walked out of my home three years and nine months ago and have never walked back into it—nobody thought that was a likely scenario. It seemed this was such an acute problem that it would *have* to be fixed. How could the government of one country go around trying to kill citizens of other countries with impunity?

And then the impossible happened: it became a longer-term problem. At the beginning, when it felt like an emergency, when there were people marching down the streets of foreign cities, carrying my picture with the eyes poked out, when we had no idea what was coming at us or how to respond to it, clearly it was necessary to say, "Okay, we're taking emergency precautions." At that time at least one could understand why one was doing so. But the longer it goes on, the harder it gets. I don't *want* my life to be led in these curious circumstances, where nobody must know where I am and people have to go through all kinds of arcane processes— as you have—in order to see me. And while I'm perfectly willing to accept the proposition that in life things generally *are* very weird, this particular form of weirdness is not one that I propose spending the rest of my life inside. I never *chose* to live with policemen.

WACHTEL That must be one of the most curious by-products of your situation. The writer's posture in relation to authority—and yours in particular—is usually quite at odds with the accommodations you have had to make. What is that like?

RUSHDIE I think there's a part of Special Branch that is deliciously appalled at the idea that one of these days I might write a book about the British secret police, which I could. I said to them, "There are very few left-wing writers who know this much about the inner operations of the British secret police." And they said, "Actually there aren't many *right*-wing writers who know this much."

The places I've been have been many and varied. Sometimes there's been enough space for us to get away from each other inside the premises. At other times we've been in quite restricted circumstances. It's odd, because what people think of as my solitude is actually a crowd. The problem is not solitude; the problem is creating solitude, creating space.

WACHTEL What are some of the restraints? One hears about your moving house a great deal, and not being able to go out. Can you walk about in daylight? At the same time, congruent with that picture of isolation and underground movement, how is it that you can travel abroad and appear in public?

RUSHDIE The problem is that the more I tell you about this, the harder it is to do it. That's one of the most difficult things about leading this kind of life: it is necessary not to share most of it. I've been trying to do what I can that is not foolish. So yes, of course I can get out in the daylight. The risk is very high but very specific—not from ordinary people in the street but from contract killers. Keeping out of the way of such people means that they not know where I live and not know in advance where I'm going to be.

Those are the restrictions. They are very big restrictions, because *nobody* can know where I live. One of the things I've learned is a very simple thing: if you want to keep a secret, don't tell anyone! Not to tell *anyone* is *very* hard. Yes, I've managed to travel around. Very few people would understand, unless they'd been directly involved in the process, how difficult those journeys have been to organize. They require the co-operation of the governments and the security forces of the countries that I've visited. It's an organizational nightmare for me to move at all, but there is no substitute for my being able to meet people directly in order to become a human being and not an abstract issue for them.

But there is a bizarre double-bind: when I was invisible and silent, people could forget the problem. Now that I'm visible and noisy it seems *that's* a way for people to forget the problem!

WACHTEL They say, "Look, he's out there, he's travelling, what's the problem?"

RUSHDIE Yes.

WACHTEL Are you afraid?

RUSHDIE It would be foolish to say that I haven't been very alarmed at times. I know this is going to sound a bit strange, but no, I'm not particularly afraid. There was a point at which I discovered that there was a "switch" you could throw and find that it's possible not to be afraid. Since the *fatwah*, several of my friends, including very close friends of around my age, have died and for rather prosaic reasons, like cancer, for example. People die. You don't have to have Khomeini's killers coming after you in order to die. Also, I think there was a point at which I felt—I *do* feel—that the only way of not being defeated by a terrorist campaign is not to be terrorized. You just have to say, "To hell with you, I ain't scared of you." Otherwise they've won. At one level it's just a survival technique. But one of these days we'll all be dead and the books will still be there. That's something I feel very good about—that we did complete the process of publishing *The Satanic Verses.* There's no way now that they can eradicate the book from the record. That's a victory.

WACHTEL By "complete the process" you mean publishing a paperback edition?

RUSHDIE I mean the English-language paperback, which was the big thing—there had been paperback publications in other languages. Really, the only way of keeping a book in long-term print in English is to have it in paperback. The hardback had already started to fade in the bookshops. A few years from now it would have been more or less unavailable, and then what the hell would it all have been for—the book *de facto* would have been banned. Now at least that can't happen.

WACHTEL Are there hardships that we can't even imagine? I can think about loneliness and intermittent fear, psychological deprivation, a sense of abandonment, losing time with your family, especially with your son, who grows up only once. Are there other things?

RUSHDIE Yes. Every day has a hundred tiny humiliations. In all sorts of areas I don't have control of my life. To be a man of forty-five and not be able to walk out the door without asking permission feels awful. That doesn't mean that I don't get on with the people who are looking after me. That's not the point. The point is I'm grown up. I should be able to make ordinary life decisions for myself, and not to be able to is like being tied down, physically. It's like being physically constrained, *held.*

It's not that I'm in an uncomfortable place. The problem is all in the head; I need to have the freedom of leading an ordinary life. Think about what you do during a day. If you run out of food, you can go to the store. If you get bored, you can meet a friend for lunch. If you want to see a movie, you can go see a movie. And it's nobody's business. In my case, everything I want to do is somebody else's business. And I can't stand it, really, but I have to.

There's another side to it, a more public problem. This is in my view a big issue of principle—but it's an issue which seems to affect only one person. It's very easy in that circumstance for people to criminalize the person, to say that it's not an issue of principle, that it's just your fault, you got yourself in trouble, and now the rest of the world is supposed to get you out; that there are many things to worry about in the world. It's very difficult to have to continually argue that there are huge issues involved here which affect everybody. They can answer, "Well, you would say that, wouldn't you?" It's very difficult, on the one hand, to be the subject of a criminal attack, and on the other hand to be treated like the criminal. That is one of the humiliations.

WACHTEL You have described a television show, where studio audiences were asked for a show of hands on the question of whether you should live or die. And there was a national opinion poll about whether you should be murdered. What's your reaction to that sort of thing? Anger? Do you feel wounded?

RUSHDIE Both of those, yes. I've been very angry about many things. But you have to learn a "Buddhist" attitude—that anger is not helpful. I've decided that I'm going to defer anger. I'll be angry later. Right now I've got to fix something. I don't propose to spend the rest of my life like this. Already I'm not spending my life quite as I did at the beginning. I don't sit locked up so much, though that's not because anything's safer. It's because I'm taking more risks. I felt that if I was going to remain myself and not crack up I had no option.

WACHTEL Have you ever been tempted to go completely underground, to change your identity, as the police occasionally arrange for state witnesses?

RUSHDIE No, not for a moment. That would be worse than death. I couldn't see my friends, my family. I couldn't be a writer. What the hell would I be?

WACHTEL You'd be alive.

RUSHDIE I *am* alive. But what I want is *my* life. I don't want somebody else's life. Just silencing me as a writer would be a fantastic victory for them. They're not going to win at all is my view; they're going to lose. The consequences of their winning are catastrophic, for many people—notably myself but also others. This is only the best-known of a number of attacks against progressive thought in many Muslim countries right now.

To lose this—if I got hit—what would that say to writers and intellectuals in Muslim countries? It would say that all the might of Western security couldn't protect him from the wrath of Islam, so what chance have you people got? It's a new form of terrorism, remote-control terrorism. If it works, there's no question but that it will be repeated. Muslim writers and intellectuals in many countries are well aware of that, and that's why they have frequently spoken up in my defence.

And next time it doesn't have to be Islamic fundamentalists. Anybody who has the inclination and resources can do this, if it's demonstrated to work. This becomes a test case. Freedom of speech is not just the freedom of writers to write. It's also the freedom of readers to read. It's the freedom of publishers to publish and booksellers to sell books and journalists to write journalistic pieces and newpapers not to be censored by governments. It's not so enshrined anywhere in the world that it doesn't need defending.

WACHTEL One result of religious persecution—or, as this is, a combination of religious and political persecution—is that it creates martyrs. Some part of society would make you a martyr. How do you deal with that?

RUSHDIE There is a problem when you acquire a symbolic role— as either a demon or a martyr. I can't pretend that this incident doesn't have high symbolic content. My problem is that I'm not a symbol; I'm a person. It's very difficult for symbols to write novels, and I'm a novelist. I have to accept that while there's this public thing on the one hand there's also a private self, but above all a private *working* self which has to somehow maintain continuity with the previously existing working self. I'm still the same writer, or I need to be. One of the things that is very hard to live with is this weight of abstraction. The best thing I can do is to continue to be as much myself as I can. Another victory for me is that they haven't turned me into someone else. I haven't cracked up. I haven't changed beyond recognition.

WACHTEL You said once that you feel as if you've been plunged like Alice into the world beyond the looking glass, where nonsense is the only available sense, and you wonder if you'll ever be able to climb back through the mirror. Are you permanently changed?

RUSHDIE I think an event of this size has to change you. I've gone through a great deal more pain than I ever thought I would— emotional, intellectual pain. That changes you. I've had to learn a lot about a lot of things that I didn't particularly expect I'd ever have to learn about.

I've also had to learn something that has been quite useful. I've always been a satirical, comic, more or less dissenting writer. If you're that sort of writer you spend most of your time saying what you're against and making jokes about it, pulling faces. It has become very clear to me in this situation that it was easy to say what I was against, but that that wasn't sufficient. I didn't choose the war, but given that I'm fighting this curious war, it has become very important to know what I am fighting *for*. That's a thing most of us don't have to do, to sit down and actually discover the values that you're fighting for. You simply write or live from those values. You obviously have to examine them a little bit but you don't have to formulate them.

Religious fanatics have declared repeatedly, in attacks on the novel as a form, on my novels, on me, on novelists in general, on the intellectual life and on secularism: "You guys don't believe in anything. We believe in lots of stuff. We've got heaven and hell, and we've got holy books and laws, and we kill people if they break those laws, but what have *you* got? You've got AIDS. You're a decadent culture. You're finished, empty."

I thought: You've got to answer that attack. You've got to say that your morality is anterior to religion, that it comes before it. Good and evil come before their codification in religious practice. You don't have to have a religion to have a moral view. You don't have to be a *mullah* to be an arbiter of values or to have values of your own. There *is* a bedrock, in this society and in this way of looking at the world, which is as important to *me* as their rather cruel values seem to be to them. I'm prepared to defend it, if necessary, with my life. And I guess that's the bottom line.

There is a profound conflict between people who value literature and people for whom it has no value at all, who think that godlessness is immorality. And on a simpler level between people who have a sense of humour and people who don't. *The Satanic Verses* is a comic novel. There's a part of me which thinks that what's happened is one of the greatest failures of sense of humour in history! At one level this is a battle between people who understand what it is to be comic and people who can't take a joke.

I remember one of the leaders of the British Muslims being asked quite soon after the *fatwah* whether he had any knowledge of *The Satanic Verses*, which needless to say he didn't. He was then asked by the journalist: "Mr. Rushdie's been quite a well-known writer in this country for over a decade. Have you read anything that he's written, any book or anything at all?" To which he replied: "Oh no, books are not my thing."

At another level, that's the problem. Here's a fight between people for whom books *are* their thing and people for whom books are not their thing. Between the sacred and profane text. That's one of the subjects of *The Satanic Verses*. Parts of that novel now read with ridiculous, pathetic accuracy.

WACHTEL From reading your recent essays and speeches it seems to me that you are taking a very different approach and looking at questions of literature and religion and politics in a much more direct way. You raise the issue of "secular fundamentalism," which is an odd twist.

RUSHDIE That's a kind of nonsense, isn't it? An attempt by religious fundamentalists to claim that they are somehow being persecuted by secular culture. The answers to this are so simple. For example, the First Amendment to the American Constitution guarantees freedom of religion as well as freedom of speech. The point about these freedoms is that they are joined. Of course people should have freedom to worship. At the same time, people must have the freedom *not* to worship. There is no sense in which the language of religion can be privileged above any other language. If it is, then its supporters have a disproportionate freedom; they have the freedom not only to believe as they believe but also to prevent other people from disagreeing.

That is the basis of the American Constitution. It's the basis of John Stuart Mill's ideas on liberty, of the entire fight of the Enlightenment writers. It's a basic presumption for most people who wish to create a free society. It's important, and necessary, to point out that Islam has never created a free society. Anywhere. Ever.

People's ideas are always in conflict. The idea that *any* society can be homogeneous, composed of an agreed-upon view of the world, may once have been true, but it certainly hasn't been true for a very long time. Societies move forward by friction between ideas. The problem is when one side in the argument decides to use physical violence, for in a way it destroys the argument. Of *course* there's reason for dispute over *The Satanic Verses*, which takes a non-religious—although I think quite respectful—look at revelation. Of course there's an argument against this view. There's a way of disagreeing with anybody who says anything in any book. I would have been perfectly prepared to have that debate. That's how intellectual processes work normally. The moment the idea of murder and book-burnings enters the story you can't have that conversation anymore. That's only one of the bad things that the *fatwah* did. It forestalled any kind of serious discussion.

WACHTEL You've described yourself as having been a secular man since your teens. Yet one of the questions you wanted to explore in *The Satanic Verses* is the question of faith—the nature of revelation and the power of faith. Why are you drawn to that question?

RUSHDIE I'm by origin Indian. India is a country in which God isn't dead. There are gods everywhere. I remember thinking at the time I was working on *Midnight's Children* that one of the reasons for writing in the way I did in that book—and the way I have continued to develop since—is that you're writing about a reality in which the idea of the miraculous is an absolute truth. It's not a metaphor, it's absolutely real. The miraculous and the everyday coexist; gods are real and intervene in human affairs; miracles happen. So you have to develop a form which doesn't prejudge whether your characters are right or wrong. You have to create a form in which the idea of the miraculous can coexist with observable, everyday reality. The way I've always written has been shaped by the everyday fact of religious belief in India—not just Muslim, Hindu, Buddhist and Sikh, but every belief.

After writing two novels which were more or less historically grounded, I wanted to write a novel *not* based on history but on the deep workings of the soul and the self. *The Satanic Verses* takes, as its engine, what happens to the human self when it is transported across the planet, and then what happens in the act of migration. The opening, with people dropping out of the sky, falling out of an aeroplane and landing in Britain, is only the most dramatic act of immigration I could think of! You have to leave a lot of your luggage behind, and a lot of the luggage you bring with you looks different in the new place. The roots of the self—language and culture—are lost. Everything about you has to be renewed. If that novel is about anything, it's about the reiterated question in literature: How does newness—whether it be migrant groups or new ideas or whatever—enter the world?

I wanted to look at every aspect of the outer and inner lives of people like myself, people of different classes, people to whom this extraordinary twentieth-century event—mass migration—

had happened. One aspect is the spiritual material, the stories, the beliefs that they bring with them. How does that look in the light of the New World? The stories which informed their lives are re-examined in the light of Western culture, and in what Milan Kundera called the defining form of European culture, which is the novel. You use the language of one culture to look at the language of another. And that's a serious effort, but it's also—as we've seen—explosive, because it means disagreeing with the first principles. If somebody asks me, do I believe that the angel Gabriel appeared to the prophet Mohammed and stood upon the horizon and filled the sky and dictated the uncreated word of God, the answer is no, I'm very sorry, excuse me, but I don't. Do I think that that's a rather beautiful story? Yes, I do. Do I think it's a powerful metaphor that actually works on my imagination? Yes, I do.

One of the interesting things about this whole affair is that many of the people who are making the fuss haven't really studied it very closely. Much of the description of revelation, in my novel, is actually very close to what the prophet Mohammed said hap-pened to him. He doesn't say that he always saw things. He says that sometimes he didn't see them. Sometimes he seemed to see some things, and other times he seemed to hear noises, voices, a voice. At other times he said it was physically very painful, the process of revelation. He would feel that something was tearing at his gut, that something was coming out of him.

These are the forms of mystical experience we know about through the history of mysticism. All I was doing was using that. Of course, I was using it from the point of view of a non-religious person, which is that good and evil are not external to us, in the form of God and the Devil, but internal. The Angel and the Devil are both inside us. And the question about whether verses are angelic or satanic is very difficult to resolve. That was the point of view from which the book came. That seems to me to be perfectly serious, and in a Western context not even that new. The idea that these stories can be interpreted metaphorically and don't have to be taken literally has been accepted in the Judaeo-Christian culture for quite a long time.

The problem here is the use of a literalistic language. If you don't believe that the archangel Gabriel stood on the horizon and filled the sky and dictated the uncreated word of God, then you should be killed. This gives me a problem.

WACHTEL How did you become a secular man? You've said that you realized when you were in boarding school in England, at Rugby, that you didn't believe in God.

RUSHDIE There was not a lot of religion in my family. Mercifully, I had an almost entirely religion-free childhood. My father would take me to the mosque once a year, the equivalent of going to church at Christmas, and otherwise never had any interest in religion. In retrospect, I'm very grateful to my parents for having brought me up in that way. It didn't at the time seem exceptional to me, and it was also how most of my friends of all religious backgrounds lived and thought.

Growing up in a city like Bombay, I didn't live in an exclusively Muslim environment. It was a multi-faith—or multi-nonfaith—community. But everybody in India says they belong to this or that religion; it's a definition of community as much as anything else. If I'd been asked I suppose I would have said, in some unexamined way, that I was Indian Muslim. I certainly have the memory of having ceased to believe in God soon after coming to England, and having eaten a ham sandwich to prove the point.

WACHTEL A very unfulfilling way, I would think.

RUSHDIE It wasn't a very tasty sandwich, but it felt sensational. After fourteen years of being told that the pig was unclean, it didn't seem that unclean to me! There's a kind of surreal version of this ham sandwich in *The Satanic Verses*. When Gibreel Farishta loses his faith he goes off to an International Hotel and stuffs his face full of pig, in a much more operatic version of this little biographical incident.

I've simply not felt the need for God. It doesn't seem to me to be an idea which I need in order to explain the world I live in.

WACHTEL Yet the vocabulary has stuck. You've talked about a need to fill God-sized holes in your life. "I want to write," you've said, "in part to fill up that emptied God chamber with other dreams." It's a curious inversion, like one of those double-perception tests: the vase is here and the exterior of the vase remains.

RUSHDIE Anybody who is seriously interested in this whole area is affected by the stuff. Acceptance and rejection are not that far apart. The thing that's far removed is indifference. If I were indifferent then I'd write about other things.

One of the things that really interested me about Islam is that it's the only great world religion whose origin is found inside recorded history. If we're trying to look at what a religion is, how it comes to be and how it comes to mean what it means, the only one we can study is Islam. The rest is myths and legends. You can't see the texts of Christianity and Judaism as history books. But Islam has a lot of historical material. For me, that made it absolutely fascinating—the way in which a great idea would grow out of the circumstances of its time and then become universal.

I think it a great tragedy that a lot of the historical research which has been done in this century about the life of the prophet Mohammed is banned in Muslim countries. It's very sad that the people who live inside the aftermath of one of the great phenomena of world history should be the only people who are excluded from understanding it.

WACHTEL You've talked about wanting to develop a form of fiction in which the miraculous might coexist with the mundane. One could say you approach the miraculous through a kind of fabulism, or what's sometimes called postmodern fantasy, where people do fall out of the sky, and that the mundane is where you polish your political satire.

RUSHDIE I don't accept that at all. *The Satanic Verses* is a novel about London. Much of its character comes out of a fairly closely observed description of reality. The largest section in the novel is called "A City Visible But Unseen." In other words, there is here, in London, a world, ways of life, which exist—you can go see them, I can give you their addresses—but which are not looked at because they're not given value by the majority culture. So it was an entirely realistic attempt to say, Let's look at this city that is visible but is not seen.

I also don't like all this postmodern fabulism stuff. When *Midnight's Children* was written and everybody in the West responded to it as a beautiful fairy-tale, everybody in India responded to it as a history book. I've often said I think part of the confusion is that people have this idea that realism in literature must follow a set of rules. If you write in a certain way—He stood up, went to the door, opened it, got himself a glass of whisky, drank it—somehow that's realism. I don't think that kind of mimetic naturalism has anything to do with realism. Realism to me has much more to do with the intent of a work. If what you're trying to do is to find a way of reflecting as much as you can of the way in which you perceive the world in which you live, that's an attempt at realism.

The world is not very naturalistic these days. The world is operatic and surreal and grotesque. I think the quiet little novels which pretend that it isn't are the fantasies. Those are the fabulist fictions, because that certainly is how the world is not.

WACHTEL Some would argue that the profane is in the ascendant in your writing, though there's always been an element of political engagement and political satire. Indira Gandhi wanted to sue over her unflattering portrait in *Midnight's Children*. Benazir Bhutto was wickedly satirized in *Shame*. The book was banned in Pakistan.

RUSHDIE But not because of her. It was banned in Pakistan because it satirized the general who happened to be the dictator at the time, which I guess is not surprising.

It's true that both *Midnight's Children* and *Shame* have political content. But they are not political novels in the sense that they're not about a political issue or whatever, in which case they'd self-destruct the moment the issue faded. When I wrote *Midnight's Children* I certainly wanted it to have enough durability to transcend the moment of Mrs. Gandhi's power and make a sharp political point, because that moment would pass. There had to be other things to hold up the architecture of the book.

I thought *The Satanic Verses* was the *least* political novel I'd ever written. It didn't rise out of that kind of historical process, but out of an attempt to try to understand the process of my own life. I'd always felt that at some point my writing would have to make the same move that *I* made. It would have to move from the East towards the West. That's what I thought *The Satanic Verses* was about, that kind of very personal, *inner* novel. It turns out to be the *most* political novel I ever wrote. This just goes to show how wrong writers can be.

WACHTEL How do you feel about fate, about the way in which your writing has led you to this point? I went back to page one of *Midnight's Children*, published in 1981, and I couldn't read it without being aware of a certain resonance. It's a book about children born, as you were, in the year of India's Independence, 1947. The narrator says he has become "heavily embroiled in fate. At the best of times, a dangerous sort of involvement."

RUSHDIE It also ends with a terrible curse. It's the privilege or the curse of Midnight's Children to be unable to live or die in peace, to be both masters and victims of their times. In an earlier draft the opening sentence of the novel was, "Most of what matters in our lives takes place in our absence." The line's still in the novel, but I pushed it inside because it seemed too *Anna Karenina*-like a beginning and it wasn't a Tolstoyan fiction. I suppose in the Tolstoy-Dostoevsky divide my writing comes down towards Dostoevsky rather than Tolstoy.

But I did think that sentence was true, especially in the modern world where our fate is really decided in rooms that we have no way of entering, places where currency rates are set, places where political decisions are made. Most of what shapes our lives does take place in our absence. It's a statement about life in the twentieth century, about the point of conjunction between the individual and history. To what extent do you have control over your own life and to what extent do other people have control over you? That's something I've always tried to write about.

WACHTEL I know that you don't want to be the Rushdie Affair, you want to be Salman Rushdie the writer. You've talked about how literature is situated on the "frontier between the self and the world," that the world flows into the artist and the artist flows into the world. What sort of world is flowing into you now? If you don't want to write a book about the British secret police, how can you write, and what are you writing now?

RUSHDIE I've got a lifetime of material; I don't have to write about what happened last week. The history of prison literature or exile literature demonstrates that writers can keep going for very long periods of time on the basic fuel of their experience of life, not just their immediate circumstances.

At the same time, there's no question that this *thing* has left a very deep residue in me of what, sometimes, I think of as damage, and other times education. It will no doubt affect what I write. I'm writing a novel now, some of which takes place in India and some of which takes place in Spain. A lot of it is about painting. I feel very nervous talking about unfinished books. One could say that it was recognizably derived from what's happened to me, in that it's about somebody expelled from, cast out from, what he had always thought of as his natural life, but for entirely different reasons. And in place and time it is entirely different. But having to reconstruct a system of values, and indeed a way of life, more or less from scratch is part of what it's about. People may see some parallels there, but it's very rash to decode a text allegorically.

I've always been a writer who has written from some place reasonably close to experience, but it's always *used*, turned into something, put somewhere else, made something of. It comes alive when you do that to it, not when you write about it autobiographically. So yes, of course what I write will learn from what's happened to me, but it won't just be an allegorical account of what happened. Any more than *Haroun and the Sea of Stories* is an allegorical account, although you can clearly see in it the marks of what happened. But that's not all it's about; it's one of the echoes in it. I guess that will go on being an echo in my writing until I've worked it out for myself.

WACHTEL For a time you talked about a novel you were thinking about writing and couldn't write. How much are you able to write now?

RUSHDIE The last couple of months I haven't written at all. I've been running around being a politician. My own feeling is that this particular phase—of trying to kick open the doors of government rooms—is very brief. I think the law of diminishing returns applies. If I were to come back to Canada in six months' time and try and kick open the same doors, they probably wouldn't be opened. There's a shock value in my arriving in this way which enables me to gain access to high levels of government. That's something in this campaign that people cannot do on my behalf. But in the end the Canadian government will be influenced by Canadians and will act to the extent that there is Canadian public pressure on them to do so, not pressure from me.

That process is almost over now. I've been to a lot of places, talked to a lot of people and it's getting to the point where there are enough wheels in motion. I think that very shortly I'm going to stop and go and write my book. It's that odd thing. Writing is my gift. It's the thing that I can do that other people can't do in the same way. It would be absurd not to do it.

WACHTEL You often write about characters who are divided inside themselves between good and evil, secularism and faith. It seems to me that you must be divided between hope and despair.

RUSHDIE Yes. It's like being on an emotional roller-coaster. Some days I feel very bad, some days I feel better. But we're all divided selves. It is in the nature of modern life that the self is a very plural, fragmented bag of selves. It may be dramatized by the act of migration, by having the self placed in conflict, in the way it's happened to me, but if it weren't true of everybody, it wouldn't be interesting to say.

WACHTEL I have to ask you a question you've been asked before. Do you regret having written *The Satanic Verses?*

RUSHDIE No. That's it. No. I'm very proud of the book. It's the most ambitious book I've ever written. In my mind, it's as good a novel as I could write. Why would I be ashamed of it?

WACHTEL But knowing what has happened as a result of your writing it, do you regret having written it?

RUSHDIE No. The world is what it is. You do your work and what happens happens. Clearly, I would much prefer the things that have happened not to have happened. But as horrible and demeaning and painful as this has been, at least in my mind it's not the wrong fight. It's a fight in which all the things that I value are ranged against all the things that I don't. It would be much nicer for one's life not to contain these great operatic conflicts, but if such a conflict does intrude and distort the centre of your life, at least it ain't the wrong fight. It's not meaningless, which a lot of wars are.

WACHTEL Two years ago you said, "Our lives teach us who we are." And that as a writer you accept your condition and try to learn from it.

RUSHDIE Yes. I thought I'd stopped going to school some time ago, but it seems I'm still being taught. I've learned a great deal, and not all of it nice.

WACHTEL About who you are?

RUSHDIE About who I am, and about who other people think I am. The worst part of this has been to discover the very unpleasant descriptions that have been imposed on me. There's been so much untruth and vilification. Quite often I've felt that when people meet me, somehow I have to fight past all those other false selves before they actually start seeing *me*. That feels awful, like a defeat. To an extent, one doesn't recover from that.

WACHTEL What have you learned about who you are?

RUSHDIE One of the things I've learned is that I'm a little harder to destroy than I might have expected. If you'd asked me four years ago if I'd still be in one piece, I'd have said no. But I am. As it turns

out I'm quite stubborn, though I don't feel particularly exceptional.

WACHTEL Do you think you'll ever be free of this persecution?

RUSHDIE Oh yes. One can't afford to lose, therefore one has to
win.

December 1992

interview prepared in collaboration
with Anne Gibson

Diane
Wood Middlebrook
on Anne Sexton

In 1974, wearing her mother's old fur coat, a fresh glass of vodka in her hand, Anne Sexton committed suicide by asphyxiating herself in the garage of her home. She was forty-five. In the years before her death, Sexton was honoured as a major American poet. She won the Pulitzer Prize, she was awarded honorary degrees, received Guggenheim and Ford Foundation grants, and yet during this time she was often severely depressed, suicidal and dependent on alcohol and prescription drugs.

Anne Sexton used poetry to save her own life—for as long as she could. The poet Maxine Kumin, a close friend, said at her death that Sexton would have cracked long before 1974 without the rigor and solace of poetry, and the enthusiastic public response to her work. Sexton wrote poetry that was personal, intimate and female—raw and close to the bone.

Diane Wood Middlebrook, professor of English at Stanford and herself a poet, spent ten years researching and writing *Anne Sexton: A Biography* (1991), at the invitation of Sexton's daughter and literary executor, Linda Gray Sexton. Middlebrook had already co-edited a selection of Sexton's poetry, but it was during her biographical research that the controversy over her use of tapes recorded by Sexton's psy-

chiatrist began. Middlebrook discovered that Dr. Martin
Orne, who saw her from 1956 to 1964, had kept 300 hours
of tapes of their sessions. Four of these tapes were already
among Sexton's papers to which Middlebrook was given
access. But now, all this new material was uncovered. Linda
Sexton wanted all of the medical and psychiatric records
made available to her mother's biographer. In one instance,
Linda went to court to obtain the material, and won.

But when Dr. Orne released the tapes, there was a furor.
The American Psychiatry Association, *The New York Times*
and *Newsweek* all questioned the ethics of the doctor and of
Sexton's daughter. Sexton's nieces wrote to *The New York
Times* condemning Middlebrook's book; writers Erica Jong
and Maxine Kumin rushed to its defence. Poet Katha Pol-
litt, in her review of Middlebrook's biography, pointed out
that compared to the other kinds of abuse that Sexton
received at the hands of her psychiatrists, these posthumous revelations of her conversations were a peccadillo.

Diane Wood Middlebrook treats her subject with compassion and fairness. And it's especially reassuring to know
that she saw virtually all records of Sexton's life, given her
subject's skills as a performer and self-inventor.

WACHTEL Your biography opens with a description of Anne Sexton at a poetry reading, "an actress in her own autobiographical
play" is how she put it once. Did you ever see her perform?
MIDDLEBROOK No, but that characterization of her in the preface
was the one I had settled on as the character I wanted to present.
Sexton as an actress, because she was very, very good at concealing
how sick she was. By the time she died, she was no longer capable
of writing her poetry. So the self-invented public persona was the

one that lasted the longest. In many ways I found that character almost heroic in her ability to conceal her misery and terror in order to perform in front of an audience right up to the end.

WACHTEL What was an Anne Sexton poetry reading like?

MIDDLEBROOK She always dressed in very sexy clothes. At one of her last readings she wore a sexy red dress. It had buttons all the way down the front and she would always leave a couple of them open at the top and a couple of them open at the bottom. She would walk around as she read, kicking her legs so that the buttons started to come undone from below, and she would shrug her shoulders so the buttons would start coming undone from above. The audience was riveted, waiting to see whether the dress would unbutton itself entirely before the end of the performance. This was a trick Sexton pulled often; her clothes were part of the show. She had the body of a fashion model, and the spectacle she presented—deliberately provocative, deliberately a tease, but very much her own woman—was part of her personality. She also carefully rehearsed her readings, and at every reading she gave one poem in which she would break down and weep.

WACHTEL Do you think this was a conscious ploy, or would she just get into a state?

MIDDLEBROOK From what I understand about method acting, performers work to induce in themselves the emotion they're supposed to project, and I believe that Sexton was very good at that. Of course, the emotion was initially hers, but that's not the point for an actress; the point is to be able to summon the emotion at the moment when it's going to be dramatically most effective. And that was what the rehearsing was about. I don't believe that having rehearsed it made the poems any less sincere or the delivery any less spontaneous; she simply had an actress's powers.

WACHTEL Not only did people throng to an Anne Sexton reading or performance, but her books were also very popular and sold well. In the epigraph to your biography, you quote a fan who says—and this is ten years after Sexton's death—"I don't read poetry, but I read Anne Sexton."

MIDDLEBROOK That was said to me more than once. The first time I heard it, I thought it was very negative. What I heard was, Well, I don't read poetry, Anne Sexton isn't really a poet, which is why I read her. The question as to whether Sexton was a major writer or was only a "popular writer" was for me one of the fascinations of this project. I was dumbfounded when I learned how well her books sold—almost half a million copies by 1988. That's a lot of books of poetry. So one of my questions in pursuing my research was, who reads Anne Sexton and why? Of course, the other meaning of that epigraph is that Anne Sexton's poetry is so powerful *as poetry* that it's the only poetry the people who read her care about; she says the things that they go to poetry to hear. For me, the double meaning in that claim put together the paradox of Sexton's force as an artist, both that she was popular and that people had problems with her.

WACHTEL In the preface you put the question, "Why did her work appeal to poetry avoiders?" How were you able to answer that question?

MIDDLEBROOK First of all by reading the fan letters she received, and kept. Sexton didn't ever throw anything away, as far as I can tell. I found that people wrote to her because they identified with her, either because they themselves had been ill or because somebody in their family was ill and Sexton's poetry had helped them to understand the illness. Or because they were women who felt stifled—or men who felt stifled—by the conventional roles their families or their communities had enforced on them. Sexton used to say, "People only hear you one at a time." And those letters came one at a time, saying, I hear you, and you say the things that I need to have put into words. This, I think, was among her most important experiences as an artist, and I think it's what gave her the confidence to ignore the bad reviews and the put-downs, and her own internal insecurities, and develop in the radical way she did.

WACHTEL You admit that at the start you didn't really like the Anne Sexton persona, but still you were drawn to her as a biographical subject. Why was that?

MIDDLEBROOK Because it was a fabulous project. There was this enormous treasury of manuscripts, Sexton's own working papers, her worksheets, some of which are reproduced in the book. She made carbon copies of all the letters she sent to people and kept them in the same files with their letters to her, so that there is a complete array of correspondence. And, of course, she was in touch with some of the major poets in America in the late fifties, sixties and early seventies; she had friends and mentors who were central to American poetry. Then there was the fact that she might very well have died instead of becoming a poet, so how did she do it? How did she rescue herself from that terrible illness? Also, there were the difficulties of her lack of education. And she was female in what the British would call a very "blokish" environment, the poetry scene in Boston in the fifties and sixties. All of those things made me interested in Sexton, and I just hoped that the fact that I was initially put off by her was not going to be a tremendous difficulty.

WACHTEL Every literary biographer has to deal with the relationship between the life and the work. Sexton's poetry was so boldly autobiographical, not simply "confessional poetry," like the poetry of Robert Lowell and John Ashbery, but also publicly tied to her mental illness, that this would be a particularly tricky situation for a biographer. Sexton herself was inconsistent about how she used her own experience. You quote her saying, "I use the personal when I'm applying a mask to my face, like the rubber mask that the robber wears." How do you distinguish what actually happened in her life from what she invents in the poetry?

MIDDLEBROOK In that metaphor she's telling us that what sounds most authentic in a work of art may very well be stolen. You think that the mask is her real face but she is an artist first and foremost, so whatever needs to be in the poem, whatever truth the poem needs, becomes the truth she tells. That's why it was so important for me to keep Sexton's persona in front of me; she had invented somebody to perform the scripts she wrote. The performer and the words behind the performance—the script and the performer together—are the work of art. Then, behind that, somewhere else, is the life on which Sexton is drawing to write her poetry. That division between her art and her life is as firmly held as it is by any of the poets who would describe themselves as "impersonal," such as Eliot and Pound, who were the principal figures in poetry preceding Sexton.

WACHTEL Her family had a history of mental illness and suicide, and also a history of alcoholism. Your biography traces some of the roots of Anne Sexton's madness to that and also to some disturbing influences in her family. What kind of home did she grow up in?

MIDDLEBROOK Anne Sexton had a powerful attachment to her childhood. She idealized her mother's parents and the cottage in which they spent their summers every year from the time she was a little girl, on Squirrel Island in Maine. That, for her, was paradise; it had an almost fairy-tale, magical quality. It was a big, warm extended family, in contrast to the distant, cold and isolated life she led inside the family house, where she lived with her father and mother. She was cared for by a nanny and didn't, according to her anyway, have very much day-to-day interaction with her mother.

Her father's father had had what was called "a nervous breakdown"; her father's sister, who was considered extremely eccentric, later became an alcoholic. On her mother's side, her most importance influence was her great-aunt, who had a breakdown when she lived with Sexton's family. Anne witnessed her, out of her head and screaming, being carried out of the house by doctors and taken to a mental hospital. This experience was a spectacle so influential on Sexton's psyche that I believe she committed suicide in order to avoid having it happen to herself; she very much identified with that woman. So there were acknowledged precursors in Sexton's own family to her breakdown. There was also, obviously, an extremely complicated and very important family dynamic going on around her. I tried to pull all of these things into perspective in the book.

WACHTEL Her obsession with suicide seems to have begun after the birth of her second daughter, when Sexton was in her late twenties. This was when she sought long-term treatment from a psychiatrist, and it's also when she started writing poetry, which is an amazing story. Where did she find the confidence to express herself through poetry?

MIDDLEBROOK How did she find the confidence to rescue herself through poetry? That, I think, is the mystery of human strength. I don't know where it came from but I made some guesses. For one thing, she identified with her mother, who was thought of in the family as a writer and was the only child of a writer, the editor of *The Lewiston Evening Journal* newspaper in Auburn, Maine. This grandfather was a terribly important figure to Sexton's mother—I think in a way she competed with her mother to be the one who inherited the writer role. They both had the middle name Grey, which was very significant to Sexton, which she passed on to her own daughter, who is also a writer. So there was a competitive spirit towards her mother, and in a certain way I think her mother almost grudgingly recognized that Anne really did have the gift.

Sexton's father was a salesman, and the kind of poet that Anne Sexton was depended a lot on salesmanship. I'm laughing because this seems so unlikely, but I believe that Sexton's performance skills, her sense that you had to have a signature, you had to be a recognizable person, you had to be able to charm the audience— all of those things she learned from her father, and they stood her in very good stead during her career.

So I think I found the secret ingredients that Sexton drew from her family, but why they combined in the way they did in her case is mysterious and has to do with a kind of inner spiritual strength. Her spirit just refused to be killed. She said at one point, "Suicide is the opposite of the poem." Writing was what she lived to do, but she never lost the intense obsession with suicide that I think drove her every single day of her life, from the time she broke down in 1956.

WACHTEL Anne Sexton saw herself as a fifties suburban housewife transformed. She was remarkably driven as a poet, and there are ways in which she fits the paradigm of the pre-feminist fifties woman—the frustrations of a housewife expected to take naturally to the roles of wife and mother, and the ways in which she was kind of crazy in her own right. You yourself put the question, "How did a mad housewife become a star?"

MIDDLEBROOK Sexton had a very lucky life in many ways, and luck played a great part in helping her to use the resources she had. She lived in Boston, where poetry is a respected enterprise, and there were plenty of people around to teach her how to write. Among her peers were people like Maxine Kumin, who was in much the same boat but just enough ahead of her to be helpful as a mentor. It was an environment that valued literature and poetry, and made resources available for writers. Of course, the key person in connecting her with this resource was the doctor who said to her, your problem is that you don't believe in yourself, you need to do something that you yourself value. He said, why don't you try writing? That was the luckiest thing of all.

WACHTEL He suggested this just after Sexton told him that one thing she might be good at was being a prostitute, helping men feel good about their sexual powers.

MIDDLEBROOK Yes, but being a prostitute is not what he had in mind! He was the first person to tell me that story, but later I saw how it fit into the puzzle of Anne Sexton. She had a tremendously self-destructive drive that was expressed through her sexuality, but also a great deal of pride and sexual curiosity. She was a very sexual person, and the range of her sexual expression and her sexual investigation was, again, exemplary of a woman of her time.

WACHTEL Anne Sexton met Sylvia Plath at a writing seminar given by Robert Lowell. Plath is another suicidal, tragic, confessional female poet and you point out that her later suicide provoked a complex reaction in Sexton, that Sexton felt that something that was hers had been taken, that death had been appropriated.

MIDDLEBROOK It's disturbing, isn't it, that Sexton saw Plath's suicide as a career move, one that had been taken from her because

Plath beat her to it. The best thing Sexton could make of it, first of all, was to try to enhance the identification between the two of them. She more or less prevented Lois Ames, Sylvia Plath's biographer, from doing her research on Plath by asking her to work as Sexton's *own* biographer. And because Sexton was afraid of travelling by herself, that meant following her around, taping her classes, being pretty much at her beck and call—and all of this successfully undermined the project of getting Sylvia Plath's biography written.

So there was a real sense of rivalry in Sexton. The person who meant the most to her in this regard was Ernest Hemingway. She saw suicide as a kind of death that had a lot of resonance for a literary career and also helped with the marketing of the work. Her prediction about Sylvia Plath came true: Plath was relatively unknown when she killed herself, but shortly after that she became the best-known woman writer in America and probably in England as well.

WACHTEL You describe the experience of writing this biography as "a moral education." What do you mean by that?

MIDDLEBROOK I had to confront an awful lot of my own biases about Anne Sexton. I disapproved of her, disapproved of the fact that she'd committed suicide first of all. I'm a teacher and I had avoided teaching the work of either Plath or Sexton in my courses because I thought it was bad for young people to get the idea that creative women always killed themselves. So they were off my list. I held that against her.

Her hysterical personality really gave me the creeps. I had spent an awful lot of time in my tender youth and young womanhood being an honorary man, and Sexton was simply too female for me. I realized, when I started to really think about what it was I didn't like about her, that she confirmed the worst anti-feminist attitudes that I held—shamefully deeply, it turned out—so that coming close to her was a way of recognizing my own biases. That's what I meant by moral education.

WACHTEL Perhaps the best-known controversy surrounding your

biography is your use of more than three hundred hours of taped therapy sessions released by Sexton's primary psychiatrist, Dr. Martin Orne. Sexton's daughter and literary executor helped obtain these and other medical records for you. Did you have any qualms about using them?

MIDDLEBROOK This question comes up whenever the issue of the tapes is raised, and I think it has helped me to sharpen my own focus on the difference between the ethics of biography, let's say, and the ethics of psychiatry. I believe that Martin Orne acted very judiciously. He deliberated for some time about giving me access to these tapes and consulted both the family and, according to him, ethical advisers in his own profession, who agreed with what he himself thought. These records were regarded by the family themselves as belonging to the literary archive. In Sexton's case, I think there's an almost unique pertinence in the psychotherapeutic records because she not only wrote about them but she learned about writing from them.

I've never had any qualms about listening to the tapes. When I reflect on why this is, I think it's that in order to write a biography at all, you have to be willing to be extremely intrusive and voyeuristic with respect to somebody else's life. It's a fundamental invasion of privacy. I freely read Sexton's mail, something I would never do with my own family. But the biographer is a licensed snooper, invested with a particular kind of invulnerability to censure of that kind. You're *supposed* to find out as many things as you possibly can. So the primary ethical question about biographies is, Should anybody do it at all? If you decide yes, writing a biography is ethical and it provides a valuable contribution to culture, then the next question is, Should you use everything you find out?

By the time I got around to listening to the tapes I'd spent months decoding Anne Sexton's own notes on the tapes, so it wasn't as if I didn't already have access to some of the material before the tapes were in my hands. But I discovered how very much more there was to be learned from listening to her talk about herself than I had even dreamed. No, far from qualms, I felt that, alas, listening to them was going to take a long time, but it was going to be worth every minute.

WACHTEL You were also able to include some quite disturbing revelations from her daughter, Linda Gray Sexton, about Anne Sexton's sexual abuse of her. All of this controversy prompted one critic to call you "the Kitty Kelly of literary biography" for including this scandalous material and, unwittingly, also helping Sexton's daughter revenge herself by your collaborating in a "Mommy-dearest" type of exposé.

MIDDLEBROOK Well, I have to tell you, Kitty Kelly and I are from the same home town! But I must also say that, after four drafts and ten years, nothing whatsoever in that book is unwitting—that is my bottom line. It's all intended. I was not beholden to Linda Sexton to write the book she might have wanted me to write. The book I wrote is my book, though it was hers to grant or withhold permission to quote from unpublished materials. She sometimes debated with me about interpretations, and sometimes I learned a lot from that, but she never insisted on having her own way.

WACHTEL How were you able to completely trust the reliability of the revelations about Anne Sexton and her daughter?

MIDDLEBROOK How do you trust anything? I mean, it makes sense to you, it's consistent with something, somebody says it to you and you say, "Oh my God, it's probably true." The conditions under which Linda remembered what had happened between the two of them are for her alone to describe. But it was reading the sections of the manuscript that dealt with Anne Sexton's play, *Mercy Street*, that bore home to Linda the awful correspondence between what was happening in the play and what was happening in her own life.

WACHTEL It's astonishing to consider that, at the very time that Anne Sexton was working on material relating to her *own* sexual abuse by members of her family, she was abusing her own daughter.

MIDDLEBROOK I had a lot of trouble with that discovery. I talked about it with a couple of the clinicians I worked with closely, and here I think the clinical point of view is helpful. One of them said to me, the most generous way you could think about this is that Sexton was at her most ill when she was doing this and didn't know what it was she was doing, that she literally didn't know whose body it was. There is evidence that she experienced this very situation of intimacy with her great-aunt Nanna. That was the emotional landscape of Sexton's pathology, and you might speculate that she was in a trance when it happened and wasn't aware of what she was doing.

That was the only way I could account for what seemed to me a tremendously complex set of attitudes on Sexton's part towards her own child. She was very proud of Linda; she was also terrifically attached to her. Sexton's range of behaviours was much more extreme and pathological than I had been able to judge before looking closely at her records and also listening to her tapes, because she obviously functioned so well in other ways. In short, I think that she was not in her right mind when she did it.

WACHTEL   Later, Anne Sexton left her husband but continued to perform, to win prizes and to receive honorary degrees. Then in 1974, at age forty-five, she committed suicide. This may be one of those unanswerable questions, but, after your own ten years of "living" with Sexton, do you know why, and why then?

MIDDLEBROOK   I think I do. Sexton was very, very alcoholic at that point, and that destroyed her ability to revise her poetry. Even when she could still write it, she couldn't revise it any more, and I think she recognized that she was no longer the poet she had been. Her drinking was out of control, and was very much a response to the extraordinary loneliness of her life after her divorce. Her kids had grown up and left home, and Sexton was one of those people who could not live alone.

Then, too, there was the spectre of ending up like Nanna, going mad, being incarcerated for the rest of her life in a mental institution. For about a year before her death Sexton began preparing for it, very carefully. She got herself a literary executor, organized her papers beautifully, began preparing people for her death, and more or less committed herself to the downhill slide that she underwent. Her treatment was terminated by her psychiatrist in that environment of loss, and that too was certainly an important contributor to her sense of despair, which was very deep by then. But I see her as gathering herself together to commit suicide and doing it very deliberately and even, I would say, rather heroically.

WACHTEL Heroically? Are you changing your view of it?

MIDDLEBROOK Yes, because, unlike Dr. Martin Orne, who in the preface says that Sexton would be alive today if psychiatry had not let her down, I think she had lost the necessary conditions for her life. I don't believe that a woman of forty-five would be able to recompose the life that had supported her. Her children, especially when they were young, were absolutely crucial to her mental health because they put her in touch with her own childhood. Once they grew up, she didn't have that incredible refreshing resource any more. Her marriage had gone very wrong, and didn't have an emotional centre by the time it ended, though it certainly had a lot of other things that were very supportive.

She was also resistant to recovery from alcoholism. She liked to joke about this, saying she'd rather be a drunk like the rest of the poets than be an alcoholic because if you're an alcoholic you're expected to recover, to stop drinking, but if you're a drunk, well, you're just like everybody else. As in so many other things, she was defiant, she wanted to have life on her own terms, but this life had run out. I think that the method she chose, the day she chose, the circumstances in which she spent the whole day giving gifts to people, did not warn them that she was going to kill herself. She took her own life very deliberately and, it seemed to me, in a way that said, I meant this, it was time for me to die. And, even though I myself have a lot of problems with that, I came to see it, yes, as heroic.

WACHTEL You co-edited a selection of Anne Sexton's poetry before starting work on the biography. How has this immersion in her life affected your view of the poetry?

MIDDLEBROOK I came to think of her as an extremely important artist. That was, for me, the greatest benefit of writing the book— coming to terms with an artist whose work I hadn't studied closely enough to understand on its own terms. I kept finding wonderful things in it that I had to invent a critical perspective in order to describe. So I hope that, for some readers anyway, the critical commentary on Sexton's achievements as an artist will be valuable. I think it's terribly important for an artist to be able to change her mode once she gets something going that other people reward her for, and I watched Sexton do that a number of times. The biography tries to account for that refreshment of her own originality.

October 1991

interview prepared in collaboration
with Sandra Rabinovitch

Nadine Gordimer

Nadine Gordimer is a white South African writer who's
been described as the "conscience of her society," although
it's a label she avoids. Gordimer has won numerous international literary prizes and critical accolades for novels such
as *Burger's Daughter* (1979), *July's People* (1981) and *A Sport
of Nature* (1987). *The Conservationist* was co-winner of the
Booker Prize in 1974. She mocks foreign reviewers who
apply the word "courageous" as a literary value for South
African writers. It isn't courage that drives her to write, she
insists; she started writing when she was nine years old.

It's hard not to admire Nadine Gordimer. As *New
Yorker* critic Judith Thurman has written, Gordimer's "fury
is as shameless as her lyrical eroticism." She is intimidating
because she "asserts that it is possible to do something
about evil." Nadine Gordimer isn't easy, but she's always
interesting. She understands the nuances of love and relationships, she writes evocatively about landscape, and
despite her political priorities, she never writes didactically.

But it's not only Gordimer's writing that elicits admiration, it's her consistent, thoughtful and outspoken political
stance—fully aware of all the impossible contradictions.
Nadine Gordimer was born in 1923 and has become even
more politically engaged as she gets older. She's a card-
carrying member of the African National Congress, and

she wrote powerful, joyful journalistic pieces when Nelson Mandela was finally released from prison.

Some of her books have been banned, *A World of Strangers* and *The Late Bourgeois World* for more than ten years, but politics are an imperative. As Gordimer says, "In South Africa, there's hardly anything you do which doesn't make you an accomplice to this or that."

I interviewed Nadine Gordimer about five months before she won the Nobel Prize for Literature. When she was named there was talk of possible resentment from black South Africans, but congratulations began with Nelson Mandela, and amongst the crowd that greeted her when she returned to Johannesburg airport was Archbishop Desmond Tutu.

I had long hoped for the opportunity to meet her, and the "excuse" for my interview was the publication of her recent novel *My Son's Story* (1990). Unfortunately, it wasn't face to face, but over the phone from her home in Johannesburg. I was more nervous in anticipation of this conversation than most. I had read that she doesn't suffer fools gladly, and as one British newspaper put it, "she talks like an electric carving knife." I was daunted. But as soon as she answered the first question, I realized how generous she was prepared to be, and I relaxed.

WACHTEL Your father immigrated to South Africa as a teenager to escape anti-Semitism in Lithuania. You describe the conditions your father left behind as being closely parallel to the situation that blacks were living under in South Africa. Can you tell me more about your family background?

GORDIMER Unfortunately I know very little about my father's family background. I wish I knew more. Somehow it seemed very remote from the life I lived with my parents. And my mother came from a very different background. She'd come from England at the age of six. She grew up as a South African, and of course a native English speaker. My father's humble background was basically forgotten about. So I wish I knew more, but I do know that one of the reasons why he—and then other members of his family, his siblings—came was because in Lithuania Jews were not allowed to go to high school, and there were all sorts of other problems at the time. My father, who was one of eight or nine children, was brought up by his grandmother and grandfather back in the village while his parents both worked in Riga. That is the parallel with the situation of many blacks here who have to work in town and send the children back to rural areas.

WACHTEL Tell me about growing up in a small South African town in the twenties and thirties.

GORDIMER It was a mining town, and naturally I lived within the white enclave there. I went to a convent school, whites only, and all the other aspects of my life as a child were segregated. Children go through the early years of their life accepting the world that their parents present to them. They don't question it. The fact that there were no black children at the school, that no black child went to the movies on Saturday—this was just the way things were, the way the sun came up in the morning and went down at night. It was simply the way the world was made. I didn't realize that these circumstances were man-made. My parents were not politically aware at all. It was only in my teens that I became aware that there was something very wrong with the way we lived.

WACHTEL Do you recall how you became politically aware in your teens? What was it that triggered that awareness?

GORDIMER Oddly enough, I think it came from outside. I was always a great reader, and one of the books that was important to me was Upton Sinclair's *The Jungle*, about how the meat workers lived in Chicago. I made parallels in my mind between those meat workers and the black migratory workers in the African compounds. I lived in a town that had grown up to service the nearby mines. When I walked to my convent school every day across the veldt, I would pass the concession stores where blacks coming off shift would go to do their shopping. They were discouraged from going into town. We lived very near the mine, and I would see these, to me then, exotic-looking people—many of them came from distant parts of southern Africa, from Mozambique, from what were then Tanganyika and Rhodesia—and some of them had these clay locks. They wore blankets instead of ordinary clothes, and they seemed very exotic to me. I only realized later that I was the exotic element, the white. They were at home in their own country, and I was the child of settlers.

WACHTEL In other ways, yours was a curious childhood. You spent a lot of time with adults. You were precocious, I think, encouraged to express yourself, and your great ambition was to become a dancer.

GORDIMER I think I was a bit of a pain in the neck, a show-off, and I loved dancing and acting, the idea of the glamour of it. Of course, the cultural context in which I was brought up was so narrow. Those Saturday movies meant mainly the big Ziegfeld-type shows, so my heroes and heroines were people like Fred Astaire and Ginger Rogers, and it was that Hollywood dreamworld that seemed to me to be adult life. And dancing class was my little share of it. But I loved the dancing, and being a rather small, slightly built girl I was quite suited to it. Anyway it's a good thing I didn't take it up as a career. I don't know whether I'd have been any good, but by now I certainly would have been finished, whereas as a writer I'm not.

WACHTEL What punctured your dreams of becoming a dancer?

GORDIMER I had this vague imaginative energy that many children have, especially children who are going to grow up to be artists one way or another, so that I loved the dancing. I enjoyed mimicking people and I loved putting on little shows, for which my mother and anybody else who would watch had to be the audience. I also wrote things. I wrote my own little newspapers, invented my own news. I was writing and dancing and acting, so that it was a general feeling of vague creativity. I think what very often happens—most children have a lot of imagination, as we know, and children's games are so imaginative—is that at adolescence, people who are not going to be writers or painters or musicians lose this. It turns into something else. Quite a lot of it goes into the energy of sexual awakening, into the emotions connected with sex. But if you're going to be a writer, that's the crucial time when you don't stop dreaming, you don't stop inventing, you go right on making things up.

WACHTEL I read that a childhood health problem is what made you focus on writing rather than dancing.

GORDIMER That was one of these mysteries, you know. Later it seemed that there was never really anything wrong with me, that it was something to do with my mother's desire to keep me close to her. It's something that's better not gone into.

WACHTEL But writing seemed like the logical alternative?

GORDIMER As I say, I was writing and dancing for quite a time. I was doing all sorts of things. But I read more and more, and became more and more aware that there was the possibility of expressing myself in words.

WACHTEL You were always an avid and eclectic reader—from *War and Peace* to *Gone with the Wind* when you were twelve—but among the writers you mention as influences, Marcel Proust stands out. You describe his influence as so deep that, to quote, "It frightens me, not only in my writing, but in my attitudes to life." How did Proust shape your attitudes to life?

GORDIMER I think in the sense that I was reading him before I had much experience of life. Especially his attitude towards love, that it could never be entirely successful, that the desired object would always slip through one's grasp. I think he influenced me in that way, though once I began to experience these things for myself I didn't quite agree with Marcel Proust.

WACHTEL You had more successful experiences?

GORDIMER Yes. In that wonderful book, which funnily enough

I'm just re-reading now, the beloved is always out of reach.

WACHTEL Why are you re-reading *Remembrance of Things Past?*

GORDIMER Well, I read it every few years. And now, for the first time, I'm painfully and slowly reading it in the original.

WACHTEL Your work is so very much identified with South African life and politics. You've said that you were a writer before you became politically aware. "It was learning to write that sent me falling, falling through the surface of the South African way of life." Can you tell me more about how writing led you to political consciousness?

GORDIMER Writing is always a voyage of discovery. I didn't begin to write out of political awareness. I'd been writing since I was nine years old. I published my first adult story when I was fifteen. But if you're going to be a writer, you first of all have to develop unusual powers of observation. You're very contemplative of other people, as well as yourself. I was always an eager eavesdropper, and I still am. That's one of the ways a writer teaches herself or himself to write dialogue, to write direct speech. You have to have an ear for the way different people speak, for the way they express them-selves, for the pauses that indicate what is not being said. This sort of instinct is something that a writer subconsciously begins to teach herself.

The political awareness came through looking very closely at the people around me, in other words at my own society, and at myself and my place in it, my reactions, their reactions. When I described this as falling from layer to layer, I meant falling through layers of illusion and coming slowly, stage by stage, to certain truths. Coming through what was false and searching for what was true. This process of falling through all kinds of sophistry, all kinds of mistaken ideas, is something that has gone on all my life, and still goes on. This comes from being born and brought up in this sort of society, where from the time you're a small child you're living so many lies.

I talked a little earlier about how I didn't question the fact that I went to a school where there were no black children. So what was the lie there? The lie was that I just assumed that black children didn't want to go to that school. It didn't occur to me that they were not allowed to. The same with the cinema and the library. If I had been a black child, I couldn't have been a member of that library, and I assure you I'd never have been a writer. These are the sort of lies that children in this kind of society are brought up in— to think that blacks were so different that they weren't human, that they didn't want the things we had. These are the early layers you fall through, and it goes on and on, all sorts of prejudices to be sloughed off. You could call it an onion peeling, you could call it falling.

WACHTEL But the layers get more complicated and subtle, and you've always been very hard on yourself as well as everyone else in terms of not finding it a comfortable place. Being very aware of the contradictions of privilege at the same time that you resist and reject the society that creates it.

GORDIMER Of course I don't consider it being hard. I think that people do themselves a disservice, and a writer does society a disservice, by continuing to cover up such things, that the really helpful thing, the thing that makes you grow, is trying to peel away these misconceptions.

WACHTEL You've written about the tensions between a writer's need for privacy and the necessity for political engagement, what you call "creative self-absorption versus conscionable awareness," and you suggest that it's that very tension or dialectic that can make a writer. How have you been able to negotiate this dialectic in your own life?

GORDIMER It hasn't been easy, but I think it's essential. It's a kind of balancing act. As I say, my political awareness came rather late when I think of the political sophistication demonstrated, for instance, in '68, in France, in America, maybe in Canada as well, by such very young people—school children, certainly high-school children. At that age I wasn't interested in politics at all. I didn't know it existed. I was absorbed in poetry and in writing of a very different nature. And I wasn't reading political tracts. I wasn't reading politics at all, and I didn't belong, when I was eighteen, nineteen, and could have, to any progressive group discussing left-ist politics. I wasn't interested. So I think that when I finally did become aware that politics wasn't just like taking up golf or tennis, something that you could take or leave if you were a white South African or if you were any kind of South African, it was then that I began to be politically aware. This grew with the widening of my contacts as I had more and more black friends and became involved in their lives, and they were feeling the hard edge of apartheid on the other side of the colour bar. So then as a human being, as a citizen, I became aware and, as the years went by, involved.

But I've always kept for my writing something that has only to do with me. I have never tried to shape my imagination to any kind of political line. I've never allowed myself to write propa-ganda, however strongly I've felt for the people on my side, on the side that I've attached myself to as a citizen and as a human being. I have fought to retain that freedom to write what I like, how I like, and not follow any line, because I think that the first impera-tive duty, if one wants to use that word, for a writer is to be true, to preserve the integrity of whatever talent he or she has. This is the one thing you have that matters, and your first duty to yourself and your society is to develop it. You're constantly teaching your-self to write, you're constantly seeing where you failed at the things you've tried to do, you're constantly working away at developing your ability and finding the right way to tackle more and more complex themes. I always remember something that Gabriel Gar-cia Marquez said a few years ago, on being asked the same kind of question as you're asking me now. He said, "In the end, the best thing a writer can do for his society is to write as well as he can." And that, of course, is a lifetime's task.

But living in South Africa as a white, I couldn't simply shut myself in an ivory tower and say I'm a writer, finished. In the other part of my life I've become active in a way that really goes against my nature. I'm not a joiner, I'm not a person who likes to sit on committees or to get up and speak on public platforms. But I couldn't live as a white South African in South Africa and not take part in some kind of active protest, so that's how my life has developed. But, of course, a writer's life anywhere is the tension, as I've said, between doing and standing back and contemplating, so that, in an odd way, the things that have taxed my energy have also fed my writing. Because I've experienced things that if I had shut myself away and said, I'm not going to do anything but write, I would never have experienced, and so they wouldn't have enriched not only my life but my writing.

WACHTEL You've become more radical over the years. There's a wonderful line in *Burger's Daughter* that defines loneliness as to live without social responsibility. Obviously your writing has been forged by living in a place where, as you've said, one *must* write about injustice, about the political situation.

GORDIMER I think you can't help it, because what does anybody write about? They write about the texture of the life around them. This country has always been so absolutely imbued with politics, riddled with politics, whatever you like to call it, and indeed—I believe this profoundly—black, white, all of us have been shaped from the time we were born by the strictures of our society. I often think of it in these terms: when a child is born and comes down the birth canal, it's then that its head is shaped. If you're brought up within an apartheid society with all its strange restrictions, you know your skull is not quite shaped; it goes on being shaped by these pressures.

WACHTEL For you, this meant moving from a kind of liberalism to a real radicalism.

GORDIMER I was becoming aware that there are actions and attitudes appropriate to one historical period that are not appropriate to the next. Another demand comes up. The liberal position might have been all right in the fifties, but as things developed, it was a kind of impotence in the sixties and seventies, and has remained so ever since. So what the historical situation you live in demands of you as a human being changes, and you have to find out whether you're equal to it or not. Some people have proved themselves magnificently equal to it and have gone through extraordinary changes, much more profound than my own, but everybody responds in the way that he or she is capable of.

WACHTEL Do you ever long for a writer's vacation, in a sense, long to have a holiday from repressive South Africa?

GORDIMER Not really, no. Oh, I sometimes despaired—but not now, because now, you know, there's this turmoil, but there's change. But perhaps ten years ago there was just a feeling that nothing was ever going to change here, and that was very frustrating and depressing. I don't think a writer can really take that kind of holiday, because you're going to carry your experience around inside you. And people who write fiction carry these experiences for a very long time. You never know when they're going to come up and go through the process of your imagination and your creation, and come out as part of something that you're going to be writing twenty years after it happened. Writers are notoriously dependent upon early impressions, and constantly hop back to them. It's a kind of process of comparison that goes on all the time. I suppose that enables us to create characters of a completely different age group, because we've gone through it or we've observed it very closely in others. Otherwise we couldn't write from the point of view of children or young people when we're old, or old people while we're still young.

WACHTEL One of your decisions early on, and no doubt a decision that you may have had to make on a number of occasions, was not to leave South Africa, that it was better to resist from within than to live in exile, and despite opportunities to leave you've always chosen to stay there.

GORDIMER I think it was Jean-Paul Sartre who said, "If you go into exile, you lose your place in the world." I believe he meant an inner world as well. But, of course, many people have been forced into exile. It's very interesting now to see the process of adjustment among my colleagues and comrades, among writers, black writers who've been in exile and who have now come back. It's very difficult if you've gone away young and lived twenty years or so of your adult life away, and you have a picture in your mind of home and the people there. It's difficult, but I think some very interesting writing will come out of it, because now this is an experience that doesn't fit the dream of coming home.

WACHTEL Does it sadden you that your children have chosen to leave?

GORDIMER Yes. One chose to leave. But with the other one, it's just happened. The girl simply fell in love with a Frenchman and had to go and live in France. It wasn't a conscious choice with her. For my son it was, but maybe he'll come back now. It was very difficult for men. We sent him out of South Africa to go to school so that he wouldn't go to a racially segregated school. He went to school in Swaziland and lived among black boys, white boys, boys of all grades of colour. And then there was the choice for him of not coming back here at all, or of doing his army service. He did his army service, and it was a big shock to him to see the attitudes of some of the people who were with him in the camps. Then came the time when people were being called up once a year, or whenever there was an emergency, and sent into the townships, with dogs and tear gas and guns. He had been to school with blacks, and for him it was an incredible thing to be sent in, in this way. That is really why he left.

WACHTEL You have since actually advocated that whites think twice about doing military service, that white boys resist.

GORDIMER I don't know whether my son would have been prepared to go to prison for five or six years, or whether I would have been prepared to see him do it, but the fact is that quite a number of people did it. And I think it was an extremely brave thing to do. It was a revolutionary thing to do.

WACHTEL One of the consequences of your staying in South Africa and being politically involved is that three of your books, including one of your best-known novels, *Burger's Daughter*, have been banned, at least temporarily, for periods of several months to fourteen years. You've said that censorship is a brand on the imagination that affects a writer forever. How have you been affected by the banning of your fiction?

GORDIMER First of all, there's that strange kind of hiatus in your relationship with your society. For years two of my books were not read by my own people. I think that's something you don't forget; it's a kind of gap which can't really be bridged. Some people whose books have been banned have begun to write differently or have gone through a period of self-censorship. I was fortunate. I didn't do that. By the time my books were being banned I already was known in the outside world, so I knew that they would be read somewhere.

WACHTEL Do writers rely on some kind of reaction from their society? Do you need to have some feeling of community?

GORDIMER Yes, I think so. The only book of non-fiction I've ever published is called *The Essential Gesture*, which is a quotation from Roland Barthes. For the writer, his work is the essential gesture he makes to his society, the hand he puts out. Writing is a very solitary occupation. You don't sit with other people to do it; it's something you work at on your own, so you haven't got the kind of working comradeship that exists in other forms of activity, and you communicate essentially through the book's being read.

WACHTEL You've said that sex and politics are the greatest motivators of people's lives. In *My Son's Story*, sex and politics certainly coalesce in complex ways. The central figure, Sonny, is a so-called coloured schoolteacher who becomes a political activist and then has an adulterous affair with a white woman, a comrade in the struggle. That situation ultimately undermines him, in his work and in his view of himself. Is this mix of sex and politics inevitably fraught?

GORDIMER To a certain extent, yes, I think so. In the case of Sonny and the woman Hannah, the colour difference is almost irrelevant. You may remember that in one of his darkest hours, Sonny has, to him, the ironic thought that he wishes that such a relationship had still been forbidden by law. This would have been the case a few years earlier, before the so-called Immorality Act was rescinded. He feels that if that law had still been in force, he would never have risked his political career by going to prison for a love affair. And it's a terrible thought for him.

I think this whole business of sex and politics, and the complications that sexual emotions cause in politics, comes about because of the enormous demands that political activity makes on people, and the tremendous intrusion into their private lives. Almost without exception, all the full-time political activists I've known simply don't have time for family life. They're sent all over the world; they pass in and out of prison; their families, whether it's their children, or wife or husband, tend to be left alone for long years. Other emotional attachments come up. It makes normal family life and love relations very, very difficult, because people's lives are so invaded by the demands of a liberation struggle that is ruthless, taking all people's time and energy. And when there has to be a choice between some sort of private responsibility and a responsibility to the movement, if you really are dedicated to the movement, then the movement must prevail.

WACHTEL There's a way in which, in *My Son's Story*, the sexual liaison erodes Sonny's ideals.

GORDIMER I would contest that. Sonny's a bit of a prig in the beginning. He's a goody-goody in the sense that he has a very narrow morality and he wants to function within that to be useful, to be decent, to be progressive. He's really trying at the beginning to be a good schoolteacher, to be helpful within his community but to go no further than that. Yet Sonny grows to take on much bigger demands, even to the extent of ruining his marriage. The trouble with that marriage is something that I think is quite outside the political context—people marry very young, and then one partner outgrows the other in the spiritual and intellectual sense, and that's what happened to Sonny. Why is he attracted to Hannah? It's not just a physical attraction but because she really can keep up with him and his ideas, and she is truly devoted to the same cause he is. So it's a mixture between a political-intellectual attraction and a sexual attraction.

WACHTEL Yet Sonny, who is a basically good man, loses a lot in the course of this book: he loses his family, his lover and even his political position in the struggle. Why do you punish him so much?

GORDIMER I don't know that he really loses his position. You see, there again, there's a subtle truth that has to be faced, and I see it again and again. In a liberation struggle, people serve a certain purpose at a certain time, and then that time is over, the struggle moves into another stage and others more capable of dealing with that stage take over. I think it was Lenin who said that at the rendezvous of victory there will be room for all, but I don't know whether that's quite true. We've all seen how the people who make the revolution get pushed aside when victory comes. In some cases they even get destroyed, as they did in the French Revolution and as some did in the Russian Revolution. Sonny responds courageously and grows, but somehow he is not going to be up there among the top leadership. At the end of the book he's in prison again, so he still counts obviously, otherwise nobody would bother to detain him. Certainly in his personal life he has lost everything; that's a sacrifice he's made for the struggle.

WACHTEL What struck me in *My Son's Story* is that in a way, the others who take over, or who carry on, are the women. His lover, his wife, his daughter. They move forward and carry on.

GORDIMER Yes. But, they're not in the movement with him. His wife Aila is, but the others are not. Hannah goes off with the United Nations Commission for Refugees. And how busy she must be now. I sometimes think of her. But in the movement, his other comrades are going ahead. He's just become slightly peripheral. Not right up with the top ten.

It's odd to me that most people don't talk about what, to me, is central to *My Son's Story*, and that is the relationship between father and son. So much love there and so much conflict. Sonny manipulates the boy, partly because of political pressures and partly because he wishes to, because of this love affair and because he wants to protect himself. The boy's resentment grows—his being an adolescent, his sexual jealousy of his father compounded by love of the mother, feeling that the mother is being betrayed. To me that's so important in the book.

WACHTEL The very title of this book gives a sense of expectation from one generation to the next, and this comes up in some of your other books too. Sonny wants his son Will to become a writer. Children measure themselves or define themselves against the values of their parents. Rosa, in *Burger's Daughter*, is the daughter of a very politically engaged—in fact, martyred—man, and she reacts against that and has to work through it. Do you feel that this kind of generational tension is particularly strong in a country like South Africa?

GORDIMER The so-called generation gap takes on a very interesting form among politically active and aware people in South Africa. One phenomenon that I was exploring in *Burger's Daughter* was that very often this total devotion of their lives to political activism passes from generation to generation. I can think of one particular case that involves three generations of the same family, in which each generation has devoted itself to all the risks and all the deprivations that come with being politically active in South Africa. The grandparents have been active, their children were in and out of prison as things developed, and now the grandchildren are living the same, very difficult life, having passports seized, unable to travel, being detained, being debarred from certain careers that they would like to have taken up. It's like an extraordinary faith, almost like a religion, that has a hold on people from generation to generation. So the children don't rebel against the kind of life imposed upon them by the parents. I think that's a new wrinkle on the generation gap.

WACHTEL Returning briefly to where we began, do you ever look at your own life in these terms? Do you ever measure yourself in relation to your parents, as the daughter of Jewish immigrants who came to South Africa for freedom and opportunity?

GORDIMER Oh yes, of course. As I say, I know very little about my father's background and not much more about my mother's. I suppose this isn't exceptional; it's probably true of most people whose parents have immigrated, who are the first generation born in a country. But I never felt, or was made to feel, that there was some part of me that belonged somewhere else. I was born and brought up here and this is my home; I'm not a European. So I didn't have any sense of a split. In any case, as I have said, my parents came from very different backgrounds, and very different countries. The one from London and the other from a little village outside Riga.

My life has been vastly different from that of my parents. There is a far greater difference between my life and my parents' life and the milieu in which I spent my early years than there is between my life and the life of my now-adult children. I don't know why that is. I think it has something to do with this country, and with the social and political pressures here that brought about a kind of awareness that my parents didn't have. But then of course, they were different people. Sometimes the genes get together and throw up somebody who is a real cuckoo in the nest, and that's what I seem to have been in my family. There's certainly no tradition of any writer or any artists in the family as far as I know.

WACHTEL Rosa Burger says that it's strange to live in a country where there are still heroes. Many people call you a hero. Does that make you uncomfortable?

GORDIMER Oh yes, because it isn't true. It isn't true at all. What is true is that I myself have that feeling—that it's strange and it's also wonderful to live in a country where there are still heroes. It's inspiring, despite all the terrible things that happen here, that there are such wonderful people. It's a privilege to have known and to know them. I think in many parts of the world there's a kind of evenness, a level of awareness, of courage and so on, among people. Great demands are not made on them, so that you don't see who is going to be exceptional and who isn't. But, in this country, even with the waves of people going into exile, going into prison, there are always others coming up. Always. So that there are people here, individuals whom I revere. I don't know whether I would feel that way if I lived in America or in England.

May 1991

interview prepared in collaboration
with Sandra Rabinovitch

Margaret Atwood

The first interview I ever did was with Margaret Atwood. I was book review editor at *The McGill Daily* and a new book of poems arrived called *The Circle Game* (1966). Given the classic, Anglophile education I was receiving at the time in honours English, Atwood was one of the first Canadian poets—one of the first living poets—I had occasion to look at. But the poems in *The Circle Game* had an immediacy and an accessibility that drew me in. The first poem in the book, "This is a Photograph of Me," is an evocative image of the poet (or alter ego) disappearing into the landscape, drowned in a lake. But "if you look long enough," Atwood writes, "eventually / you will be able to see me."

It was the mid-sixties and Atwood was teaching at the other English university in Montreal, Sir George Williams, now known as Concordia. I called her up and we met at a small Greek restaurant on Park Avenue and drank cups of tea. She talked about writing poetry. And then she became famous.

I've interviewed Margaret Atwood many times since then, usually for radio when she's published a new novel, but the publication of *Selected Poems 1966-1984* (1990) was the first time in almost twenty-five years that I had the chance to talk to her again about her poetry. The selection spans nine collections—from *The Circle Game* to *Interlu-nar*, published in 1984.

Her seven published novels include *The Edible Woman* (1969), *The Handmaid's Tale* (1985) and *Cat's Eye* (1988). Many readers familiar with Atwood's novels aren't aware of the poetry; others, often writers, say they favour the poetry. Fortunately one doesn't have to choose—both are there to be enjoyed in abundance. But the poems often yield clues and themes that emerge in the prose. I welcomed the chance to go back to them.

———————————

WACHTEL You produced your first book of poems when you were seven—which, you said, didn't indicate promise. Why did you start writing poetry?

ATWOOD Because I was writing everything else at the time. I started a novel about then. It featured as its central character an ant. Don't ask me why. I did not finish that book, but it started off quite well. And I was writing other things as well—I think our main form was comic books. We probably did more of those than anything, but I also did a play around that time. I think children—this is the pre-television generation—imitate the art forms they see around them. I had a large book of Mother Goose—you know, the Collected—and other poems as well, so it was just a natural thing.

WACHTEL I was going to ask you what kind of poetry you were reading.

ATWOOD At the age of five?

WACHTEL Well, we could start there, and we could move on a little bit. When did you really start reading poetry seriously?

ATWOOD I didn't really start reading poetry seriously, apart from the stuff we had to do in school—you know, *Poems Chiefly Narrative* and things like that—until I started writing it. The poetry I was exposed to was not written in the twentieth century. I didn't even really know that there was such a thing as modern poetry until I was at university.

WACHTEL Which is when you really started to write poetry.

ATWOOD No, I started when I was sixteen, in high school. It all sounds like Edgar Allan Poe on a very bad day; you know, Byron with a hangover. It all rhymes and scans. Actually, it's rather startlingly bad poetry. It's written by a sixteen-year-old; what can we expect?

WACHTEL Is it full of angst?

ATWOOD Lots of angst. I looked back through some of it, which I still have, and noticed I had written a poem about the Hungarian uprising of 1956 which I had quite forgotten. But there is a reasonable amount of angst, more so as I hit the coffee shop. Let's face it, once you hit the coffee shop—once I hit T.S. Eliot—then lots of empty vessels appeared in my poems, you know, empty cups.

WACHTEL I remember measuring out my life in coffee spoons around that time.

ATWOOD They had a big impact. Also, the fact that you could put garbage in a poem very much impressed me because, if all you had was nineteenth-century poetry, that had no garbage in it. It was much more noble. But once you hit the twentieth century —

WACHTEL What kind of garbage?

ATWOOD Garbage, you know, garbage blowing around on the street, the kind you have in garbage cans. So I put some of that in my early poems, and leaves, decaying leaves, not spring leaves.

WACHTEL What draws you to poetry both as a writer and a reader?

ATWOOD I go through long phases of neither writing it nor reading it. Then I'll go through a phase in which I really can't get enough of it. I go to the bookstore and I catch up on all the books of poetry I haven't read over the past three or four years. It's like another life, or let me put it this way: it's another language. I always have the sense of opening up a box and finding amazing things in there which are suddenly very attractive—you know, coming across something you had hidden away, finding it again. I think for me it has a lot to do with the rediscovery of language or concentration on the word.

If you're writing a novel, you're concentrating on much larger units—not that you don't pay attention to your sentences et cetera, but the potency of the individual word tends to be more spread out. You're really concentrating on starting something on page 30 that you finish on page 250. The wavelengths are a lot longer, the pattern much larger. Poetry is a very concentrated form, and therefore the explosiveness of each word becomes much greater.

WACHTEL You say you go through periods of not writing poetry at all, while at other times you write a lot. Do you know why?

ATWOOD I have no idea, nor do I try to predict or have any opinions about it, because I think once you start indulging in too much self-observation you interfere with the process.

I'm superstitious about writing in general, maybe a little bit more about poetry—I've started again after some time. I was writing the entry about Gwendolyn MacEwen for a Commonwealth biographical dictionary, and that really put me back into being twenty again, when we used to read at the Bohemian Embassy in Toronto. Gwen was a couple of years younger than me, and she was just a phenomenon—this eighteen-year-old kid who had quit school to dedicate herself to writing and here she was already with a fully formed style and a manner of presentation that was completely professional. I was thinking back to that, and I was thinking what an astonishing thing it was to make that leap, to take that risk. I got sentimental about all of that and I started writing poetry again.

WACHTEL The first poem in your latest selected poems, "This is a Photograph of Me," is from *The Circle Game*, which came out back in 1966. I've always liked that poem a lot, even before I realized that it touches on a number of themes that you've returned to or developed. One is in the line, "I am in the lake in the centre of the picture just under the surface." It's a very evocative image, being in the photograph but invisible, drowned, and I wonder, what is it about photographs that you find so fascinating?

ATWOOD Photographs are stopped time. All that they can portray is appearances. You see the moment, you see the instant when that photograph was taken. But the camera cannot take a picture of your thought, it cannot take a picture of what was really going on. It's a completely odd phenomenon when you come to think of it. Photographs are frozen light. There is always either much less in them than meets the eye or much more.

I adore looking at photographs. They're mysterious. They purport to be very flat and visible, and they have no depth on the page; they're just a flat surface. But if you look into them rather than at them you can go underneath the surface of the photograph. That sounds creepy. I find them a very Gothic form.

WACHTEL There is the cliché that a photograph steals your soul. But I was wondering if it can also save your soul—because it fixes you, or it holds something.

ATWOOD Let's leave souls out of this.

WACHTEL All right, it just saves an image of your body.

ATWOOD It saves the image of light being reflected off the surface of your body. That's what it saves. But if you want to get metaphysical about it and talk about the fact that matter and energy are equally convertible, your body is made of light.

WACHTEL There's another tantalizing line in the poem, at the end where you write, "If you look long enough, eventually you will be able to see me." I know the "me" isn't necessarily you, but you are very elusive in your poetry. George Woodcock described your poetry as "inclined to an almost Buddhist objectivity."

ATWOOD I don't know exactly what is meant by those things. I suppose some people when they write poems create dramatis personae for themselves. They write roles for themselves, which they then play in the poems: me, person who drinks a lot; me, who wears loud, plaid shirts; you know, whatever their thing happens to be, whatever the costume happens to be. And there is another kind of poem in which the narrator really is the reader, the "I." Because the "I" is not described and is not specific it becomes the reader, so that the reader, instead of viewing the poet, as if the poet were cavorting about on the stage, is able to enter the poem as a co-creator.

WACHTEL Is that a deliberate strategy? It sounds suspiciously postmodern.

ATWOOD No, I think it's just the way it works, and it's not postmodern. I was already old by the time postmodern came along.

WACHTEL A lot of readers think they recognize you in your novels.

ATWOOD You know what they really recognize? They really recognize themselves. When they write letters, it tends to be not, "Gosh, that was an interesting description of your childhood," but "Gosh, that was *my* childhood."

That's what we do when we read books. We enter in. They know, from wiring up people's brains, that when you watch television there is less activity than when you are asleep. But when you read a book there is a great deal of brain activity, because you, the reader, are creating all the sound effects, all the visuals; you are making that world. That's why people are deeply influenced by books in a way that they are not by TV. You can have a momentary interest in TV, but try to remember all the TV shows you've seen, and now tell me the plots. I double-dare.

But you could tell me the plots of quite a few books because you have lived those plots. They also know that reading a book is, in terms of brain activity, the nearest equivalent to actually doing it, whatever *it* is.

WACHTEL The poem "This is a Photograph of Me" also picks up the idea of a human figure in relation to nature—in this case, quite literally submerged in nature, underwater. You spent a lot of your early childhood close to nature. Your father was an entomologist and your family spent a lot of time in the bush. How do you think that affected you?

ATWOOD I also spent a lot of time in the early sixties looking at Canadian paintings, among them the paintings of Jack Chambers, and one of the things that Jack Chambers was very interested in showing was the human figure disappearing into a landscape. In fact, the whole tradition of Canadian painting and how and where figures enter landscapes was very interesting to me at that time. It connected with my own experience of growing up in the North, and the fact that if you are watching a figure in that landscape, one minute you see it and the next minute you don't. It disappears among the trees, it goes around the corner, people dive. There is a constant metamorphosis going on between human figures, foliage and water surfaces in that sort of landscape.

WACHTEL Was your childhood a kind of bush idyll?

ATWOOD I don't think it's quite like that in the Canadian North. It's a large place, it's easy to get lost and there is always the possibility that something may come out of the woods. It's a landscape with a lot of spiritual resonance. How can I say that without sounding pretentious? Well, I can't, so we'll just keep that, that phrase.

WACHTEL Did you feel that even as a child?

ATWOOD Who can remember what they felt as a child, precisely. It was my home, so all those home feelings you have—this is familiar, that's familiar—all of those kinds of feelings I associate with that landscape. I also knew that one false step and... You had to watch where you were going and what you were doing. It was not a feeling of complete safety, but on the other hand it wasn't the kind of paranoia you get living in the city.

WACHTEL You've written a lot about survival and nature, and as you have observed, it's a theme central to Canadian mythology. It's also central to an earlier poetry collection of yours, *The Journals of Susanna Moodie*. Is that what drew you to her story?

ATWOOD Her story was my story backwards in a way. She was a cultivated Englishwoman coming into the bush and suffering all kinds of mishaps. She fell over a lot of logs and got bitten by mosquitoes and encountered skunks and many things she found very difficult to deal with. I was in a way the reverse. As I said, I thought of the North as home. The alien thing for me then was urban life, not that I'm not acclimatized now. I can take a taxi just the same as anybody else, but that isn't what I grew up with. I think we're back to photographs here: Susanna Moodie was a kind of negative, or positive, if you like, of my own experience. That is how I speculate in hindsight; but you don't think these things through ahead of time; something just comes along and grabs hold of you, and you feel that this is a completely insane thing to be doing, but this is what I have to do right now.

WACHTEL I read somewhere that the Susanna Moodie poems started in a dream for you. You dreamt you were watching an opera that you had written about her. Are dreams fertile ground for you?

ATWOOD They often are, but they're not at all dependable. Sometimes they can be just about failing to catch the train or finding that you're back in high school and have to write an examination and it's all written in Chinese and you can't understand any of it. Or my other favourite is the wardrobe dream, in which you have to go out to some event and you're looking through the wardrobe and none of the clothes are yours, and they're all either too big or too small. What horror! If I dream about things other than clothing, there's more of a chance I'll turn them into a poem.

WACHTEL Your 1971 collection, *Power Politics*, with its unforgettable epigraph, "You fit into me / like a hook into an eye / a fishhook / an open eye," really captured the *Zeitgeist*. How do these poems look to you now?

ATWOOD Pretty interesting. But again, any time you're looking back on things you have done, they don't *seem* like things you've done; they seem like things somebody else did. You can sort of remember having done them, but they don't really feel like you now. When I look at them I look at them more as somebody else's work.

What I was doing, believe it or not, was writing something that was the equivalent of or that I felt to be cognate with sonnet cycles, both Shakespeare's sonnet cycle and works like *Sonnets from the Portuguese* or *In Memoriam*. I was, after all, a Victorianist in an earlier incarnation. In other words, there is the idea of a number of short poems connected together in a narrative way. And the book is arranged so that the first section is personal, the middle one is political and the third one is mythic.

WACHTEL   The overall impact, especially because of that powerful epigraph, is of sexual politics.

ATWOOD   That's what the time was about; it's what the book is about. It was a little early, coming at the beginning of that period rather than at the end of it. I think it was one of those moments in which something I was interested in doing coincided with something that it became possible to do and interesting to do and that other people found of value.

WACHTEL   After those poems you move from that world, from the world of personal politics, into the world of public politics and torture in collections such as *You Are Happy*, *Two-Headed Poems* and *True Stories*. This is not easy stuff to read, and I imagine it must not have been easy to write. In fact, you have a sequence of poems called "Notes Towards a Poem That Can Never Be Written."

ATWOOD   When I write about things like that, I try not to make anything up. What some human beings have done to one another needs no embroidery, it's all just horrific the way it is.

What you concentrate on first as a poet is gaining some sort of control of what you're doing formally. And then, if you're a young person, you're interested in your own emotional contacts with the world or with other people, so you concentrate on those. Then you wake up and realize that the world is a lot bigger than you thought and that there are a number of things going on in it that are extremely unpleasant.

Now, if you had grown up in some part of the world other than Canada, you might have known this at a much earlier age. But it was as if Canadians, especially of that time, lived in one of those little gardens you grow under glass bells—you know, a contained biosphere, a contained emotional biosphere, quite cozy, and who should knock it, because this is presumably the goal towards which we all should be striving, rather than a world in which everybody is poor and miserable and killing one another. We should not spit on Canadian niceness; but we come to realize that this is not the whole world, that there are things going on elsewhere that really require attention. I came to that partly through Amnesty International and partly, strangely enough, through what was interesting me as a novelist.

WACHTEL Does drawing from reality make it easier for you to write on these difficult subjects?

ATWOOD I don't think it's easier or more difficult. I think one of the questions that always confronts you at that moment is, What the heck am I doing sitting here writing poetry about this stuff?

WACHTEL There is a line in the poem "Notes Towards a Poem That Can Never Be Written" in which you say, "In this country you can say what you like because no one will listen to you anyway." In Canada, are the risks in writing poetry all aesthetic?

ATWOOD I used to think so. That may apply to poetry. I don't know whether you would call them aesthetic. Nobody is going to shoot you for writing poems, almost no matter what the poems say. If, however, you write newspaper pieces on subjects such as free trade, you will come in for a certain amount of attack. I saw a piece in the newspaper the other day in which a man was saying, Why do we assume that just because people are writers they know something about anything? Why should their name on a petition carry any weight? But that's not the point. The point is, why are they so frequently asked? They're so frequently asked because they have the freedom to take a public position without being fired. A lot of other people would like to do the same, but there is too much risk for them.

So I don't think the risks are entirely aesthetic, not once you recognize that being a poet makes you a member of a large community, a community of writers, which extends into the past and also extends very much outside your own country, and you feel the compatriot of those people. So when those people are under threat, which they always are in any sort of totalitarian society, you have a moral responsibility towards them.

WACHTEL I want to change the subject completely and talk about love.

ATWOOD That was about love. But let's talk about love.

WACHTEL A different kind of love. You've written some beautiful and remarkably tender love poems, poems such as "Variations on the Word Sleep." It's such a compelling image, to want to be like someone else's breath, "that unnoticed & that necessary." Love is the natural turf of lyric poetry, but is it hard to write love poetry when so much has already been written?

ATWOOD If we thought that way, nobody would ever write anything. We wouldn't write about politics, landscape, love or death. I don't think it's the subject; it's the verbal expressiveness. I think we were all ruined a bit in high school because we were told we had to produce précis of poems: What does this poem say in twenty-five words or less? That makes you think that poetry is really just a kind of embroidered motto—you know, War Is Hell Except That Your Love Is Golden. The poets, poor things, are inarticulate, and they have to use all these other words and fancy it up, and our job is to decode it down to one message—the précis. What is the poet trying to say? I love that. You know, the poor, tongue-tied poet, trying madly to say something, but unable to spit it out in fewer than sixteen lines.

WACHTEL There is a line in the poem "Variations on the Word Sleep," about one word that will protect you from the grief at the centre of your dream. Can words be a protective charm?

ATWOOD To a certain extent. They're not much use against maniacs with guns usually, although sometimes they can work then too. But for the individual wrestling with his or her demons or angels, yes, I would say that the way we formulate things verbally—that's how we think. We think in images, but we think in words as well. Words are our value markers. The way you formulate something to yourself can be remarkably protective or remarkably destructive.

WACHTEL The last poem in this book is called "Interlunar," and it's also the title of your last collection. In it there are the recognizable themes of being surrounded by nature and being fearful. But it's also hopeful, with the promise of safety and light. Do you feel hopeful?

ATWOOD That particular poem is a nocturne, it's nocturnal. A poem about the experience of death. It's very hopeful. I think that for all writers, even though they may end up defenestrating themselves—I love that word—at the moment of writing, even if they're writing the most pessimistic, awful thing, the act of writing is a hopeful act. On the most primitive level, you're hoping that language can communicate, that this particular language will communicate to somebody else. That's a big hope. But on another level, there is a hope that this particular language will have meaning. And surely behind every act of writing, even if the writing is about meaninglessness, there is this belief in meaning and this hope that communication is a meaningful human activity. So it's a poem about how to walk in darkness, how to see your way forward, as it were. And if you walk around a lot at night without a flashlight, you know that your eyes adjust.

Every poem is based on a physical metaphor of some kind. It's how to go forward in this world, the night world in which you can see only partial colours and partial shapes. But if you keep going into the darkness rather than trying to cut it out or counteract it with sources of light, such as flashlights, you'll be able to see your way much better, and you'll be able to come through it, if you like. The other physical metaphor, of course, is that if you keep going long enough, eventually it's morning. Yes, I'm afraid it's an excessively hopeful poem.

WACHTEL That's all I wanted to wring out of you.

Your *Selected Poems 1966-1984* looks back twenty-five years to *The Circle Game*. How do you feel from this vantage point, seeing all that work together?

ATWOOD I think a lot of poets are like people trying to walk across Niagara Falls on a tightrope with a blindfold on. If somebody ever said to them, "Take off the blindfold and look where you are," they would fall off. Much of what you do as a writer is done in that way: if you had any idea where you were going or what the possibilities for catastrophe were, you would probably fall off the tightrope. I'm still on the tightrope. I'm not in my rocking chair yet, Eleanor. I'm not at that moment where you look back over your entire life's work. I'm still walking around. Yes, I need reading glasses, but I'm still doing things, and I'm still doing things that are different from what I've done before. That's what I mean by the tightrope—you try something you think is probably a recipe for complete disaster but you have to do it anyway.

WACHTEL When you see a book like this, does it give you a sense of how your work has changed?

ATWOOD It's changed a lot, yes.

WACHTEL Could you say how?

ATWOOD It's such a simple thing: I'm older. When I look at the poems at the very beginning of the book, these were the poems of a young person, and they were poems that I can now see indicated things that I was going to do later on. I have hindsight. When I was writing them, of course, I had no idea that this particular poem might lead to something else five years later or that it might lead into a novel or a story. It was the work of the moment, what I was interested in. Those wonderful insights you can have looking back were not mine to have. At the time I was living in a remarkably cheap apartment in Point Grey, Vancouver, and I was writing my poems and stories, and indeed, later, my novel *The Edible Woman*, in UBC exam booklets. Very handy, neat lines.

WACHTEL A sense of small satisfaction as each one is finished?

ATWOOD No, things were more chaotic than that. When people see the nice books with the nice white pages and the nice black writing, what they don't see is the chaos and the complete frenzy and general shambles that the work comes out of. I mean, you are not to picture a nice little desk with a little chair and me sitting writing neatly on the lines. It's not the way it was. You should picture a room with papers strewn all over the floor and in piles that only I could make sense of, and an apartment with hardly any furniture in it because it was only partly furnished and I didn't have the money to buy any other furniture. My dining-room table was a card table lent to me by Jane Rule, bless her. She lent me the plates too. And there I was with my pencil. These were poems written in pencil, scribbled, as like as not, not on the lines but diagonally across the page. That tells what an optimist I am: I start at the left and I slant up.

WACHTEL You slant up? There we are, that explains everything.

September 1990

interview prepared in collaboration
with Sandra Rabinovitch

Amy Hempel

When I first read Amy Hempel's book of stories *Reasons to Live* (1985), I was so struck by the mixture of pain and comedy—the sense of loss and bereavement and the surprising wit and quirkiness—that I immediately wanted to find out more about her. The stories are set in San Francisco, so that was a clue. One of my favourite lines occurs during an earthquake, while a woman is on her psychiatrist's couch. Suddenly the couch is moving. She jumps up and says, "My God, was that an earthquake?" And the doctor says, "Did it *feel* like an earthquake to you?" As the story's narrator says, "You have to look on the light side."

Amy Hempel was born in Chicago in 1951, grew up in San Francisco and now lives in New York and on Long Island. Her second slim collection, *At the Gates of the Animal Kingdom*, was published in 1990. Both volumes could easily fit between the covers of a single short novel, but size doesn't measure impact. One reviewer compared these powerful stories to the miraculous exactitude of observation and execution you find on a couple of inches of carved ivory or porcelain. Hempel's writing is elegant, compact and unsettling. She writes tantalizing first sentences: "The year I began to say *vahz* instead of *vase*, a man I barely knew nearly accidentally killed me." Or, "Are you here for all the things that I don't have?"

Amy Hempel writes about resilience because—as I learned when I talked to her—resilience is important in her own life. But she arrived in the studio talking about other writers, such as her former teacher and editor Gordon Lish, whom I had interviewed a few months earlier. Lish is a controversial teacher, but one whom she clearly admires. Hempel is acutely conscious of what she does in her fiction, of her own style and that of her contemporaries.

WACHTEL You write stories that are funny and sharp and well-observed. They're also often very short, but powerful and moving. You've been called a "minimalist tough cookie," though I think it's more accurate to call you a "miniaturist." But that aside, does the label surprise you? Do you think of your work as tough?

HEMPEL It can be tough. The brevity comes from distilling. I like distilled stories and condensed poetry, which I'd be writing if I could, but this is the next best thing I can do. I know there's a certain stance in some of these stories that is unlike my own—in real life I'm not at all tough, but on the page you strip things away to uncover the core material, and that can make you sound tough.

WACHTEL What is it about distilling and paring down that appeals to you?

HEMPEL It's getting at the essence of something. I used to define minimalism as leaving out the boring parts. It's very attractive, as in poetry, to get at the essentials of a situation, of a moment, of a story, of a person's life.

WACHTEL Is it actually a process of paring down? Do you start with all the boring parts?

HEMPEL That's a good question. I don't start with volumes of material and just tear it off as I go. I might ask myself, what is it about this person, what is the one thing that will reveal everything about this character? That's the interesting piece of description that I'll use.

WACHTEL You've talked about the influence of Mary Robison, Barry Hannah and Raymond Carver—writers who use this kind of compression and distillation to tell the truth in shocking ways, you say, because that gets to the heart of things. Truth is such a hard word to tackle, but what kind of truth do you want to capture in your writing?

HEMPEL A harder truth. How to explain that? I want to say something truer than the obvious observation about a person—go deeper. My editor uses a model, when he's talking about writing, of stories that move vertically rather than horizontally: instead of moving horizontally on the page, stay with the one moment or revelation and go down-down-down, vertically, deeper into complication, keep going down and uncovering harder things to say about the same thing.

WACHTEL Your editor, Gordon Lish, was fiction editor at *Esquire* and is now a fiction editor with Alfred A. Knopf. He's had an influence on a number of writers, on those just mentioned, Anne Beattie and others. Does it bother you to be part of a group of writers that revolve around him?

HEMPEL It doesn't bother me at all. Years ago I identified him as the arbiter of short fiction. I felt that he knew more about short fiction than anybody in the United States, and when I heard he was going to teach at Columbia I made sure I was in that first class. Certainly there's room to be allied with him in a publishing venture and still sound like yourself. He publishes so many writers who have such range. I mean, we're not all the same.

WACHTEL To go back to this idea of truth, you've said that your first collection of stories, *Reasons to Live*, is not autobiographical, but that the whole book is true. What does that mean?

HEMPEL It means that not everything happened to me, although most things did, but even the things that didn't happen seem true to me in a way that sometimes things that really did happen don't. I guess that's what I mean!

WACHTEL Tell me a bit more about the actual autobiographical aspects of your writing. You've said that your twenties were miserable.

HEMPEL Oh, the worst. The Lost Years. My twenties turned out to have been "research." I really felt as though it was a wasted decade and yet, when I started to write after that, everything I wrote about came from that awful time. It was a way of recovering some of that.

WACHTEL Why was it so awful?

HEMPEL Oh God, everything you could think of happened. I was in two very serious accidents, there were two suicides in my family, there were earthquakes in California—disruption and calamity everywhere. I felt very beaten back by it. You know, you walk out the door in the morning and you're looking up to see if there's a safe falling out of the sky on you. It was just very hard, but it's better now.

WACHTEL How did you climb out of it, or did the events of your life just change?

HEMPEL No, I changed them. I worked very, very hard for a long time to recover a small measure of control over my life. I suppose some of it had to do with the writing, although I think personal catharsis is a terrible reason for writing fiction. It's a great reason to keep a diary but a lousy reason to write fiction, because really, who cares? What reader cares that I feel better for having written this story? They want to know what's in it for *them*, how are you going to make *them* feel better. And that's a perfectly valid response.

WACHTEL What did the writing do for you? What were you able to get out of it for yourself?

HEMPEL I came to a realization that I found pretty remarkable, which was that things that I knew already, experiences I'd had, were valuable. They could be made into something valuable. For the first time I felt a kind of entitlement—I am entitled to tell this particular story in a way no one else can—which is a kind of power.

WACHTEL I think you tell stories in a unique way, and you tell them with power and with tenderness, especially towards young people who are trying to cope with loss. For instance, there's the teenage boy, Big Guy, in your story "The Most Girl Part of You," who does these odd, endearing things after his mother has killed herself. You show a lot of compassion.

HEMPEL I hope so. That story—of a boy finding his way in the wake of his mother's suicide—actually came from the best friend of my little brother. His mother killed herself around the Christmas holidays one year, and I was very taken with these two thirteen-year-old boys, my brother and his friend, just trying to make some sense out of something like that.

WACHTEL You have written a couple of stories about mothers, or the children of mothers, who've committed suicide. "Tom-Rock Through the Eels" is about a woman whose mother has killed herself. In the course of the story the woman does a kind of inventory of mothers while trying to remember the good times with her own mother. Tell me about mothers and daughters.

HEMPEL Speaking for myself, it was an extremely rocky experience. My mother and I did not get along at all, and she did kill herself when I was nineteen. I am now the age she was when she killed herself, which is something to think about. So it is a subject that concerns me, but I don't know how much more I'll write about it.

WACHTEL In "Tom-Rock Through the Eels" the narrator's inventory is really quite an affectionate look at mothers.

HEMPEL Of *other* mothers! You see? Yes! The story is about a woman who must summon up happy memories of her own mother to please her grandmother, who has asked for these happy memories and she's asked the one person who has none. So it's a scramble. If I can think of all these other nice mothers, maybe I can just pass them off as having been my own experience.

WACHTEL There's a story in *At the Gates of the Animal Kingdom* called "The Harvest" about a young woman recovering from a motorcycle accident. She's telling the story of what happened, and the reader is sharing this experience with her; then, part way through, she deliberately destroys the illusion of the fiction by saying, "I leave a lot out when I tell the truth. The same when I write a story." Here's your concern with the idea of truth again. Why did you do this?

HEMPEL I've been interested for a long time in something that turns up in a lot of writing classes. In the beginning when you start writing, it's easier to write about something that really happened, probably something fairly traumatic that left a big impression. But people are always baffled when it doesn't work as fiction. Why does it fall flat? Why doesn't it have the power that it should? So that was the initial question for me. "The Harvest" has to do with why things have to be changed and how you change the facts to get at the truth. I like to talk about Tim O'Brien in this context. He's written five or six books about Vietnam, and in his most recent book, *The Things They Carried*, he does that very beautifully. He'll say, "Here's a true war story that never happened." It's like letting the reader in on a trade secret or something.

WACHTEL But what you're doing is creating another fiction that you're really telling the truth now. I mean, how do we know the second time that you're really telling—?

HEMPEL Of course, you don't. The first part of "The Harvest," appeared in the fiction section of a literary magazine; the second part, the so-called real story, appeared in the non-fiction section of the same magazine, same issue. I could have gone on and written the third part that would address all the things I changed in the "true" version, so it's endless.

WACHTEL Did this story start with your own accident?

HEMPEL It did.

WACHTEL And then you just kept changing the details.

HEMPEL I think we do that even without trying, to demythologize the whole idea of storytelling. We do it all the time. You have a close call, and so you tell a friend about what almost happened, and without even thinking about it you embellish, you make it a slightly closer call than it was, you put a spin on it, to deepen the irony.

WACHTEL A character in another story says, "I'm exaggerating so you'll get to know me faster." Are these just the tools of the story-teller or do you also want the reader to be more conscious of the unreliability of the narrator? Is that important to you?

HEMPEL I think that the narrator has to be reliable; you have to feel that there's an authority there that you can trust or the story falls flat, it won't go anywhere.

WACHTEL But at the same time you want to keep the reader on slippery ground?

HEMPEL Yes, and I'm not sure why. In a way it makes it harder for the writer. If you put your readers on the alert that you might be playing with them, they're going to pay that much more attention and you'd better not fall off.

WACHTEL There's a restless quality to your characters. It's as if we encounter them in the act of passing through some experience—recovering from injury or loss or preparing for birth or death or an earthquake. There's no stepping back to get the big picture; you don't give us the luxury of a long view. Why is that? Why do you focus so tightly and briefly on these lives?

HEMPEL I don't have a long view of myself. I'm almost forty, but, when I was nineteen, the long view just vanished. That was when I had a very close call in an accident, and it shook me up, as one's first look at mortality will do. Suddenly it seemed presumptuous of me to believe I could think in terms of years and years and a great scope of a life. Who is to say? Then I became really interested in moments, which is what my stories are sometimes—just a crys-talline moment rather than an epic that unfolds over time. Maybe these moments are all I've got.

WACHTEL You still feel that way, even though you've managed to live more than double the age that you were back then?

HEMPEL I still feel that way, I do. And in fiction I am much more drawn to perfect moments: the small thing, the vignette that will

tell you so much about a person or a life. One of the nicest com-
pliments I ever received on my work was from another writer,
William Kennedy, who said, "You leave out all the right things." I
was so pleased he thought that.

WACHTEL The observations in your stories are often painful, but
there's always a flash of the absurd, there's always some humour.
Your story with the wonderful title "And Lead Us Not Into Penn
Station," which is a series of disturbing snapshots of urban life,
contains the line: "Today, when a blind man walked into the
bank, we handed him along to the front of the line where he
ordered a BLT." Can you always find that absurd spin on life?

HEMPEL Yes, I think so, especially in darker situations. If you
spend any time in hospitals, you discover doctors are among the
funniest people around. That particular dark, dark humour that
gets you through horrible situations—you have to have it. It's a
great gift and a great leveller, and it's always been important for
me.

WACHTEL Is it always there for you when you negotiate your way
through, say, the streets of New York or through dark moments?

HEMPEL New York is a horror show in many ways. I couldn't
stand to live there if I didn't see the absurd in it. It's odd. I've lived
in New York City for almost twelve years now and I've written, or
published, thirty-one short stories. Thirty of them take place in
California or somewhere not named; "And Lead Us Not Into
Penn Station" is the only story New York gave me. And it's only an
absurd, kind of awful vignette, so I guess that says something.

WACHTEL Your writing is full of wry scraps of philosophy—more
than one-liners, they're ironic twists on one's expectations. Lines
like, "Things get worse before they get really terrible." Or, "Hoping he would call is like the praying you do after the bowling ball
has left your hand." One reviewer said he found it hard to stop
quoting you, and I also find it hard sometimes. A favourite of
mine is: "I'll burn that bridge when I come to it."

HEMPEL I have a great love for these moments when somebody
says something in a different way, or says something I don't expect

to hear or have never heard before, especially the twist on something that already exists. I'm very drawn to that. For me, that's what writing is all about: we know all the stories, we've been around the block, we're grown-ups, so it's saying it in a new way, or asking, What are *these* people doing about it? What are *these* people doing in this situation that we all already understand? And that gets back to the minimalism question. Why describe a whole situation that everyone already knows; give the reader some credit for understanding that.

WACHTEL Your first collection of stories was called *Reasons to Live*, even though it's not the title of one of the stories in the book.

HEMPEL Originally, when I chose that title, it seemed ironic because, my God, if the people in these stories had a reason to live, it was a pretty slim one. Over time it seemed less and less ironic and more justified. It's something I really meant—that people don't have to have a very great reason, just reason enough. My attitude changed toward it. I ended the book with the one clearly optimistic, hopeful story. I did that again in my second book. So I guess I really feel that, despite a hard row to hoe, at the end I want some note of hope.

WACHTEL Your second collection, *At the Gates of the Animal Kingdom* features stories about animals, often affectionate or odd, including dogs, cats and boa constrictors. What kinds of relations do you have with animals?

HEMPEL Very close ones. They've always been enormously important to me all my life. Anyone who's lived with animals knows that they have very distinct personalities. To me they can be every bit as interesting as a person. While I may make up the human characters in the stories, the animals are all real! Everyone has heard the advice to writers, "Write what you know." A friend of mine suggested we write about what we love; it's natural for me to write about animals.

WACHTEL Are you in agreement with Colette—didn't she say something about the best kind of love is with the four-legged variety?

HEMPEL Often, often. I was in a class once where the instructor had us write down a quality that defined each one of us as a person. For example, somebody wrote down, "I am a devout Catholic"; I wrote down, "I love animals." Then he said, "All right now, write a story from the opposite point of view." So the devout Catholic had to write a story as though she were an atheist and I had to write a story as though I hated animals, which was unimaginable to me, so I wrote a story called "Nashville Gone to Ashes" about the widow of a veterinarian who resented the love her husband had given the animals and hadn't given her. That was a very peculiar experience to write as somebody who did not like animals—it was very weird.

WACHTEL The title story, "At the Gates of the Animal Kingdom," is about a woman who is mysteriously tuned into the lives of animals and their suffering around the world. Eventually she collapses—the knowledge overwhelms her. What is this animal consciousness?

HEMPEL This may be a cautionary tale. As a member of any or all of the animal-rights organizations around the world, you get frequent mailings that often include excruciating photographs and information of abuse. It's infuriating and it's horrible, overwhelming. You write your Congressman, you send the postcards, you send in the cheque and it doesn't feel like enough. And you do think about these animals, you identify with them, they're very much on your mind. I've had to fight a sort of suction, as if I'm being sucked down into something that is going to drown me in the awfulness of it. You have to fight that kind of despair and identification with suffering that doesn't go further than identification, and try to do what you can. The story was political, the most political thing I've ever done, and, as I said, I hope cautionary.

WACHTEL One of my favourite stories, from your first collection, is called "The Cemetery Where Al Jolson Is Buried." A woman is visiting her best friend, who is dying. It's another story about loss and grief that's leavened by wit, but perhaps what's most disturbing is that it's about the fear that keeps people from showing enough love and from giving enough.

HEMPEL My best friend was dying and I felt I failed her at the moment when I absolutely could not fail her. The situation was true and yet, neither of us ever uttered a word of the dialogue in the story. I feel very conflicted. We do what we can; that's all we can do, and it has to be enough, even if maybe it isn't. It's a question I haven't really answered satisfactorily for myself.

WACHTEL I hope you keep on writing to figure it out.

HEMPEL I think I'll have to.

February 1991

interview prepared in collaboration
with Sandra Rabinovitch

Bernard MacLaverty

Wars around the world come and go, but the Troubles in Ireland date back 400 years and seem destined to continue forever. Irish writer Bernard MacLaverty is an exile who writes without hope but with a lot of wit. He's perhaps best known for a screenplay he wrote based on his 1983 novel, *Cal*, the story of an innocent young man who is caught up in the ineluctable violence of Northern Ireland and becomes an accomplice to terrorism. It's about betrayal and about guilt and reparation.

Bernard MacLaverty was born in Belfast in 1942. He started working as a lab technicican, but then decided to study English, teach and write. He left Ireland in the early seventies, because it was—as he puts it—an uncomfortable time to be living in Belfast. You could be killed for what you were—Catholic or Protestant—regardless of who you were or what you'd done. MacLaverty found a teaching job in Scotland and moved there with his wife and four children. In 1981 he quit teaching to write full time. In addition to *Cal*, he has published several short-story collections and another novel, *Lamb* (1980), and has also written radio plays and film scripts.

A Catholic born in Belfast, MacLaverty takes no sides in Ulster's political battles. He's against violence, whatever the rationalization, and describes himself as living near the passionate centre.

———————————

WACHTEL You grew up Catholic in Northern Ireland, in Belfast. What was that like?

MACLAVERTY Ooh, that's a big question. I grew up during one of those peaceful times. I was born in 1942, and the recent unpleasantness didn't really start until 1969. I was a fully grown man. But there is one story I remember, of a group of us boys going up the Cave Hill, which is a mountain at the back of Belfast, and meeting four other boys coming along the path. We stopped, and there was a kind of tension in the air. One of them said, "You's Catholics?" And we said, "Yeah. You's Prods?" They said, "Yeah." There was a kind of stalemate. And some philosopher, from the back of one group, said, "Sure, it doesn't matter. We all believe in the same God anyway." This was a bit of a hefty thought. Then everybody got embarrassed with it, and they pushed this boy forward. I can still see him in my mind, with a Fair Isle pullover, V-neck. They said, "See him? He can vomit whenever he wants!" And this wee fella opened his mouth and threw up. One of our group said, "Aw, c'mon, he had it in his mouth." They said, "No, no! Do it again. Do it again, Sammy." He does. Then we turned around, we passed each other, and we galloped off in different directions. I have never been able to flip that into a piece of fiction, because it's so bizarre.

WACHTEL You've described your childhood as happy. It was during the forties and fifties and early sixties, when things were fairly peaceful. But curiously, when you write about children—and you often make children your subject—they don't have a happy time. Your children often are quite lonely and alienated, and their childhood is a difficult and traumatic time. Why do you do this to your characters?

MACLAVERTY I have no idea! But a writer I admire tremendously, Flannery O'Connor, says that the artist has a right to look at the bleak, the black side. For some reason that just seems to happen. I suppose there's a tension there, a conflict, a conflict of interests, and a child in the middle of it. I don't know why I do it.

WACHTEL Do you know why you write about children, why you go back to that period?

MACLAVERTY I suppose it's something to do with the sensual kind of details of that time. As a child you are totally aware. I mean this about everybody, not just me. The only thing you're not aware of is being aware, and that you're going around like a piece of blotting paper, absorbing sights and sounds and smells, taking it all in. In my case, the only thing I wanted to do was play football. But you look back later and you see that your antennae were out. There is that level of sense-data that you have as a child. When you sit down at a page to write, for some reason you make that connection.

WACHTEL You are also interested in parent-child relationships, especially fathers and sons, or older men and younger boys—even going back to your first collection, *Secrets and Other Stories*. Your own father died when you were twelve. Do you think that's why you want to revisit childhood, to go back to that theme?

MACLAVERTY I would say yes to that, but only in retrospect. I never really had a row with my father. He was a saintly man. Everybody has told me that. I've written about bad fathers, and I've written about good fathers or good relationships. I suppose this is a kind of creative working out of what I did not have, of the possibilities of what I did not have.

WACHTEL You said once, as a writer living in Northern Ireland in the early 1970s, that the Troubles were uppermost in your mind but the last thing you wanted to confront on paper.

MACLAVERTY I think it's because it's too close to you. It does need a distancing of some sort. My attempt to face it was oblique—if you can face something obliquely. That was in *Lamb*, which is about a man who destroys something he claims to love. It was a big image—that those people who claim to love something are destroying it. A misdirected kind of love, like nationalism or republicanism. They say, "We love Ireland," yet they're in some way destroying it.

WACHTEL Why is nationalism necessarily misdirected?

MACLAVERTY I see nationalism as being feelings that are not rooted in people, in individuals. It's national anthems, it's flags, it's wrap the green flag around me, boys—that kind of thing, I don't like that. My first novel was an oblique attempt to use an image of that. Then, having done that, I felt that I needed to look at it face on, and I wrote *Cal,* which is directly concerned with an act of violence and the whole Republican/Orange conflict.

WACHTEL After your initial reaction that this wasn't something you could confront, how did you finally feel that you could write about this?

MACLAVERTY I suppose by having a character you could believe in. My wife and I were sitting together one night, and she said something that sparked it off. She said, "There must be an awful lot of boys in Northern Ireland who have done something they will regret for the rest of their lives." I think I just tidied that away to the back of my head, and said, "That's interesting." Then another cross-current idea came up, about truth—that if the truth of some situation is told, then it will destroy the situation. Those were the two ideas; once I'd got a handle on them the writing became easier. The context was Northern Ireland, violence.

Some people say that *Cal* is a novel set against the background of the Troubles in Northern Ireland, and it's not. It grows out of the Troubles; they are absolutely essential to it.

WACHTEL Cal is a nineteen-year-old boy who's been implicated, almost against his will, in IRA terrorist activity.

MACLAVERTY Well, one incident in particular. Some people would say that is exploiting the situation, but I have been in it, and I have the right to write about that. It may be different if a journalist comes in and spends four weeks and gets some information, then sets a story there. But I'm from there; it's part of my roots, part of my very being.

WACHTEL Again you use, not exactly a child, but a callow youth. I don't wish to get into literary analysis, but Cal really is a callow fellow, somewhere between innocence and experience; he's inadvertently caught up in this experience, but he's still in many ways quite innocent. He falls in love with a woman whose husband he helped to murder.

MACLAVERTY Some people criticize the plot for being too coincidental. They see his falling in love with this particular woman, whom he has helped to widow, as a coincidence. That's a complete misreading of it. She is the only woman who will do; he wants to make reparation. This is about Catholic guilt; he has done something awful to this woman. It's not a coincidence. It's part of that thing that has grown out of violence.

WACHTEL You've been criticized for being an apolitical writer. The criticism is that a book like *Cal* is too balanced—that, for instance, by making the widow, Cal's lover, a Catholic, you're not really addressing the Protestant/Catholic split, you're softening the situation. What do you think?

MACLAVERTY I don't think you can really be an apolitical writer. If you're writing about people in a social situation, then it's got to be political in some way. Gramsci talks about that, that politics is about what has to do with people. And what has more to do with people than writing novels and creating characters, made-up truth? As a teacher I once asked a class that. We were trying to arrive at some kind of definition of fiction. This girl put up her hand and said, "Sir, sir, it's made-up truth." That's one of the best working definitions of fiction I know.

WACHTEL What about the criticism that you're not partisan enough?

MACLAVERTY I suppose the two longer pieces of work that I've done, *Lamb* and *Cal*, are motivated by a sense of anger, that institutionalized religion can do that to Michael and Owen in *Lamb*, and that institutionalized violence, state violence, as well as personal violence, can do that to Cal. You react against that—therefore that's a political reaction. The passion of the politics puts you at the centre. Maybe it's pontificating too much to say you are at the centre. How do you know? How do you know where you are? I think I would be nearly there, but I would also be passionate about it, be passionate about not killing people, be passionate about good people.

WACHTEL A lot of your characters are pretty lonely and isolated. They may have brief moments of connection with another person, but happiness is elusive for them.

MACLAVERTY I think it is elusive. If we do make connections, then that's good, that's something. But it happens rarely, I think. The ultimate kind of depression is to go silent and not write anything. If you continue to write, it's an affirmation.

WACHTEL You have written a story called "Remote," about an old woman who, once a month, makes a trip into town to mail herself a letter.

MACLAVERTY I came across that story. Somebody told me that and I thought, what a symbol. She mails herself a letter so she can get a lift home. Her husband has died, has committed suicide. Life is full of pain and tragedy, and I don't see why we shouldn't record that.

WACHTEL You left Ireland in your early thirties to take up a teaching job in Scotland, which is where you live now, in Glasgow. Did you expect, at that point, that you would be leaving Ireland for good?

MACLAVERTY No. At that time I said I'd give it a couple of years away, because it was becoming uncomfortable to live in Belfast, in the early seventies. There were people being killed all the time, and there were bombs in cars. When a car parked on the street can become a thing that delivers death, then life gets uncomfortable. There were these doorstep killings. You could be killed for what you were.

WACHTEL You mean for your religion, rather than for anything you'd done.

MACLAVERTY Oh yes. And both ways. You could be killed as a Protestant or as a Catholic. The other thing that keeps you in a place is a job, and I didn't have a job. So, like St. Paul on the road to Damascus, I thought, "I can go away." The other thing was that at about that time I was thinking of myself as possibly a writer, and an awful lot of Irish writers have gone away.

WACHTEL You're following a great tradition—Beckett and Joyce.

MACLAVERTY And Brian Moore, who went to Canada. So all those things together led me to apply for jobs in Scotland.

WACHTEL I want to go back to *Cal*. Cal reflects at one point that to suffer for something that didn't exist was like Ireland, an Ireland that never was and never would be, and that it's the people of Ulster who were heroic; they were caught between the jaws of these two opposing ideals, and their ideals were, in fact, to grind each other out of existence. What kind of heroism is possible for anyone living in Northern Ireland today?

MACLAVERTY To go on living, I think. It's one of those situations where there is no hope. The best political brains have examined it, and nobody can come up with a solution. Therefore there's no hope. This is maybe why *Cal* is a depressing novel; it ends with no hope. The thing that makes going back to the North of Ireland and to Belfast such a great experience is the people's sense of humour, this black sense of humour, and a stoicism. The people—of both traditions—are absolutely smashing. I think that's where the hope lies, the hope that people will endure, and they will laugh. I can't see any more hope than that.

February 1991

*interview prepared in collaboration
with Sandra Rabinovitch*

David Marr
on Patrick White

Patrick White was an oddity in his own country, even though he is credited with reinventing the Australian novel through visionary books such as *Voss, The Eye of the Storm, Riders in the Chariot* and *The Vivisector.* In 1973, when Patrick White became the first Australian to win the Nobel Prize for Literature, a reporter for the Australian Broadcasting Corporation interviewed him: "The Swedish Academy praised your work, saying that you wrestle with the language almost to the verge of the unattainable. But do you feel that this perhaps puts much of your work out of the reach of most Australians?" Patrick White replied: "I don't know. All sorts of different kinds of Australians read me. Most unexpected ones. It's nothing to do with class or education. It's really a peculiar kind of mind that seems to take to my books. People who live intuitively rather than rationally." He added that he wouldn't be going to Sweden because he "couldn't face a northern winter." The painter Sidney Nolan accepted the prize on his behalf, and the band played what was deemed suitable music: "In an English Country Garden" by Australian composer Percy Grainger.

The curmudgeonly Patrick White was a self-confessed "lapsed Anglican egotist agnostic pantheistic occultist existentialist." He also became a fierce anti-nationalist and anti-monarchist as well as a staunch anti-nuclear, socialist environmentalist.

Patrick White died in September 1990 when he was seventy-eight years old. Some years earlier he allowed a Sydney journalist and critic, David Marr, to write his biography, *Patrick White: A Life* (1991). (Marr, who was trained as a lawyer, had written one previous biography, a critical treatment of an Australian establishment figure, High Court judge Sir Garfield Barwick.) Although White had long resisted proposals for a biography, once he began to cooperate with Marr he became impatient to see the results. Early in 1990, with his health deteriorating, he told Marr, "I am only staying alive to read that book!" Marr asked, "Should I speed up or slow down?" White only grunted. When he read the finished manuscript shortly before his death he said, "I think this book should be called the Monster of All Time. But I am a monster." He didn't ask for a word to be changed.

WACHTEL Patrick White, like many writers, didn't want a biography written about himself and he was emphatic that he didn't want one written while he was still alive, yet he allowed you to write about his life. He talked to you and gave you access to people close to him and to his papers. Why?

MARR He didn't want a biography written of him until he'd reached the point where he hadn't the strength to write much more himself. Quite by chance, that was the point at which I approached him and said, "Look, I'm going to write this book. What kind of agreement can we have?" He'd angrily knocked back biographers from the early sixties onwards and he got a reputation for being "unbiographical." Nevertheless I decided that I was going to do it. It was sheer luck that I wrote to him at a time when his mind had changed and he had decided that he wanted this book done, while he was alive, I suppose because he wanted to both help and, perhaps, hinder if he wished. In the end he didn't hinder; he certainly helped.

WACHTEL Did you know him before you began the project?

MARR I didn't meet him properly until I started the book, seven years ago. But when I was a kid, my parents' best friends lived on a farm on the outskirts of Sydney, opposite Patrick White's farm. In fact they were great friends. I never saw or met him at the time—I was five or six years old—but he was there at the edge of my experience. I knew by the way grown-ups talked about this man, those two men, living at the bottom of the drive, that something pretty exciting was happening down there.

WACHTEL I'd like to start with his family background. Like most people, I had not realized just how rich White's family was—they seemed to have owned half of New South Wales—and just how established they were.

MARR They were lucky. The first of the Whites arrived in Australia in the 1820s, in the middle of a wool boom. They were wool farmers from the West Country, from Somerset, in England. They arrived at the right time. They were immensely skilled, dour, careful, and they remain dour and careful to this day. With a great deal of hard work and luck they acquired an enormous amount of land in New South Wales, and they chose the best land. They had splendid country, and Belltrees, which became the family headquarters, is one of the most beautiful stretches of country in Australia—a beautiful river valley north of Sydney. It was in Patrick White's imagination all through his life, an image of a kind of magical, self-possessed kingdom, and it appears in his novels as that. The Whites were a family with little imagination and few vices. Their principal vice was running racehorses, but instead of squandering their fortune on them, they did fantastically well, so the money continued to roll in. They took the precaution of never leaving any land and leaving almost no money to their daughters.

WACHTEL So it wouldn't move outside of the family?

MARR Exactly, so that the money continued to focus inwards on the men. The women were supposed to find themselves rich husbands. A couple of generations of the family had virtually no children, so for an oddly long period of time this was one of the richest rural dynasties in Australia. Now, that also made them, from some points of view, very boring. When Patrick White's mother, Ruth Withycombe—who had led not nearly as rich, established or confident a life—married Dick White, she determined to get him and any children they had out of the magic kingdom in the Hunter Valley and down into the city where there was "life." And she did. She was determined never, ever to be bored, a determination she passed on to her son. They got out of rural Australia, but they continued to live on it. Almost until the time he won the Nobel Prize Patrick White lived, as we say in Australia, "off the sheep's back."

He lived on money that had come from the land. That is not just an idle observation about the comfort in which he lived. He didn't like luxury. He lived a kind of expensive, careful life. But it left him free as an artist to work for decades absolutely the way he wanted to work, to develop the style he wanted, without needing to earn money, without needing to do literary chores. He never reviewed a book in his life. And so, in the mid-1950s, he emerged on the world scene as a unique talent.

WACHTEL Having invented himself, in a sense, as a writer.

MARR Having found himself. He was ruthlessly truthful to himself at all times. There was no invention, no pretence.

WACHTEL Your biography delineates a family portrait of the landed gentry—very proper, very conservative, aspiring, perhaps, to a kind of British respectability without being quite of that class. How would you describe this?

MARR They *were* respectable. They arrived in Australia respectable and they remained respectable, careful with both their fortunes and their position. They weren't imaginative or fashionable. However, one of the things I find really interesting about them is that they saw themselves as Australian, and they didn't keep in contact with their relatives in England. It may perhaps have been out of fear that their poor relatives would continue dunning them for money, but they broke all links with England, and by the beginning of this century they saw themselves as thoroughly Australian.

Late in life Patrick White would say that they were not aristocrats. They weren't aristocrats in any British sense; they were, however, one of a very small group of families of wealth and power in Australia from about the 1880s through to about the mid-1920s. They knew what rule and power meant: it meant having a seat on the local shire; it meant having a position which ensured that you got a high-level bridge to your property so you could get the wool out in any weather; it meant advancing the interests of the district as well as the state.

WACHTEL Patrick White's parents were quite old when they married—his father was forty-two, his mother thirty-two—and they were second cousins. His father didn't seem to have to do much for his money, except run racehorses. His mother was a society lady; she wanted to have a good time. White blamed his mother for his asthma and for his homosexuality. Why do you think his relationship with his mother was so fraught?

MARR They were very similar, I'm told. As his old nurse once said to him, "The trouble, Patrick, was that you both wanted to be stars." When they were in the same room, or indeed the same city, the sparks flew all the time. She was a fabulous woman; a monster, but fabulous. She loved good music, she loved good cooking, she loved the theatre, she loved fine furniture and houses; she was, as her son was, a genius of elegant domesticity. And she read. She introduced Patrick White to Australian authors and to Katherine Mansfield, one of the passions of his reading life. I loved hearing about her and I loved talking to people about her. I said to him once, "Patrick, she was terrific," and he said, "Yes, but she wasn't *your* mother."

He was very, very unfair to her. He fibbed all his life to hide the fact that his mother was his great promoter. He always cast her as the woman who had stood between him and his career as a professional writer. I believe he was shrewd enough to know that he had to fend this woman off if he was going to survive as a separate and whole human being. He had seen men, particularly homosexual men, who had not been able to get clear of their mothers. These broken figures were traipsing around society when Patrick was a boy and a young man, and he was determined not to be one of them. He therefore decided that the best possible place for him was on the other side of the world from his mother. He remained immensely attached to her, however, and they wrote to one another every week while she remained alive, and she lived to a tremendous age; she was eighty-four or eighty-five when she died. He kept all her letters but, alas for the biographer, finally burned them.

WACHTEL That illustrates the contradiction you describe—how, for instance, White would get furious if a letter didn't arrive from her.

MARR Yes, beside himself. Of course, each of his books contains a portrait of his mother. In one guise or another he struggled with her in every work. Right at the end of his life he wrote a very beautiful series of three little short stories, prose poems, called *Three Uneasy Pieces*, and in those he's still struggling with his mother.

WACHTEL Does she ever come off well in his books?

MARR There are times when she comes off better in the books than in his own recollections of her. He will give her more intelligence and generosity in fiction than in fact. She was not a tremendously intelligent woman, but she was generous and, so long as she liked people, enthusiastically kind-hearted.

The great fictional portrait of her is Elizabeth Hunter in *The Eye of the Storm*, which is really a 600-page death scene. It begins with her dying and ends with her dead. It takes 600 pages to review her life, and it is Patrick's mother's life very thinly but beautifully turned into fiction. He gives her a humour he denied her in life, resilience, bravery. He also allows her to be more unconventional than she was in life. Ruth Withycombe was a very conventional woman. He also has her commit adultery. It took me some years, but finally I knew I had to do it, and I asked Patrick one day, "Patrick," deep breath, "Patrick, did your mother ever commit adultery?" There was one of those appalling silences, and then he shouted, "No!" in a voice that could have been heard halfway across the park. I mean, he *defended* his mother's honour to me.

WACHTEL Patrick White more or less accepted his homosexuality from an early age, although he felt it probably doomed him to loneliness and alienation. How did his family feel about it, and at what point were they made aware of it?

MARR I don't know the answer to that question. Today, when candour about such things is valued more, it's hard to imagine a time when a family's acceptance of such a situation was civilized but inarticulate, in that they knew but did not acknowledge and would never have discussed it. As far as I know, from talking to Patrick and to Manoly Lascaris, his partner, about this, he never discussed it with his mother, though the reality was quite clear to her, I think. One of the treasures in my book was a letter given to me by a friend of Patrick's, a letter written by Patrick's mother in the middle 1950s, after meeting Manoly Lascaris for the first time. They had been together for seventeen years by that time, but Manoly had not met Patrick's mother. She wrote to this friend, "We took him to our hearts and we all loved him."

WACHTEL White acknowledges the male and female sides to himself. How do you think his homosexuality affected his writing?

MARR He was one of those homosexuals who see themselves as part feminine, as well as masculine. That's not a view that all homosexuals share, but Patrick saw himself as able, therefore, to write about the female as well as the male, and able to draw more strongly than he might otherwise have been on instinct, which he saw as a female quality, as opposed to intellect. He didn't mean to denigrate women by this, and he never did denigrate women, but he tended to see that kind of stiff, academic, intellectual stance as a masculine characteristic. He condemned it as a masculine trait, and he trusted more to instinct.

I think this gave him the imaginative freedom to range over a much wider field of gender than he would have been able to had he not been homosexual. I'm not for a moment saying that the imagination of the heterosexual writer is in any sense limited. That's a matter for each writer. But it gave White the confidence to range—and range, I think, successfully—across a wide spectrum not only of male-female but also of heterosexual-homosexual experience. However, it was only later in his career that he began to write more candidly about homosexuality. Homosexual figures had always been there, though often unidentified—Patrick referred to them as "veiled brides"—but later he becomes much more candid about them, and I think his writing is better for it.

WACHTEL Of course, he also writes about people who aren't sexual at all. His "spinster women" is the phrase he uses.

MARR That's a very important part of Patrick White's literature. He was fascinated by the sexless figure, and the spinster is, as you say, one of the recurring figures in his writing. They were fabulous, absolutely beautiful figures, figures of wisdom and dry, commonsensical, practical goodness, figures who lived up to his notions of love as expressed through service, through doing things for others. They presented no sexual threat whatever to Patrick as a kid and as a young man, and they were people he always felt comfortable with. They were also, of course, figures of freedom in the class in which he lived: the spinster with a bit of money was free to move, to travel, to live her own life, in a way that married women were not. His godmother was one of these women. She travelled the world on tankers and cargo boats. Patrick loved that as an image of freedom, and she became the figure of Theodora Goodman in *The Aunt's Story.*

WACHTEL One of the strengths of your book is the insight it provides into the connections between his fictional characters and the people in White's own life.

MARR There are two steps here, and probably the second is more important than the first. The first step is to find that raw material of his inspiration. The rule I set for myself was that I would identify no sources unless Patrick endorsed them. So every identification of a real person as the source for a fictional character is endorsed by the author. That's step one. Much more important is step two: that is, the way in which the genius of the man transforms that observed reality—the people he knew, his family, the garden in front of his house, the property on which his father was born and brought up—how those are transformed into art. It's that power of transformation, not the power of observation, that makes White a great writer.

I set out to find the sources of his art, and part of it was detective work, but part of it was to try to understand Patrick White's mind and the way in which he transformed his material. I came to the conclusion that Patrick's method of writing was essentially theatrical. Characters and situations were formed in his mind in a self-consciously theatrical way; his mind was a stage on which they moved. He talked about the characters that were always in his mind. Sometimes they collided, and that might be the start of a novel. Those collisions took place in the theatre of his imagination, in which he was the prompt, the scriptwriter, the producer, all of the actors and the audience, all at once. From that process, which sometimes took years, a book would come.

He always thought about novels for a long time, years and years, before he wrote them down. He began to work on *The Aunt's Story* before the war. I've now found a fragment of diary which shows he was working intensely on *The Aunt's Story* when he was stationed with the South African Air Force group in the Sudan in early 1941. When the war ended, this was the first of the novels to pour out.

WACHTEL Why was that something he would think about, so far away?

MARR He wrote the book as he was coming to the conclusion that he must return to live and work in Australia, leaving the Europe he adored, and America, where he had thought he would go to live after the war. He had thought of becoming an American citizen in the early months of the war, but he came to realize that to be a great writer he had to return to his own soil. It was an insight of enormous courage, because Australia was a pretty rough place in those days, and a particularly rough and difficult place to return to with his lover.

In *The Aunt's Story* he looks back at the Australia he'd left fourteen or fifteen years before. He also looks back at Europe in the years before the war, a time that is marvellously, sometimes unbelievably complexly reworked in the central section of the book, "The Jardin Exotique." He made the journey home, but he abandons his character Theodora Goodman in New Mexico, and leaves her going mad. When I asked him why, he grumbled and said, oh, he'd have to read the book again if he was going to answer a question like that. Then he got a bit more reasonable and said, well, there was no place for her back in Australia, but there was a place for him.

So he returned to Australia with his book, which had been enthusiastically reviewed in New York—though not so enthusiastically reviewed, it turned out, in London—and he imagined that it would immediately establish him as the great Australian writer. In fact, in that parochial Australia the book was virtually ignored. The principal newspaper in Sydney gave it three paragraphs at the bottom of the literary page, in Melbourne it received four, and that was it. He was so wounded by that that he never really recovered from the sense of outrage, of being unfairly slighted. He loved that book all his life; it was the one that he wanted people to read and to know and to love as he did.

WACHTEL Before we leave Theodora Goodman going mad in America, why did he write about people who were going mad?

MARR He feared going mad himself. He feared that he might crack under the immense stress of the work of creation. This was particularly so during the ordeal of writing *The Tree of Man*. He was a wild man during the writing of that book: he drank very heavily; he brawled with Manoly Lascaris. He despaired of ever being able to finish the book. Of course, it was an international triumph.

He talked to me about his fear of madness. I said, "What kind of mad, Patrick? Do you mean barking mad or insane?" He said, "Worse than barking mad." That was all he'd say. He talked of suffering diseases. He called writing a disease, and, while he was very circumspect about it, in gloomy moments he also talked of his sexuality as a disease. You mustn't forget that madness was rather a cliché of modern fiction, and lots of pieces of his are not very good about people going a bit loony. But the madness of Theodora Goodman is astonishingly convincing.

WACHTEL What was it about disease that was so compelling for Patrick White? He talked not only about writing as a disease but the disease of foreignness, the disease of memory—he couldn't forget things.

MARR The disease of memory. Isn't that a fabulous notion? Disease was a central fact of his own life. He was asthmatic from birth, and it conditioned his whole life; therefore, I think, he tended to see any condition that afflicted him in the same way. It was a metaphor. He used to say he wished he could forget, but in fact he prized his memory. Of course, it is the great storehouse for a novelist; a novelist who can't remember hasn't got the raw materials to draw upon. White could remember, and the strength of his memory made it possible for him to be the capacious writer he was. But he did have this image of himself as flawed, and diseased.

He also had the notion, and this is the next step, that his talent came from the flaws—not from what was good in him but from what was imperfect, unfinished in him. What people disliked in him he saw as the source of his art. He never tried to fix himself up. He was unrelentingly brutal about his own shortcomings. He never did anything about them; he just reflected on them and wrote out of them. He was asked many times, why don't you go and see somebody? He said, Look, that's a dark cave; I'm not going to enter that dark cave, because I may leave something behind when I emerge, and that something could be my talent.

WACHTEL He seemed to make a connection between love and disease by suggesting that if you care for someone who is sick, you show love in a very powerful way.

MARR I don't think that's really a link between love and disease. He believed deeply that the truest form of love was not the satisfaction of sexual passion, but service and caring for other people, and the more humiliating that was, the deeper the love. Cleaning up the shit and the vomit was a measure of your love for that person. He derived this idea, I think, from the experience that in his own childhood those who loved him most tangibly were not his parents but the servants who looked after him. The image of the good servant, the loving servant, occurs again and again in his writing. His nurse raised him until he was thirteen and went away to school in England. All his life he called his nurse his real mother. That was a calculated act of cruelty towards his real mother, but it was also a measure of how his emotional life had been formed around this idea of service.

WACHTEL Manoly Lascaris was Patrick White's lifetime companion, his lover for almost fifty years. How would you describe their relationship? I was thinking of that terrible quote of Manoly's: "It is the pleasure of the disciple to serve Christ." He comes across as a saint.

MARR Patrick White was one of those infinitely lucky human beings who find the right mate. Lascaris was a well-born, well-educated Greek-American who lived in Egypt. His mother was American from Vermont, his father a Greek from Anatolia. Manoly Lascaris is one of the most subtle, worldly, funny, wise, wicked, kindly people I've ever met.

I don't know that I've ever met a saint, but there are qualities in him of saintly forbearance and patience and strength. He met Patrick during the war. Well after the book was written and published he said to me of their first meeting: "Patrick made me happy at once, and I think I made him happy." To say, after fifty years, "I think I made him happy" is heartbreaking. But the notion of being made happy *at once* is also wonderful. What Lascaris decided in those earliest days was that this man was probably a great writer, and that it was worth his while devoting his life to this man's art. And he did.

WACHTEL You provide an evocative picture of that first meeting: Manoly is looking at a painting and Patrick comes up behind him and embraces him.

MARR Well, they went off and fucked.

WACHTEL You don't mention that in the book. Is that in a footnote?

MARR No, it's not. It was in the late afternoon, and they went to dinner that night. Only recently Manoly talked to me about that dinner. He said, "It was wonderful to be with a man you could talk to. Alexandria, you know, was a city of chit-chat." Their bond remained, for nearly all of those fifty years, physical, and Patrick White would rage when people suggested that their love had cooled down to some kind of companionship. He would shout, "We're still fucking!" He would shout it at home; it was not the sort of thing he ever said in public. Manoly Lascaris remained devoted to this man, whom he knew in all the terrible aspects of his character, and all the good aspects as well. They had frightful times, frightful rows, times when they nearly broke up; and they had times of great solid partnership, happiness—always bouts of happiness—and adventure. And they survived. In a way they became one of the most respected and respectable married couples in Australia.

WACHTEL White had a reputation for not being an easy man to be around. There are a lot of contradictions in his character that come out in your book: the shyness, the fierceness, the arrogance, the self-loathing. I was going to ask, how do you reconcile them, but you don't need to reconcile them; they're just there.

MARR The job is not to reconcile but to describe, to show how those contradictory aspects of the man locked together. They were never reconciled in him, partly because he never sought to reconcile them, because they were all lived at such passionate intensity that they were probably irreconcilable. We are all filled with contradictions. His were very vivid. They came together, but not in a reconciliation. The point at which they all focused was in his being a writer; the more contradictory he was, the more characters he had to call on. This is how he saw it. He was full of contradictory impulses, beliefs and actions, and on those contradictions he could build distinct, living, characters.

As to being an easy man to be around, a great deal depended on whether he liked you.

WACHTEL And for how long. As one critic put it, "Patrick White never hesitated to lose a friend." He seemed to shed them over trivia, a mood, a whim, even musical taste.

MARR No, they were only pretexts. When the friendship was dead he waited for a pretext and then, because he wanted everything to be dramatically expressed and final, the breaches were brutal, and all the more brutal for being unjustifiable.

WACHTEL There appears to be a kind of callousness. For instance, White seemed to be particularly interested in knowing Jews when he was writing *Riders in the Chariot*, and he started to shed his Jewish friends when he finished writing that book. Is that a fair account?

MARR It's not quite complete. He was interested in knowing Jews in Sydney because, in the early 1950s, they were the most stimulating people around, a lifeline to the European culture he still loved and valued and needed. In that shaggy fringe of Sydney where Patrick White lived there were several Jewish families who taught him a great deal about European culture and he loved them for that; he loved them for themselves. Out of knowing them grew the plan to write *Riders in the Chariot*. There were many other sources as well, but they were essential to it. Having written that work he decided to put novels behind him for a time and re-enter the theatre. He shed many, but not all, of those friends, quite brutally, yes. He was an artist. He believed that he had to keep the decks fairly empty in order for the voyage to continue, in order to take on fresh passengers, and he did.

WACHTEL At one point White himself said that a novelist needs to like people because they're his material. Did he?

MARR Yes, he did, but he was always much happier complaining than praising. Complaining, in any case, is easier and sometimes more vivid. He used to say that writing about a good person is the most difficult thing to do. Yet all of his novels are, in one way or another, an investigation of goodness, which makes them so unusual in twentieth-century writing. He is trying to identify what is good, what is saintly and what is truly valuable.

WACHTEL In a context of ugliness and violence and deterioration.

MARR That's right. But his view was that you had to accept the whole of the world, and that included ugliness and violence and deterioration and squalor. Later, when he became a kind of Christian, or certainly a religious believer, he believed it unfair to God's creation not to look at the squalor and to write about the squalor, because that was what was truthful. Patrick's quest for truth meant pursuing it through many uncomfortable and squalid byways.

WACHTEL Patrick White seemed to have a kind of love-hate or even hate-hate relationship with Australia. He was an outsider, yet it was his homeland; it was in his bones. But then he would write essays like "The Prodigal Son," in which he condemns Australia as a country where intellect was not valued.

MARR He loved what his country might be and despaired at the way it continued to fall short. He loved the country that he remembered from his childhood, which was a kind of perfect Australia where the hedges were clipped and the gravel was raked and the servants were polite and the bush was wonderful and free, where he could live like a completely wild kid, riding his pony and mucking around with other kids, and hunting and swimming and just being alone, and come home at night to a perfectly ordered existence, with nannies and servants and beautiful food and good hot fires. But he left that Australia when he was thirteen years old. He didn't experience adolescence or early manhood in Australia. The Australia that was most deeply planted in his imagination was that perfect country of childhood, all the more perfect for being the country of childhood. He used to talk about childhood as the purest and deepest well from which a writer can draw, and he continued to draw from that well.

When he returned after the war he discovered a very different Australia. Had he always lived here, he would perhaps have been able to accept the incremental changes year by year. But it was a shock. It was a tough, philistine, physically very beautiful, but intellectually rather arid place. There was writing, there was wonderful painting and there was always splendid music in Sydney, so it was not entirely a cultural desert. But it was still a shock after Europe, and hard to reconcile with those childhood memories.

For the rest of his life, when he was writing about Australia, and in one way or another he wrote about the country all his life, he never ceased to urge the country on to the kind of wonderful place it might be if it adopted its own character instead of aping either the United States or Britain, if it set out to be free and independent and if it valued what was best about itself. He hammered away at the themes of public honesty and public good sense, getting rid of the prevalent ugliness of so much of Australian city life, not because he hated the place, but because he loved what it might be, and because he was a passionate perfectionist. That, of course, meant he was at war with himself as much as with his country, all his life, to the end.

WACHTEL You suggest that it wasn't as simple as the country's not accepting him for many, many years and then switching tracks when he won the Nobel Prize in 1973. In fact, his first novel, *Happy Valley*, received an award in Australia, and while it's true *The Aunt's Story* did not get good reviews, other books were embraced. How was Patrick White regarded, and how is he regarded now in Australia?

MARR Always as a controversial figure. There was a body of readers who, for perfectly respectable reasons of taste, disliked his style, disliked his approach. I hope I've respected those people. The book is in fact dedicated to my father, who could never read more than two paragraphs of Patrick White's work—he just loathed it. He quite liked the man when he met him but absolutely loathed the work. And that's a perfectly respectable difference of taste. There were also people who knew him and hated him; and there was also a body of second-rate writers who resisted as much as they could the style of this new writer.

As far as most of the Australian public was concerned, from the release in the mid-1950s of *The Tree of Man*—which was an enormous success in North America and in Europe, and was translated into God knows how many languages—Patrick White was accepted as a great writer. But Patrick's odd psychology demanded that he continue to see himself as an outsider and a foreigner and as misunderstood, as *needing* continually to prove himself. With each act of creation, each novel, he would say, "This time I'll show 'em." Even when critical opinion was engulfing him in good will, he would pick out a hostile review and birch himself with it. This was his way of moving on.

WACHTEL He turned down various awards offered to him and with the money that came with the Nobel Prize he set up a fund for senior writers in Australia.

MARR He always turned down civic awards. He turned down knighthoods once or twice—the notion of Sir Patrick White is hilarious. He turned down honorary degrees, medals and so on. He accepted literary prizes for a while, then gave orders that his books were no longer to be entered in literary competitions. But when the Nobel Prize came along and he was almost drowned in good will in Australia and abroad, he worked out this formula: For the people at home he used to say, "They're trying to turn me into a museum object, and I'm not going to be a museum object; I will break out and really show them." For the people abroad, he would say, "I have to show them, too, show them that this Australian can be a great writer," and that was another spur to his writing.

Then he wrote the *The Twyborn Affair*, in which he really did "show 'em." It was in this splendid and odd and terrific novel that he most directly addressed his own sexuality, and addressed it in a totally fresh and surprising way in that it was not, as most books on homosexuals are, about coming to terms with and finding happiness as a homosexual; instead it takes for granted both the homosexuality and the unfixed gender of the central figure.

The Twyborn Affair once again addresses the central issue in so much of his writing, the pursuit of goodness and purity. This was a totally unexpected way of approaching such a difficult task of sexual exploration. It's an extraordinary book. As he was writing *The Twyborn Affair* and parting so many last curtains about himself, he would write to people and say, "I'll be ostracized when this book comes out." Of course, once again he was showered with praise, and he looked around him and decided, well, maybe things have changed.

WACHTEL White not only supported your biography but read it just a few weeks before he died. He told you he found the book so painful that he had tears in his eyes.

MARR He was very old and frail, and I had the manuscript bound in four sections so that he could lift them. He told me he often had to hold up one of these sections in front of his face so that Manoly Lascaris wouldn't see him weeping.

After he had read it through, he made me sit with him—and this was the most exquisite torture—for nine days while he read it through again. I was able to watch and make notes of those passages which seemed to cause him the most distress. It wasn't possible to tell with certainty, because he had a magnificent poker face. In some of the really tough passages he sat immobile, his face like an Egyptian sculpture; he just didn't flicker. And I sat there thinking, my God, how is he going to react, because in three pages' time I'm getting to such-and-such. But he just didn't flicker. He did comment on acts of disloyalty to lovers, that did seem to give him great pain. I think he found the accounts I gave of the petty cruelties of his nature distressing, but he also laughed a lot. I asked him one day, early in this process—rather hoping he was laughing at one of my jokes—"What are you laughing at, Patrick?" It was one of *his* jokes. He was thrilled to rediscover the letters I'd dragged out of cupboards all over the world.

Those nine days went on and on, and I thought, well, when's the battle going to start? When do I start to fight for this book? He had no power of veto, but I would have been lamed if he had withdrawn permission for the letters. I just knew there was going to be a big battle. And then I realized on the last day, when we were getting to the end, that we weren't going to have that battle, and that he'd accepted it. He was an astonishing man.

February 1992

interview prepared in collaboration with Anne Gibson

Doris Lessing

Doris Lessing was born in Persia (Iran) in 1919. Her parents were English, her mother a nurse who married her patient, a First World War amputee. Lessing grew up on a remote, unprosperous homestead in Rhodesia (Zimbabwe). She published her first novel, *The Grass is Singing*, a book about Africa, in 1950, just after she had moved to England. Since then, she has written some thirty-five books.

Doris Lessing is a writer with an astounding range. *The Golden Notebook* (1962) was ahead of its time in its exploration of women's relationships, politics and choices, but it was as much about the writing of fiction, the determination to capture the multi-faceted aspects of a life, as it was any particular story. Published well before the feminist movement of the late sixties and seventies, *The Golden Notebook* was enormously influential; Lessing says that at the time, just to write down what women were thinking, feeling and experiencing was revolutionary. She consistently resisted the role of feminist heroine. With models such as Tolstoy and Stendhal, she wanted to write a social history—to record the intellectual and moral climate of the times.

In the early seventies, in novels such as *The Summer Before the Dark* (1973), Lessing portrayed a society that was both recognizable and apocalyptic. Madness or catastrophe lay just around the corner, but meanwhile her characters could lead quite ordinary lives—and Lessing was attuned to every detail. Between 1979 and 1983, Doris Lessing surprised everyone with her *Canopus in Argos: Archives* space fiction series. During the 1980s, she wrote a pair of novels about aging published under the pseudonym "Jane Somers" in the hope of being reviewed outside her reputation's "cage of associations." She also wrote two odd novels about different responses to life in modern England—*The Good Terrorist* (1985) is a bleak look at die-hard revolutionaries and *The Fifth Child* (1988)—the story of a monster child—paints an even grimmer picture.

In 1992, she published a collection of sketches and stories set in London called *The Real Thing* and *African Laughter*, a travel memoir about four visits to Zimbabwe.

———————

WACHTEL You're often described as a visionary writer. Readers have looked to you for some kind of truth about our age. You once described yourself as a searcher or a grail-seeker. Where does this questing impulse come from?

LESSING I think everybody has it. I think that's what we're on earth for, if I may use old-fashioned language. I think it is our job to find out what we are for, what our task is, but we make all these mistakes along the road. The trouble is, when you talk like this the language is rather tired and it sounds a bit soft. It's not fashionable thinking, this; it's sort of nineteenth-century thinking, isn't it?

When I said "grail-seeking," I was joking, of course. I said that my parents were both advanced grail-seekers, and they were.

WACHTEL When you say that this is what we're on earth for, I'm not sure people are generally as deliberate about their searching as you have been. I think most people—if they had to stop and view their lives in a more complete sort of way—just inch along without any, so to speak, visionary goals.

LESSING I think the strongest hunger in everybody is the need to learn. I'm sure of it. Unconsciously or not, we are all desperate to learn. It becomes clearer as people get older. You can see it. Most of the people I know well, middle-aged and older, are back at school in one form or another. This is learning on a lower level than what I'm talking about, but it's a reflection of this hunger. Everybody I know is back at night classes. I am myself.

I'm trying, in a somewhat dilatory fashion, to wrestle with Russian, but languages are not my strong point. However, it's fascinating to sit in a class in any polytechnic and look at the people there—they're all of them fairly extraordinary, and they're there for remarkable reasons. Middle-aged and old, they're damned if they're going to give up. They're learning extraordinarily difficult things. I think—this is really going way out—that inside every one of us is some kind of teacher, if you want to call it that, who propels us into useful experience, who perhaps we never become conscious of.

The first time I started thinking along these lines is when I read something Jung said, which has stuck in my mind. He remarked, almost in passing, that he'd often had the experience as a therapist of sitting with some patient who was totally at a dead end. Neither he, the therapist, nor the patient could see any way out. Yet meeting this person five years later, some quite astounding and unexpected solution had been found. (This is, of course, if the person hadn't died or committed suicide. Let's be realistic.) He was always struck, he said, by the creativeness of the inner teacher. I think it's true.

WACHTEL To return to your parents, grail-chasers of a highly developed sort, there is something sad in your writing about them. You write that their lives were destroyed, in a way, by World War I.

LESSING There's no doubt about it. I've met a lot of men—most of them dead now—who fought in World War I. They had a much worse time than anyone had, as far as I can see, in World

War II—unless they were prisoners. They were destroyed and shattered people, not least because their illusions were shattered. It sounds naïve now but they really believed that they were fighting the war to end war. There is no end to people's capacity for believing propaganda. People like my father believed it. His heart was broken—genuinely. He was never the same. He lost a leg, became very ill and died in his sixties, really from World War I.

My mother was landed in a life which was very wrong for her, unless somebody had prescribed suffering: "Maude McVeagh: Suffering." She was an enormously competent woman. Really outstanding. She was offered the matronship of St. George's Hospital in London, one of the great teaching hospitals then, when she was thirty-three. This doesn't happen to women until they're in their forties. All this energy and competence went into a ramshackle farm in the middle of the African veldt with a sick husband and children who were disappointing to her.

She was a conventional British matron. If she had stayed in London she would certainly have ended up running something like the Women's Institute. She was competent, but she had nothing to use that competence on. Now, looking back, I see how often she made little attempts to use it. But the surroundings didn't accept her. There's very little place for an immensely energetic class-obsessed British matron in a British colony of that kind. Now I find her quite heartbreaking, the way all that capacity was wasted.

WACHTEL I read somewhere that when you were born your mother was so geared up for a boy that she hadn't thought of any names for a girl, and it was actually the doctor who suggested Doris?

LESSING That's right. Needless to say, when I was young I bitterly resented this, but I've got old and tolerant. Now I'm desperately sorry for her, because she did so much want a son.

WACHTEL She got one after you.

LESSING Yes, but I was a disappointment to her. But never mind. I've forgiven all this.

WACHTEL Why do you feel you were disappointing to her?
LESSING She didn't like me particularly, and I don't blame her. That's okay. People don't have to like their children. Children are born out of the great job lot of genes; anything can happen. I wasn't right for her. My daughter would have been right for my mother—I mean that as a joke. They would have understood each other so well. But she got me, and I was a tough, intransigent, tactless, rough girl. This is how I survived.

My brother was like my father, unworldly and dreamy. He was totally unambitious. He had only one idea in his life: to spend his life wandering around in the bush. But it wasn't what my mother wanted for him. She had conventional ideas intact from Britain. She hated what I wrote which, when I wrote it, was revolutionary for that time and place. She just didn't like anything I did. She didn't like my short stories, she didn't like anything I wrote.
WACHTEL Did she dislike the fact that you wrote?
LESSING No, no. But I should have been writing something different—the biography of Cecil Rhodes, perhaps. Full of admiration for Cecil, she was.
WACHTEL You've said you were even a disappointment to your father, during World War II.
LESSING He was extremely ill, and dying. I had married a German refugee, which now sounds fairly harmless but it wasn't then. The fact that he was, by definition, anti-fascist didn't stop him from being a German. Don't forget, we had the history of World War I behind us. For me to marry a German must have seemed to my father like the ultimate insensitivity and betrayal.

I was engaged at that time in being a Red, which naturally he hated, and now I see his point though I didn't then. Also, I was busily engaged in fighting the cause of the blacks, which he couldn't see the point of. He didn't like the way the blacks were treated, but he was of his time. We're all of our time. These people believed in the British Empire. We laugh now, but they believed that the British Empire was a civilizing influence. There was no point in arguing rationally. You do not argue rationally with people in the grip of some belief. It took me years to realize this. When I was leaving the place it suddenly occurred to me that I'd been arguing for the last fifteen years and I hadn't changed anybody's mind. Was it not time to re-examine the value of arguing, I asked myself.

WACHTEL I see you as someone who's made a lot of changes in your life, and who's acted very independently. Was your independent spirit nurtured in you as a girl? Or was it in rebellion against the environment?

LESSING I think it was my nature anyway, and it was reinforced by everything that happened to me. Girls in the colonies then had a very, very independent life. Absolutely unlike anything at that time in Britain. Now it wouldn't seem remarkable, but I was able to do things that no English girl would have been able to do. It was unconventional and free. A couple of girls thought nothing of going off by themselves in a car on trips into the bush, long before this could be easily done in Britain. Or staying in what one's parents would view as appalling places, often, I would say, looking back, at considerable risk. So that was all good.

And I didn't like what was going on around me, politically. This isn't how I put it then, but I didn't know how to understand it. It wasn't an intellectual thing. I remember arguing with my parents about the blacks—not called "blacks" then, that's the okay word now; I don't know how long that'll last. Interestingly, talking about political language: now it's okay to call indigenous people "natives." In Africa, "natives" is a very bad word, which you wouldn't dream of using, because it's contemptuous. Anyway, I used to argue away about the Africans. There was such a gap between the whites' lifestyle and the blacks'. The real comparison, I've since concluded, is when the Romans came to Britain and the gap between the standards of living of us and the Romans. Did you know that when the Romans left Britain, the locals did not move into all those beautiful villas, they just left them standing and went on living in their tribal settlements?

There was an enormous gap between the Africans and us, and not very much intelligence used on our side to bridge it—to put it mildly. I don't know where to start with this subject because it's so complicated. The whole history of Southern Rhodesia was less than one hundred years. That's nothing, nothing. Their Pioneer Column came in 1890. But it shattered the entire tribal structure. It shattered everything and turned these people into servants and labourers. In a very short time there was a war of liberation, an appalling war. The convention now is whites bad, blacks good, but the fact of the matter is that the black armies were as cruel as the white. The poor villagers had a ghastly time while this war was going on. Then the blacks took power, without any training in running a country. All this in less than a hundred years. Where do you start?

WACHTEL You were saying that it wasn't an intellectual apprehension, but how did you come to question the way things were?

LESSING I didn't have the experience to know how to look at it. It was only when I went out of Southern Rhodesia and met someone who was *then* a revolutionary figure, though she was the *mildest* of liberals, who just remarked in passing that this was the most astonishing society she'd ever been in, where even the churches were on the side of oppression, where a tiny minority of whites were exploiting a vast majority of blacks and no one saw anything peculiar in it. These remarks were obvious, but I'd never heard them, brought up the way I was, and they fed new force into me.

WACHTEL You already had a lot of force. Even taking into account the latitude given an English girl in the colonies, you showed remarkable independence. You left home at fourteen to become an *au pair* in Salisbury. You've also said you got married young just to get away from home, to get away from your mother.

LESSING It was partly the war as well, because everyone was getting married. When wars start, people get married. I think biology demands it.

WACHTEL You also started writing very young—you destroyed two early novels while still in your teens.

LESSING Seventeen. They were extremely bad novels, of course, but they were useful.

WACHTEL Where did the impulse to write come from?

LESSING This is a society in which we all write. Practically every-body one knows is writing a novel or proposing to write a novel. What I *did* have, which others perhaps didn't, was a capacity for sticking at it, which is really the point, not the talent at all. You have to stick at it.

WACHTEL You once wrote that Olive Schreiner, another Euro-pean writer who lived in Africa, and you shared the perfect ingre-dients for women novelists: a practical mother and a dreamy father. Why would that be a stimulating combination?

LESSING Have you noticed how often you find this in women writers? A rather dreamy, high-minded, idealistic, impractical father and a mother who is practical, perhaps unimaginative, but who keeps everything together. Like Henry Handel Richardson (a woman writer) in Australia. Both are extremely strong in me. I recognize exactly when my mother's talking and when my father's talking. They're both there in the bloodstream, or somewhere.

WACHTEL Your becoming a utopian communist was another source of disappointment to your parents. Why were you drawn to being, as you put it, a Red?

LESSING They were the only people around. Salisbury was an intellectually benighted place. It was quite appalling. I had never found anyone to talk to about anything. I had a life entirely in my mind, about books and so on. Suddenly I met people who had read everything I'd read and who took it for granted that blacks were badly treated. The Soviet Union wasn't really the point. It was just part of the package, meeting people I could talk to. It was like going to university for someone who'd been brought up in the sticks. It *was* my university. I met some astonishing people—refugees, some of whom later returned to their countries to impor-tant jobs, and people from the labour movement in England, which at that time was very different from what it is now. It was a real political force and spawned many interesting people. It was very enlivening, the whole thing.

WACHTEL You've said recently that it was something you were not proud of. I thought you were being hard on yourself, you were being revisionist, that at the time it had made perfect sense.

LESSING I would have liked to have been a Red for, let's say, two or three years, because you learned so much about power, what goes on in groups. This is invaluable—about power struggles and how people talk one language but really mean another; they talk idealistic language but really they want to boss people. I can't imagine where else I could have learned it so quickly and competently, but the trouble is it's extremely hard to get free of an ideology or a violent emotion. Not just politics, religion or some kind of encompassing love—it takes a long time to get free of a strong emotion, and so it took me a long time. Even when, intellectually, I'd said, enough of that, it's all nonsense. You then have to sort out the ideology you're left with, the language you're left with. That takes time.

WACHTEL You didn't actually leave the Party until the Hungarian revolution in 1956.

LESSING No, I had actually left before.

WACHTEL For many people who are committed to that kind of ideology because of an understandable desire for social change, the disillusion with the Party can make adjustment very difficult. People who leave the Party often find it hard to carry on without it.

LESSING It was easier for me. Don't forget, I was only around it for a short time. The people for whom it was hard, and I knew some of them, had become communists perhaps when they were in their teens, living in extremely bad circumstances. They'd been very poor and their whole life had been the Party. Then their hearts broke. There were quite a few who committed suicide or who just quietly faded away from disappointment. Mine was just dipping in and out. It wasn't this "whole life" at all.

WACHTEL Have you been surprised by recent events in Eastern Europe?

LESSING The Soviet Union? Of course I'm surprised, I thought they were stuck in that. I'm so pleased. Friends of mine who've been over say that it is interesting how many talk democracy but still have the structure of authoritarianism in them. I understand it all so well.

A Russian came out about five years ago, and was at my house for a party. This was a passionate, violently anti-Soviet bloke. He was leaning against the wall, looking at my friends sitting on the floor, all dressed casually—you know, the scene is not exactly surprising in the West. He came to me in the kitchen and said, "Do you realize how deeply offensive this scene is to me? Why are these people not dressed better? Why are they not—?" I said, "For God's sake, you were supposed to have turned your back on all that." He said, "It's no good. I can't bear this sloppiness, *sloppiness*. I've suddenly understood that I'm a Soviet man."

WACHTEL Do you still have faith in any form of political system?

LESSING Not political parties, absolutely not. I like the idea of ginger groups—that is, people setting themselves up to achieve certain small, achievable ends and disbanding when they've done it. A small group of activists who say, We do not want this to happen in our street, or, We want cleaner water—whatever. There was a marvellous cartoon, in one of our newspapers—for the Social Democrats, I think, when they had just started up. It had two old gaffers leaning over a gate—the leaders of the party in question. One was saying, What do we believe in? And the other said, Well, let's see, we believe in democracy, freedom for everyone, equal rights for women, universal education... And so it went on, like the tale of the mouse, in *Alice in Wonderland*, getting smaller and smaller. That is what I'm afraid of—these great, idealistic parties that say, We stand for *all* this, but what happens is, of course, they don't get in, and we're stuck with yet another bunch of leaders.

WACHTEL How did you manage to pick up and leave what was then Southern Rhodesia and go to England, with a son under one arm and a manuscript under the other? And why were you so determined to go to England?

LESSING Everybody went to England in those days. You weren't brought up in Southern Rhodesia. It was the most appallingly boring society you can imagine. People sat around talking about the "colour bar" day and night, obsessed by it one way or another. It was a suffocating atmosphere, and all the people from the periphery went to the centre—to London—just as they did when the Roman Empire collapsed.

WACHTEL When you went to London, did you feel English? You've written amusingly about being in pursuit of the English, but did you *feel* English? Did you feel at home there?

LESSING Yes, perfectly (my parents were British), but at the same time not at home. I have this double vision of absolutely belonging and absolutely not belonging, which is extremely valuable for a writer. There are a great many of us—I would say at least half the writers working in Britain now are from South Africa or Southern Rhodesia or Kenya or Australia, New Zealand, Hong Kong, India or Pakistan. It's very enlivening; it's good for literature for this to happen.

WACHTEL It's nearly thirty years since *The Golden Notebook* was published and it still generates a passionate response from readers all over the world. I see you sigh and close your eyes. I know you're tired of it and you didn't intend it as a feminist novel, but women still read *The Golden Notebook* to know how to live their lives, or to see the complexity of their lives reflected in it. What do you think of the novel now?

LESSING I see it more and more as an historical document, which is how I wrote it. One of the reasons I wrote it was because there were all kinds of novels that had never been written in the nineteenth century that I would have liked to have read and I would still like to read. There's nothing like a novel to give you the feel of a time and place. The time I was living in was a most extraordinary one and was ending. I'm now talking about the late fifties. I could see it ending; it was exploding apart as I sat there. So I thought I would write a book that would give the feel of that time—the kind of conversations, the kind of people. I think I succeeded in that, and I'm glad to see that *The Golden Notebook* is now being set in history and political courses. Of course I'm delighted that women find it useful, if that is the word.

WACHTEL You don't look delighted.

LESSING I did write it a *long* time ago. Somebody said to me yesterday, "They called you a feminist and then they said you're an anti-feminist." I have never changed my position at all. I stand for the very boring attitude that women's lives are changed by economics and technology. You mentioned Olive Schreiner. Of all the women in the nineteenth century, Olive Schreiner had the biggest imaginative grasp of the psychological implications of the oppression of women. She was marvellous, far in advance of her time. But she had no idea what was going to happen because she didn't know what technology was going to bring.

WACHTEL She thought about economics.

LESSING Yes, she did, but she had no idea. Look, what has changed women's lives is, of course, birth control, really efficient birth control, a pill and all the other things. This was the great revolution in women's lives. Young women, on the whole, don't even recognize that this has happened. They do not know that theirs is the first generation of women in the whole history of humankind who can control their fertility. For some reason they have forgotten this. It astounds me!

This leads to another gripe: no one now is interested in history. It's very dangerous when people are not interested in history, because it makes them vulnerable to all kinds of exploitation and domination. They don't recognize recurring patterns when they come around.

The other thing that has changed women's lives is the introduction of labour-saving devices, none of which people like Olive Schreiner were able to foresee. What has not changed women's lives is sitting around talking interminably about the crimes of men. I think, my God, not again, because this is not the point. Women have always sat around complaining about men, just as men have always sat around complaining about women. This doesn't get anybody anywhere. What does get us somewhere is equal pay for equal work, proper nurseries, proper kindergartens—all that kind of thing is what changes women's lives. The

whole enormously energetic movement of the 1960s was dissi-
pated in words: chat, chat, chat, all over the world. What a waste
of time and energy that could have been used.

WACHTEL Did that disappoint you, or were you not expecting
much anyway?

LESSING I was enormously disappointed. We—I'm talking about
women—lost a very great opportunity, in three areas. Well, I'm
not going to criticize, because I wasn't a part of any of the politics
of the 1960s. First, it is true that the lives of a small number of
mostly middle-class women in the West were changed. But the
women's movement hasn't touched the lives of working-class
women in Britain or anywhere else I've been.

Then, the women's movement of the sixties insulted women
who wanted to stay at home and have children. It's bad enough
that these women have always had a low image of themselves and
have always been put down. Now along come these bright young
revolutionaries to insult them even more. I think that was utterly
unforgivable. You can meet a woman who will say, "Of course, I
don't do anything," and then you find out she's got four children.
It makes me so angry.

WACHTEL I think when more women saw work as a way of getting themselves into the world, those who didn't work felt very
defensive about it. I'm not sure we can say that feminists insulted
women who stayed at home. Women who stayed at home may
have felt apologetic about it because of the changing environment.
I don't know. We don't have to argue about it. The question is,
where to point the finger?

LESSING I think the feminists, if they really cared about what
women felt, should have gone out of their way to support these
sisters of theirs who were having a bad time. They did no such
thing.

My third point is controversial. It's this: Since long before any
feminist movement, women—nearly always middle-class women
who have money enough to do it—have been active in the community, and they have often got their lines into all kinds of fund-

ing, all kinds of positions of power. The point is that these women tend to be conservative, but they are enormously powerful and always have been. Had they been roped in, they could have changed a great deal. Actually, I have yet to meet a woman who is not a feminist. They certainly are not left-wing feminists, but every woman in the world knows that women have a bad time. These women should have been roped in and made use of, and asked to use their influence. But this didn't happen. I don't think it occurred to anybody at that time. I think that was a great opportunity lost. So now we have to wait for a new wave of energy from somewhere.

WACHTEL Apart from being ahead of its time in terms of feminism, one of the appeals of *The Golden Notebook* is the complexity of its structure, and your conclusion that we must not oversimplify and compartmentalize. How do you translate that into the way you live?

LESSING I try to remind myself all the time—it's very hard, because all the pressures in this society are towards compartmentalizing—that human beings, old and young, men and women, black and white, have far more in common than what separates them. I think it would be fruitful not to look for differences all the time, but rather to see what we have in common. This is what I try to remind myself of all the time.

WACHTEL Another subject you've been interested in and have written about is madness and breakdown—or breakup, which is a word you also use sometimes. I used to see this as part of the untenable nature of women's lives, that so many women were writing about madness or escape from the real world. Why has madness been a source of fascination for you?

LESSING By chance. I assure you it was not by choice. I have been associated with mad people for most of my life. It took me quite a long time to realize this. I thought, hang on, wait a minute, how is it there's always some lunatic in my life? I came to the conclusion that *I* was quite clearly mad and exteriorizing my own madness on the people who turned up in my life. What other conclusion can you come to? So, I'm usually in the situation of being a boringly sane person while somebody else is fairly crazy.

WACHTEL When asked if you're this character or that character in one of your books, you reply that you're all the characters. But you identify with three types in particular: the detached storyteller, the sensible, practical woman and the rather crazy girl. You're saying you actually live out the sensible, practical woman, while —

LESSING All writers have a cast of characters that keep turning up under different names and different sexes. Have you ever looked at Dickens from this point of view? In my books you'll often find a crazy or delinquent or inadequate person. Clearly this is somewhere in me, too. It turned up again, of all places, in Jane Somers, a crazy girl. When I plan novels, I think, "Not again," but there she, or he, is. I take the view that we're not one character but rather we're all composites of different characters who pop up at different times. Sometimes these characters can surprise you; sometimes they go past so fast you often don't notice them.

WACHTEL You say you live out the "boringly sensible sane person," while surrounding yourself with all these mad people—

LESSING No, no, just there's always one in my life somewhere, if not actually in my house, somewhere close to me.

WACHTEL What have you learned about madness?

LESSING For some people it's a way of achieving wholeness. This is not a new idea, I know. The idea was floating around in the fifties—that's when I first started thinking about it and observing it. You see it clearly in a person who has been very bigoted about some idea or other, like communism or religious fanaticism. These people break down and are usually much improved by the experience. I'm not talking about depression, because a couple of my friends are real depressives. I don't mean, Oh God, I feel so depressed today. I mean real depression. That is so awful. I just say, there but for the grace of God. I suppose I could easily have been a depressive. That, I think, is probably the worst.

WACHTEL Do you really think you could have easily been a depressive? You seem so sturdy.

LESSING Yes, I think I probably could. Yes, I do. Then, of course, one knows people with tinges of schizophrenia. We are programmed by nature to take in very little, just enough to survive and not much more. We take it for granted that what we see and feel is all there is to see and feel. Sometimes schizophrenics break through this protective barrier and subject themselves to the most appalling violence. I don't know if you've ever been with a schizophrenic person when they're really suffering. It must be extremely painful. All these voices they hear—they come from different parts of the psyche, of course. One of the common voices is what I call the self-hater. That's culturally induced, put into someone in their early childhood. The self-hater can destroy someone if they're not detached from it.

I have—who hasn't?—a friend who has paranoid breakdowns from time to time. He turned up only two weeks ago convinced that the whole of the Home Office was out to kill him. I saw myself in that familiar role. "Do sit down. Have a cup of tea. Come on, now! Are you quite sure the *entire* Home Office really wants to kill you?" Yes, said Ned. This went on for the whole afternoon.

WACHTEL When you say "who hasn't?", I think a few of us don't have people who drop in on them in that way.

LESSING Well, maybe I attract them.

WACHTEL You've always had what could be called an apocalyptic vision. I was struck by something you wrote twenty years ago—in a later preface to *The Golden Notebook*. You said, "I am so sure that everything we now take for granted is going to be utterly swept away in the next decade." The change or revolution anticipated then—are we in the middle of it now?

LESSING I think so. But a couple of weeks ago I saw a television interview I'd given in the seventies, and I suddenly realized I was then in the grip of a state of mind that I'm not in now—the "big bang" state of mind. The "big catastrophe." I've been wondering where it came from, how it was bred into us. I don't have that any more. My theory is that it is the result of too much war. People of my generation were brought up in the aftermath of one war and then had to live through another. Everything was coloured by that. We are now living in a time of such accelerated change that we're not taking it in, though we do try hard. Perhaps only later will we see how extraordinary it is.

Today we face a lot of separate dangers that at least we seem to be aware of and are trying to do something about. That is hopeful. We have a new kind of awareness of the need for a global responsibility. This is new in the world, and it's very powerful and growing, and will have to save us.

WACHTEL Your last two novels, I think, are in a way complementary, although they're very different. *The Good Terrorist* is about die-hard activists who go sour and violent—I'm simplifying and reducing it, I realize—while *The Fifth Child,* concerning upright traditionalists who produce a monster, has the opposite of this cast. It's as if either way of trying to cope with the world or advance some sort of political or personal solution is inadequate, naïve.

LESSING I don't think these books are linked in any way. *The Good Terrorist* was written about a common phenomenon at that time—a houseful of people who called themselves revolutionaries, living in the style of revolutionaries, even though they need never *do* anything. This is by far the most interesting book I've written from the point of view of the response I got.

I got a lot of letters from people who had been terrorists—of course it had to be "had been." One of them was from an Italian who said he had been in at the beginning of the Red Brigades. But, he said, by good fortune he'd had to leave Italy for some reason, and all the people he'd been associated with were now either dead or in prison. *The Good Terrorist,* he said, described exactly the very beginning stages of the Red Brigades, when they were chaotic and incompetent, before they became efficient and ruthless. But the point that interested me was that he said they were captured by the language they used, this debased and stupid political language. Political language is always oversimplified and stupid. I've been thinking about that ever since.

When I wrote this book, I wasn't aiming to describe the beginning of terrorist groups. I was writing about things I knew, through people I knew. The character of Alice increasingly fascinates me. I've known her all my life in one form or another. She can be a consciously good person and know that she's good.

WACHTEL She's the sensible, sane one. She tidies up.

LESSING But she's mad, crazy, around the bend. What fascinates me is that people don't even notice that Alice is mad. She cares for whales and baby bears and timber and things like that, but at the same time she will say, "Well, of course you can't make a revolution without breaking eggs, and we have to kill five million people." This is a combination that didn't strike me as extraordinary when I was young, but now I find it increasingly amazing.

WACHTEL You say those two books—*The Fifth Child* and *The Good Terrorist*—are completely unrelated. Could you go along with me for a moment in my interpretation of their being complementary?

LESSING But what has *The Fifth Child* got to do with the solution to anything? It's a development of the changeling story. There are changeling stories all over northern Europe, where the little folk, the little people, the fairies, the gnomes, the trolls or whatever, steal a human baby from its cradle and put in one of their own, and this child grows up in a normal family. It is a story embedded deeply in the northern European psyche, which may be why this book was such an enormous success in Germany. But it's got nothing to do with any solution to anything.

WACHTEL Do you see us just projecting our politics onto your books?

LESSING Yes. This book has nothing to do with politics. People said, Oh, of course, this is about the Palestinian problem; or, it's about genetics. I say it's not about anything. It's a story.

WACHTEL But it describes a disintegrating, unpleasant environment in modern England. That's the context, and at the end this changeling —

LESSING Why is it unpleasant? This is an extremely nice, middle-class household with four children in it, all of whom are rather satisfactory.

WACHTEL The child is a monster, but he isn't simply an anomaly, a monster to be looked after or institutionalized; he finds a milieu in which he is not so strange—among the punks and alienated youth of modern England, a *Clockwork Orange* type of environment he feels at home in. How could we not see that at the end of the book?

LESSING This particular society of alienated youth is found in every country in the world and always has been. It's not exactly a new phenomenon. People go on as if these young people are some new invention of our society. They're not. They're in Dickens, they're everywhere. I was not writing a political tract. I was writing a version of a legend.

WACHTEL I know, and it doesn't read as a political tract, but it reads very powerfully, and it's sort of an after-the-fact act of the reader to analyse the effects —

LESSING Literary education, which practically everybody I meet has had, teaches you to analyse what you've read in an intellectual way and to find a message in it. But the point of the story is that it makes an impact on levels that are not intellectual. This is what literature is. I could have sat down and written an article about alienated youth, or an article about the Palestinian problem, but I didn't. I was writing a story, which talks to you on a different level. Perhaps it's a mistake to analyse too closely.

WACHTEL Okay, point taken. In recent lectures you have talked of the equally strong forces of reason, sanity and civilization, as you were saying a few moments ago, of there being some hope, some sort of awareness now. What kind of hope do you have, as the end of the century approaches, for social transformation?

LESSING We have to start thinking long term, instead of short term. As far as I can make out, the only people in the world who are thinking long term are the Japanese, who don't think in terms of the next four years of an electoral period. We've got to think long term. If we don't, I really do think our civilization will collapse. We are threatened by so many different things, from ozone depletion to the filth in the North Sea and our poisoned rivers. I could sit here and produce a list of fifty threats that we all know about, but that isn't the point. The point is that we are evolving different ways of looking at ourselves. It's a way of looking at ourselves as a global society. I think this will save us yet, if we can just be a bit quicker.

WACHTEL In the preface to a recent selection of your work, *The Doris Lessing Reader*, you admit that selecting from half a lifetime's work is a strange business, but that, in fact, you don't see much difference between parts of your first novel and, say, parts of the space fiction series. This might surprise some of your readers, who see you going through all sorts of changes and phases. What makes your work all of a piece?

LESSING I think every writer has what I call a tone of voice you can recognize, but what that is I don't know.

WACHTEL You've just turned seventy-two, and you've written some famous tragicomedies on aging. One of your most anthologized stories, "Habit of Loving," is about an old actor trying to hold on to young love. You've written books about older women under the pseudonym Jane Somers. Do you think much about aging?

LESSING It depends on what mood I'm in. Sometimes I don't give a damn about getting older. I just forget about it for weeks at a time. And then I suffer the most terrible pangs, which I regard as childish, but one does. Particularly if you look in the mirror and remember what you used to look like, and you feel the most frightful loss. But on the whole it's not too bad. It even has advantages. If you're a young woman and attractive, as I was, you're always on the defensive in one way or another. It's very hard to be natural. A friendly impulse towards some man or other can easily be misinterpreted. When I was young there were suddenly no rules, and as a result people were continually misunderstanding each other.

I was remembering the other day a rather famous person—a

man who was then about sixty while I was about thirty-five—I'd known him for a long time and never at any moment had there been a whisper of anything to do with sex or romance or anything like that. He took me out for dinner for some reason, where he said with a great courtliness, as I recall, "I think I ought to tell you that I am no longer interested in sex, I am only interested in food, just in case you might get the wrong idea." At the time I was so angry I could've killed him. Now I think it's the funniest thing. He didn't know how to behave; I didn't know how to behave. Once upon a time there were rules and you kept to them.

Now, if suddenly I like a man, he's not going to think I'm after him and I'm really longing to drag him into bed. It is so funny, isn't it? The natural instincts that used to govern different societies were replaced by laws and rules, and now there's nothing. There are impulses or *ad hoc* arrangements that always confuse everybody. I thought this dinner declaration was terribly insulting at the time, but it wasn't insulting at all. He probably thought, "Oh dear, I hope she doesn't think I'm after her body. What can I say to set her at her ease?" I can imagine him thinking this, straightening his tie before the glass; and I was thinking, "Oh well, I like this old chap. He's a nice old chap." What a comedy.

October 1991

interview prepared in collaboration
with Sandra Rabinovitch

Mary Gordon

Before she was thirty, Mary Gordon had achieved striking success with her first novel, *Final Payments* (1978). In it, a woman leaves her home in Irish-Catholic, working-class Queens for the first time at age thirty after devoting her youth to caring for her overpowering, devoutly Catholic, invalid father. After his death she embarks on a life of her own, via the lingerie department at Bloomingdale's.

Mary Gordon is a feminist who writes about modern women in a Catholic environment—women struggling with families or the constraints of the church to find their own identities. As one reviewer wrote: "Two recurring obsessions chime as regularly as the Angelus Bell through Mary Gordon's novels—the Irish-American community and the Catholic Church."

Gordon followed the success of *Final Payments* with *The Company of Women* (1980), *Men and Angels* (1985) and an immigrant family saga of five generations, *The Other Side* (1989). In 1991 Gordon published a collection of essays, *Good Boys and Dead Girls*, in which she discusses other writers, moral issues and her own religious upbringing, and includes informal fragments from her journal about pregnancy and motherhood. She writes with the kind of wit and intelligence you'd expect from someone who once identified her "avocational interests" as theology and musical comedy.

When I spoke to Mary Gordon from the CBC's New York studio, I focused on the glimpses of her life and work offered in *Good Boys and Dead Girls and Other Essays*. Her most recent book is *The Rest of Life* (1993), a collection of three novellas.

———————

WACHTEL The experience of growing up a Catholic has provided material for some of the best literature in English—funny, poignant, even frightening. You've explored this world in your fiction. In fact, you've been described by one critic as the "pre-eminent novelist of Roman Catholic mores and manners." Now you're writing about it more directly in your new essay collection *Good Boys and Dead Girls*. Here you observe that there is a silence, an absence of the Catholic voice, in American literature. Is that a role you yourself have chosen to fill?

GORDON I would never choose a role. For a writer to choose a role is a doomed, perhaps self-defeating and self-deceiving project. As Flannery O'Connor says, you learn everything important that you need to write about by the age of six. By that age, most of what I had learned was imbued with an intense kind of Catholicism, which is what shaped my whole family. So it's not anything I've chosen; rather, I think it was visited upon me.

WACHTEL You grew up in a devout Catholic household, but I was interested to discover that your father, who died when you were seven, was a convert to Catholicism, that he was originally a "left-wing, Jewish intellectual."

GORDON That's right. He did something that I don't know of anybody else having done and, if for nothing else, that made him noteworthy. My father would be ninety-three in March. He went to Harvard in the middle of the First World War, in 1917 and 1918.

He was an enormous liar, and most of the people who knew him are dead, so in a sense I've created a fiction about him, trying to use the facts, but they could be wrong. This is what I put together from what I know and can surmise.

He went to Harvard and he dropped out. He then went to Europe. After that, he seems to have taken a political turn to the right, which was very unusual for a Jew at that time. I was greatly helped by Cynthia Ozick, who told me that probably the experience of having been one of the few Jews at Harvard was so scarring that he wanted to adopt an identity diametrically opposed to the identity expected of Jews. So, after many side-trips in literature and politics, he became a right-wing Catholic. My father had many, many lives (at one point, in the late twenties, he started a girly magazine), all of which came together in his passionate devotion to the right-wing church.

WACHTEL Did you ever question the spirit behind his conversion? Did you come to understand the strength of his faith?

GORDON It wasn't until I was at least a teenager that I questioned it. Despite the fact that he was an intellectual, he had a real romance about the working class, particularly the Irish working class. That is the community he placed me in, so I grew up in a world dominated by a very insular, working-class Irish Catholicism. I had no access to any voice that would have led me to question my father's commitment or his choices. In the context of the environment in which I was brought up, his commitment was considered heroic by those who took it seriously; other people just thought he was a nut because he wasn't practical and he didn't make money. But nobody would have questioned the conversion; that would have been honoured and valorized.

WACHTEL You're very candid when you say that the only thing your parents had in common *was* Catholicism.

GORDON That's right. They were wildly mismatched. My mother is Irish and Italian, although the Irish seemed to have drowned out every other ethnic strain. We were brought up in a very Irish Catholic community. She's a very working-class woman. She was a secretary, not very well-educated, certainly not intellectual but highly religious. My father arrived speaking seven languages and giving study groups about Thomas Aquinas to women; they met through a priest. The only thing they had in common was this extremely intense religious life.

WACHTEL And they both loved you more than each other. Did you feel that when you were a child?

GORDON Oh yes, there was no doubt about that. You didn't have to be subtle to pick it up.

WACHTEL In an essay called "Getting Here from There: A Writer's Reflections on a Religious Past," you talk about the relationship between Catholicism and your writing. You describe the impact on you of some of the rituals of Catholicism and the way they affected you as a writer. And you say, "The celebration of mass was an excellent training ground for an aspiring novelist."

GORDON It was good for a couple of reasons. If you went to daily mass—as my mother and I did—you were in a very quiet, dark place, very early in the morning, with some extremely marginal types. What better situation for a novelist; it was made in heaven! When you went to church on Sunday—this was the fifties, so they were crowded—you got to see the whole social parade, again in a closed room, where you could be very observant. It was the perfect place for an observer. Also, there was the aesthetic form of the Latin mass. One paid a price for that: it was exclusionary and was certainly biased in favour of Western ideas. Nevertheless, it had a kind of austerity and richness of form and language and sensuality that was wonderful training, that really created a standard of aesthetic formality.

WACHTEL Were you conscious of that at the time?

GORDON No, I was utterly absorbed in it. Religious Catholics would be ashamed to talk about the beauty of the mass, as if it were a work of art. It was utterly functional; it was the vessel that housed the truths by which you lived. To consider it a species of beauty rather than truth, rather than an utterly sacred vehicle for a transformation that they believed to be real—they actually believed that bread and wine were turned into the body and blood of Christ—to reduce that immensely powerful and important experience to mere beauty would have been unthinkable. That would have been something people like my father would have had *complete* contempt for.

WACHTEL How did you overcome that? The church is not necessarily supportive of creative expression, especially by women.

GORDON My father was enormously supportive of my intelligence. He trained me to be a little scholar as a very young girl. He taught me to read at three; he taught me French; he taught me Latin before he died. He always gave me the sense that I was gifted with words and that I was more gifted than anybody. It would never have occurred to him that there was anything I couldn't do because I was a girl. That just was not in the equation. So I grew up believing myself to be quite gifted. Then the sixties came along, and it opened up the world. As Pope John XXIII said, "It opened the windows and the doors." I began to see that there was a larger world, a world to which I could have access and to which I wanted to have access. I think it was a combination of personal and historical accidents that enabled me to do this peculiar thing I do with my life.

WACHTEL You always look back. You even find models of heroic women in Catholicism.

GORDON You don't expect me to look forward, do you? You think I'm crazy!

WACHTEL In "Getting Here from There," you say that the church of your childhood is gone, but there is still something there. How would you describe that?

GORDON As I say at the end of that particular essay, I don't know where I am. Sometimes I'm in, sometimes I'm out; it depends on whom I'm with and what the church is doing, and how badly they're behaving, and how much toleration I have for their bad behaviour. Do I look back? I think most people with a literary sensibility look back, or else they'd be making rock videos. The relationship to the past is one of literature's great subjects.

WACHTEL You've certainly mined it successfully. Where did you find heroic women in the Catholic tradition?

GORDON One advantage that Catholicism has over other religious traditions is that there was always the example of women who did *not* define themselves through marriage or their sexual or maternal roles. Women like Teresa of Avila and Catherine of Sienna who stood up to bishops and popes and who accomplished things that had nothing to do with being sexual or maternal. These were people you prayed to, people children were named after. We also had the figure of the nun, who was unmarried, unconnected to a man, yet who operated in the world. I think that accounts for the disproportionate number of Catholic women who have actually achieved. It's a very double message because Catholicism does go in for a lot of repression. Nevertheless, there was a subtext there, a subversive subtext—though they didn't realize it—of women who did not play the game according to the rules that men set down for the female body. I think there is a way in which Catholic women do have models that are helpful, in a strange way, in counteracting the enormous repression of a church run by celibate males.

WACHTEL You grew up in what you describe as a rather closed community—the predominantly Catholic section of Queens—and you have said that it served you well when you did turn to writing fiction, because your natural subject became the secrets of the Catholic world. What kinds of secrets?

GORDON I think that there was a secret language, and that language created categories of thought. There were ideals of behaviour, by which I don't mean rules of behaviour but ideals that had one foot in eternity and one foot very solidly on the ground; these were codified and given their own festivals and colours. There was a way of behaving, and there were subversive tactics.

Most of the Catholics I knew became very adept at getting around authority. It's one of the things that Catholics laugh about—how adept a liar being involved in the church makes you, and how you learn all these end runs. But at the centre of it, for many Catholics, there was an enormously serious issue, which is, how do you become a saint? How do you save your soul? And that shaped everything in a way that was very unlike other religious traditions.

WACHTEL Is there a way in which it's traitorous to expose the secrets within your own community?

GORDON Oh, sure. As many people as there are telling me they're very grateful for what I've done in telling their stories, there are others, particularly in my family, who think I'm a slut, because I've opened the door and told what *they* think is a distortion of the truth.

I don't very much like those people in my family who *don't* like my books, so I really didn't care about their reactions. But there were a couple of very sensitive, thoughtful souls who were really grieved or uncomprehending about what I had done. That was painful, but not enough to stop me. I think I got enough satisfaction out of outraging the bad ones. Also, in a rather touching way, some of the people who were saddened by my work continued to love me. There was some odd bond of understanding there that couldn't be severed.

WACHTEL You write that there *isn't* a tradition, or not much of a tradition, of Irish-American or Irish-Catholic writing. The Irish, you say, like to tell stories, but they don't actually want to reveal anything and they don't value writers. I found this a very surprising notion, but I realize that you're right.

GORDON People think that the Irish-Americans are like the Irish, and they have these fantasies of the Celtic twilight in Ireland. They forget that most of the writers of the Irish Renaissance were either Protestant or supported mainly by the Protestants. Joyce left Ireland for a very good reason: he wasn't appreciated there. There's an added issue with American-Irish: they left Ireland because they were the practical ones; survival was their business. Telling stories about the clan is not a very great help to survival. They didn't, a lot of them, respect anything that was not going to push them ahead in America. In addition, because Irish Catholicism has so many secrets, they're a little phobic about expressing *any* emotion.

They're very, very sexually puritanical people, on the whole; they really are phobic about any kind of sexual transgression. Also, the Irish have been very hard hit by alcoholism. Alcoholics have to keep a lot of secrets. I think those are the two major areas of secrecy: sexual transgression, which is bound to happen in such a strict, enclosed system and which the Irish have very little toleration for—they're very different from Mediterranean Catholics in that way—and alcoholism. These are by definition going to create a secretive culture.

WACHTEL You have also written that women are more prone to reveal these secrets, and that for women to write intimately is considered taboo. Yet when this taboo is broken, their work is judged either trivial or an embarrassment.

GORDON I was brought up short on this topic again when I read the biography of Anne Sexton and thought about the response to her work, which was very intimate and self-revelatory. People were terribly embarrassed by it at the time, in a way that they weren't by the work of Robert Lowell or John Berryman, who were equally self-revelatory. There's something about a *woman* speaking intimately that presses the light of embarrassment, in a way that doesn't happen when men writers do it.

WACHTEL You were schooled in the idea that the writer should strive for distance, but you say that what *you* love to write is "radical closeness."

GORDON That was the way I was trained. And the values I believed in for a very long time canonized Henry James, for example—whom I adore—as *the* paradigm of how one ought to write. That finished, distant relationship between author and subject matter, and emphasis on formality. My early training in the church made formality and distance things to be enormously desired. Remember, our sacred figure was the figure of the priest, who *never* got close to ordinary life. I think I must have transmuted that ideal of the distant priest to the ideal of the distant artist. Women were the ones who messed about in the muck of life and I didn't want to do that; for a long time I really struggled against that. I thought if I did get too close or too intimate, people would think I was writing like a girl. That was something I was afraid of. Then I realized, I *had* to write like a girl, I *was* a girl; that it would be enormously distorting to try to write like what I was not; and that in fact these models, in their monolithic nature, were extremely distorting and destructive.

WACHTEL You mention that your father wanted to be a writer and was interested in scholarship, in learning, and that that was a form of support for you then. Do you think your father would understand or appreciate your work now?

GORDON I can't imagine that I would be doing the work I'm doing now, if my father had lived. I think if there is a heaven, he thinks I'm the greatest writer in history. But I would be an enormously different person had he lived; I don't think I would have fought him. I would probably have been seduced into being the good daughter, which is an enormously powerful lure for women. I'm not sure I would have been able to shake it off. I think more women are held back by being good daughters, or good girls, than by many more obvious forms of oppression.

WACHTEL You write that you've also come to realize that you're not only your father's daughter but also your mother's daughter, in terms of the influence on your approach to writing: metaphysics from your father's side and the kitchen table from your mother's.

GORDON Yes, and the more I look, the more I see how difficult a child I must have been for my mother, although I was a very, very good child—I was pathologically obedient. I spent hours worrying about being good. I literally lay in my bed, worrying about it. I was never really disobedient. Now my mother sees my daughter—who tells me exactly what she thinks I'm doing wrong in florid detail, and why there is absolutely no reason for her to brush her hair—and says, "Your mother was never like that. Your mother was such a good child. How come you're such a bad child?" And I say, "Yes, that's right, she's a bad child, thank God!" Although she's not, she's a very good girl. But I was, as I say, pathologically good.

I was really worried about being perfect. In that way, I was an easy child, but my mother must have felt that some bird laid a strange egg in her nest. When I was very young, she must have looked at my father and at me and decided, "She'll do better with him." Spiritually, she gave me over to my father, and held back and didn't try to change me, which I think was an act of enormous love. She supported me in an endeavour that she really didn't understand. I don't know whether I could do that for my child. I think it's really extraordinary. My mother also had a lot of pizzazz. She was very snappy, very funny, and she knew how to tell a good story. My father was, too. Thank God, I had two funny parents. But my mother also had a real interest in the dailiness of life that my father didn't have. I think that, too, was a gift to me as a writer.

WACHTEL Do you think that part of your desire to be good had to do with the reality of reward and punishment, heaven and hell, saints and devils, and things like that?

GORDON Absolutely. I really was in fear for my immortal soul a lot of the time. But there was also the idea of an infinitely loving God whom you were disappointing, whom you were hurting, when He had never done anything but love you. That sense of fear of the Loving One's disappointment was in some ways much more potent than fear of hell-fire.

WACHTEL Although you tell your daughter that the devil is more like the Loch Ness monster, or a banshee.

GORDON Yes, I cannot, with any conviction, muster up the devil. Although recently, my son—he is having a sleeping problem— kept wanting to wake me up. I said to him, "We really don't want you to do that." I explained the subconscious mind to my seven-year-old, and I said, "We really want to trick your mind, because there's a voice telling you to sleep, and there's a voice telling you to wake up. We want to trick the voice that's telling you to wake up." He said, "Yes, there's my good voice that says, 'Go to sleep, go to sleep.' Then there's my devil voice that says, 'Try to get into the bed with your mother!'" I really, really didn't tell him that!

WACHTEL You are a feminist with progressive views, and yet you also regret some of the changes that have happened in the church since you were young. How has the feminist in you managed to get along all these years with the Catholic in you?

GORDON Because there are enough women I know, and men too, who are like me, and because it seems to me I wouldn't be a feminist except for my early training as a Catholic. I was brought up to take issues of justice very seriously. And what is feminism except a desire for universal justice not bounded by gender roles? I don't understand how anybody could be a Catholic and *not* be a feminist. I don't understand how anybody could read the New Testament and support a sexist position. It doesn't seem to me that *I'm* in conflict. I think *they're* wrong, and I'm shocked.

WACHTEL There are a lot of them, though.

GORDON Well, many people believed in slavery for a very long time. They were wrong. These guys are wrong. Even though there are a lot of them, they can still be all wrong. I don't really see a conflict. I don't know how they can sleep at night. I'm sleeping fine.

WACHTEL Do you still go to church?

GORDON Sometimes. I can't say it's something that shapes my life in a central way. It's not that I never have a desire to go, or that I feel nothing when I go. I like hearing the gospels read, and I like feeling that I'm in a room with people who at least pretend to believe these words that are of great beauty. I like being in a large room with a lot of different kinds of people. Most of my life now I meet rather upper-class, literate types. I like being in a room with people who are very different from me, all of whom have their hearts tilted towards one thing which, at its best, I find very beautiful.

October 1991

interview prepared in collaboration
with Sandra Rabinovitch

Amy Tan

Amy Tan was born in Oakland in 1952, just a few years after her parents came to California from China. *The Joy Luck Club* (1989)—about Chinese mothers and their American-born daughters—is her remarkable first novel. I was not alone in my attraction to the book's cross-cultural mix and its exploration of the way children of immigrants are pulled in conflicting directions. *The Joy Luck Club* was on the bestseller list for months and paperback rights were sold for $1.2 million. But Amy Tan, who had worked as a language development consultant for disabled children and as a freelance business writer, seemed amazed by her success. True, her mother had had high expectations of her: when she grew up, Amy was to be a neurosurgeon—and a concert pianist on the side. She was to speak Chinese and stay close to the family. But Amy herself wanted to be like her American friends. She told me that she used to sleep with a clothespin on her nose so she would look more American.

The Joy Luck Club was based on stories heard from her mother, who insisted that her next novel be devoted entirely to telling her mother's own story. The result is *The Kitchen God's Wife* (1991), in which Tan focuses on her mother's life in China just before and during the Second World War. It's a painful and moving story. Remarkably,

273

this second novel is even better than its highly popular pre-decessor—which was itself a tough act to follow.

———————

WACHTEL Your first novel, *The Joy Luck Club*, is a book about mothers and daughters—about four Chinese mothers trans-planted to the United States and their American-born daughters. Your second novel, *The Kitchen God's Wife*, explores some of the same tension between the two generations and the two cultures. At one point during *The Joy Luck Club*, one of the mothers says that she wants her children to have the best combination possible: American circumstances and Chinese character. What happens when you put the two together?

TAN In the case of the parents, they oftentimes don't mix, like Coca-Cola and soya sauce. My parents ended up feeling they'd have to sacrifice one thing or the other for the sake of our survival in the United States. Often it was the Chinese character that had to go, although they fought very hard to keep those qualities. This mainly had to do with family, your responsibility to family. West-ern values concentrate so much on individual freedom—disobey-ing your parents, making up your own mind. My hope is that, over time, American circumstances and Chinese character will mix, and that you can regain this sense of family and the values that go with that while still taking advantage of the opportunities of the new country. I think my mother believes this is possible.

My mother felt great sorrow that she couldn't expect that I would ever speak Chinese. She also had to give up the idea that I would marry somebody Chinese. She resigned herself because we ended up living in neighbourhoods where there were no other Chinese, so I had no opportunities to meet Chinese people.

So she thought, "Oh, probably I'll have to deal with having a foreign son-in-law," which she did. We turned him into someone who's Chinese, so it's turned out okay. He was Italian when I first married him, but he's now Chinese.

I think that what was most wounding to my mother was my lack of this Chinese responsibility to the family. She couldn't understand why I would want to be with my friends more than with her or with my family. All teenagers want to be with their friends and to have as little to do with their families as possible. Those values she didn't understand. It's taken time. Now she can laugh about it; we can both laugh. In fact, she says if there's anything that she learned from me, raising me from childhood, it's extreme patience. She could get through anything in life because she got through waiting for me to come to my senses.

WACHTEL You've talked about how when you were younger what you really wanted to do was to emphasize your American side, to merge into an American way of living. It took a while to accept your Chinese identity.

TAN It was that peer pressure, which starts off in a very insidious way. When I was six years old, somebody called me Chinese in what I sensed was a derogatory way. I was trying to figure out *what* made me Chinese. The only thing I remember of that experience was looking at my leg, my calf, and asking myself, "Does this leg look like it's Chinese as well? How does this Chineseness run through me? Can I change this? If I eat more American food will this leg look different?" It's a very silly notion of cultural identity, but that's how it starts off: trying to figure out what parts of you—literally, in your body, the things you put inside of you—make you one thing and not the other. It was this conscious effort, growing up, to put as many American things into me as I could, as if I could finally change that. And some day, when I grew up and was old enough, I could dye my hair and the transformation would be complete!

Fortunately, that identity problem went away over time. Looking back, I realize that it changes. The issue of your identity—whether it's cultural or just having to do with one's self, one's self-esteem—changes over time. And the issues change also within society. There's no final answer. It's there with me even today.

WACHTEL Do you remember if there was a specific moment or time or situation that turned you around, that made you more accepting of, or more interested in, the Chinese side?

TAN I think it was going to college. But also when we moved to Switzerland one year when I was a teenager, shortly after my father and brother died. We went to a school in which we were the poorest family. These were kids of ambassadors and wealthy industrialists from different countries. They were *all* different. *I* was very different. At that time, being Chinese in Europe was very unusual. The men thought I was exotic. Looking back, that wasn't necessarily great, but I was desirable suddenly. I had felt ugly and unwanted in high school in the States. I realized that it *can* be a good thing. I realized later, when I came back to the United States, that it was not so good to judge myself by how other people saw me. I could be bouncing back and forth, back and forth, according to whether or not somebody liked me. It was a good lesson for me, to experience these extreme responses.

WACHTEL In your writing, when we look at the Chinese mothers through their American daughters' eyes, the mothers seem in some ways familiar, but also a bit extreme, almost comical figures at times. They're excessively ambitious for their children; and they're anxious to improve their luck; they seem superstitious. Is that how you saw your mother when you were young?

TAN I did, but I think what I saw were only the things on the surface. My perspective of my mother was very flat, just like the daughters', very stereotypical—of an intrusive mother, an intrusive *immigrant* mother.

What I find interesting is that shock of discovery, the revelation you get when you enter in one door and then find yourself going into many rooms that you did not know existed. That's essentially how I feel with these characters. I will take feelings that *I* have had in looking at my mother—or another person of whom I have only a quick impression—and then go in and get to know that person through what *they* have to tell, through what *they* have to reveal, without judging, without having the opportunity to judge. You just sit back and observe, and listen.

WACHTEL How did your mother gain dimensionality for you? How did you get to see her differently?

TAN I had a very interesting lesson in what it means to truly listen and observe. I got a video camera a few years back. I'd been listening to my mother's stories for quite a while, but I set this camera up and I started to ask her questions. I found myself constantly interrupting or making judgments: "Why didn't you cry? Why didn't you do this? Didn't you think that perhaps you could've left?" I noticed how I would interrupt the story, and she might change it, might shorten her story somewhat. In the next video I asked her to talk about a certain situation and I said nothing. I just listened. I got so much more out of that. She revealed so much more to me. It was a lesson on how to listen with your heart, not making judgments and observations.

She was talking about her life and what had happened to her with the terrible man she'd lived with for ten years; she was married to him. I could never understand why she didn't leave him earlier. My American assumption was that it must have been love. She kept insisting, no, it wasn't this way, and trying to explain, in fragmented, different examples, why it couldn't have been love. Finally I could hear not only what my mother was about but what had *made* her, the circumstances in her life that had contributed to this lack of resistance.

Actually, it wasn't a lack of resistance; it was a lack of choices. She resisted, emotionally and mentally, in so many ways—some very funny ways, too. She had real strength and wit in outmanoeuvring him. They were arguing once. Her husband asked her if she liked the dish that was served. She said no, it was bitter. So he served it day after day after day. My mother said, "I could have told him, 'Today, oh, it's delicious!' and that would have been the end of the argument. But if I said that, wouldn't that be like saying my life was finished, he had defeated me? So every day, for weeks and weeks, I ate that bad cabbage. I would rather eat the bad cabbage than tell him that he had won, that he had conquered me in that way!"

That kind of fighting spirit differs from what a feminist today might say about how you should fight back, but the choices were so much more narrow back then. You had to use other resources to fight to preserve your own will and integrity.

WACHTEL That story has a familiar ring, because it appears in *The Kitchen God's Wife*. Before we talk about that, why did you decide that you wanted to videotape your mother?

TAN I wanted to preserve these stories. She is such a natural story-teller, and I was afraid that, through my interpretation of her story—hearing something and then translating it into something else—I would lose what was really her story, her life. I also wanted it for her grandchildren. I have a niece whom my mother adores. We call Calgary the centre of our universe because that's where my little niece lives. I wanted Melissa to have these stories forever, so she could pass them on to her children, if she chose to have children.

WACHTEL What first made you interested in your mother's stories?

TAN A number of different things, over time. Certainly, the most important was when, in 1978, she decided to go back to China for the first time in almost thirty years to be reunited with her three daughters. I suddenly developed a very keen interest in China. I had these sisters that my mother was going off to meet. She might, I thought, decide she was never going to come back, and she might say, "God, I've been living with this terrible American daughter, and I've got these three great daughters in China. I'll just stay with them!" She was gone for several months, and wrote me letters—very funny letters. When she came back I was so relieved that she still loved me, that she was happy that I was her daughter. I thought, I'm happy she's my mother and I should get to know more about China and her other daughters, about her life, what she gave up to come here and what she still misses.

I think all daughters go through a period—when their mother

is aging—where they suddenly take on the role of caretaker or mother, the roles reversed. When you take on the protective role you lose your mother in one sense, because she is no longer the one who completely protects *you*. That happened to me when my mother remarried—her third marriage—and it didn't work out. She was unhappy and called me up and said, "Will you come and save me?" I drove to where she was living, helped her pack everything up and we drove away. She was grateful, but I was sad. I thought, we've just come to terms with our mother-daughter relationship and now we're changing. I'm becoming the mother. I wanted to recapture that daughter role again.

What for me is so wonderful about writing fiction is that I am able to bring back the past, where she felt she was the mother, giving me advice, telling me the stories, the gift of her life. I also have something to give in return, but *as* a daughter, simply listening and giving back these stories to her.

WACHTEL Listening to you talk, I hear fragments of stories from both your books. The half-sisters in China come into *The Joy Luck Club*; the bad first marriage is in *The Kitchen God's Wife*. It's fascinating to see the fragments that are put together to build your fiction.

TAN People often assume that if something is autobiographical, it's wholly autobiographical. I like to use my imagination to try to reconstruct how certain details from my mother's life might have felt. I also wanted these stories—especially in *The Kitchen God's Wife*—to be a tribute to my mother and in that very deepest sense to document a life that she has had, changing many things, but keeping the essential core of how she suffered and how she grew and became strong, how she knows what she knows, those most important things. It didn't have to coincide completely with all the dates or, as my mother said, "In that house, we only had two stoves, not four!" Or, "I didn't know anybody named Peanut! Why do you have this character named Peanut in here?" I obviously changed things, but this is the reason I write—at least it was the reason I wrote these first two books.

WACHTEL I think what you do—especially in *The Kitchen God's Wife*—is restore a wholeness, a complete life to your mother, something it's very hard for children to do with their parents, especially while their parents are still alive. Sometimes it takes the death of a parent to realize they had a whole and independent life.

TAN It's amazing to me that for so long I knew nothing about my mother's life. To reconstruct it was, in part, to learn the difference between having no sympathy and having sympathy, but also to have empathy for what she had gone through. For fifty years it was as though people dismissed what had happened to her: "Well, that was China; everybody had to go through that." You just accepted it.

She could never get this sorrow off her back. She could never talk about it. But in the telling of it, finally she could let go of so much pain that she'd always carried with her, even to America. That is why the last chapter is called "Sorrow Free." In the telling of stories something happens, your whole perception and memory of things begins to change and you can let go of what you have just told—you *give* it away.

WACHTEL One striking aspect of *The Kitchen God's Wife* is the complex and painful reality that you reveal about women's roles in traditional Chinese society. The mother is not only a submissive wife, she's also an abused wife. What's worse is that this is publicly acceptable. Was it hard for you to write about this?

TAN I found myself in tears at times, writing about things that I knew had happened to my mother. But I also didn't want it to seem as though my mother was purely a victim. She was a victim, clearly, but it's not as though she was not aware of it. And there was a lot of resentment that went on behind that. There's a line in the book that explains the thinking of the time: you didn't necessarily blame men for the kind of enslaved life that women led; you blamed other women who were weaker than you were for giving in and letting you get slapped around.

She blames the husband's mother for raising him to be a bad man. You are afraid, and you blame those who are more afraid or less afraid than you are. It's that fear that supports the society, and that's what she comes to realize. Why did this man have so much power? He wasn't that smart; he wasn't that handsome. Yet he had power over men and women; he knew how to manipulate the fears in people that flourish in such a society. It was an interesting time for me to write that—as the events were unfolding in Tiananmen Square. I wanted to understand *why*, if Chinese people were so smart, they didn't do this a long time ago? Why didn't they rebel, demand certain freedoms?

WACHTEL This is the American side.

TAN Yes, this is very American thinking. Just like with my mother: why didn't she leave this marriage so much sooner? You really have to understand what it is like to live in that society, how you have fears and you begin not to even question where they come from. That is the reason for the title: *The Kitchen God's Wife*. The kitchen god himself is this god from fable, who is like a Santa Claus, a spy who watches over the household and determines whether or not you're going to get good luck or bad luck, depending on how nice you've been during the year. He judges your morals.

Nobody ever stops to think about things like kitchen gods, or other things that govern our notions of what it means to be successful or good or competent or happy in life. You stop questioning these things. How did he become kitchen god? *Why* is he the kitchen god? He is the kitchen god because long ago he wronged his wife, ran off with another woman, spent all the money, let the farmlands go to waste and fell into poverty. He lost the woman he ran off with and it was his wife who came back to save him. In his shame, in not wanting to face her and say sorry, he jumped into the hearth and burned up. When he went up to heaven he told the Jade Emperor what had happened. The Jade Emperor said, "Well, for having the courage to admit you were wrong, I make you kitchen god, watcher of people's morals."

I thought, what happened to the wife? She was the forgotten woman. Not to say that she should have been deified. It's just that we forget to question why we believe what we believe. I'm not just talking about Chinese superstition. It could be Western propaganda, or the way we are taught as teenagers what will happen to us if we don't behave, "old wives' tales" or fables. So many of these offer wonderful parables for life, but it can be dangerous if we don't learn to question why we believe these things. This is another kind of repression.

In *The Kitchen God's Wife* almost every chapter has some bit of fable or "old wives' tale." There's an apocryphal tale used to keep women in their place in China—that a woman who is too strong will drain her husband during sex and end up killing him. My mother told me that story. To this day she believes it's true. I said it couldn't be true, it's medically impossible. She said, "I know this is not common—maybe only one in a million—but I know somebody this happened to; somebody told me." That's why we were told we couldn't be too strong!

WACHTEL Once you understand how deeply that kind of oppression of women is grounded in folklore, in the structure of the society, I guess all you can do is what you did in this book: you honour the wife of the kitchen god.

TAN To honour the wife of the kitchen god is not a simple thing. You cannot suddenly deify the forgotten woman. Rather, it's the realization within each person. It's the realization within this person, Winnie, of all these things that she came to believe, and her dismissal of those beliefs. Winnie does not just say, "Oh, my God, I've been victimized all my life. I should be angry now." She says, "Okay, I've told my story. Now I see where these stories come from, how I believed all this. I had these hopes, I had this innocence, I wanted to believe." At the end, she has to become stronger for her daughter too. She lets go of all this and moves on.

WACHTEL *The Joy Luck Club* tells us that through the generations mothers and daughters are, as you put it, like stairs, one step after another, going up and down, but all going the same way. There is the idea that despite the remarkable differences in life and environment and culture, there are these bonds and similarities that exist between mothers and daughters.

TAN I find it amazing that these traits have been passed on to me. I don't think it's just her nurturing of me; it's also in our nature. When I met my half-sisters, even though they'd been separated from my mother for thirty years, I found they had the same characteristics that my mother had: their sense of humour and the things that made them angry. It amazed me. What makes both my sisters and me most angry is when somebody is being nice, but in a condescending way. It's almost worse than if they're just downright rude. Our sense of humour, our playfulness is the same. We also share traits I know have been fostered by my mother—ideas about loyalty and friendship. What does loyalty really mean? What are you looking for in your friends, or in your family, a husband, a wife? Why, for that matter, should you get married? These are questions that my mother always asked.

WACHTEL The mother in *The Kitchen God's Wife* died in 1926, when her daughter—your mother—is six years old.

TAN There are the emotions of that loss, of losing one's mother, trying to hold on to the things that were most beloved about them and finding that it keeps changing as your memory changes. The person seems to change over time, even though they've been dead all these years. That's how I think my mother feels about my grandmother. My mother recently told a relative, "No, my mother's *not* dead. She still comes to see Amy all the time and tells her these stories." I have this image: my mother imagining my grandmother, in her 1926 garb, standing next to my 386 computer, saying, "Hit the delete button on that sentence, it didn't work!"

WACHTEL This idea of continuity between mothers and daughters, from one generation to another—does it inspire you or is it a little disconcerting, or both?

TAN It definitely interests me, but I don't think it's the only thing I can write. I don't want to become a teller only of mother-and-daughter tales, as though I'm some kind of psychological expert on that area, because I'm not. In fact, if anything, I write about it because I *don't* understand it, because it *is* such a mystery to me. If it ceased to be a mystery, and if I were an expert on it, I wouldn't write about it. I like to write about things that bother me in some way, that I have a lot of conflict with. I certainly have had conflict with the fact that my mother had another life in China. I write about these things for my own reasons, not for literary reasons. Like every writer, I have literary ambitions to do something different, to take what I think are the strongest elements of my writing from the first two books and then try something a bit more challenging or different.

WACHTEL Another source of tension between the mothers and daughters in your books is the idea of fate or chance or luck. The mother says, "Chance is the first step you take. Luck is what comes afterwards."

TAN I wrote this book because I didn't know what really was happening in life. If you're raised in two traditions, you're bombarded by conflicting beliefs. My father was a Baptist minister, so I had this idea of God's will, and miracles and prayers changing your life. Things like that, on top of Chinese luck and superstitions. Also Western logic: you do this and this happens as a consequence. Then there was the very big philosophical question of what is fate and what is simply random chance. What do we actually control and what can we change?

I found the Chinese way very comforting; you end up picking what is most practical, what works the best for a given situation. There is no one answer; it changes constantly. Sometimes fate decides, and you shouldn't worry about taking responsibility for it. But sometimes you can determine that an outcome was caused by something else, such as misplaced attention, and you can correct this by setting up a charm. The charm is a way to focus how you think about this problem in your life. That's basically how I see it.

In 1968, when I was about fifteen, my oldest brother and then my father were stricken with brain tumours, and they both died that same year. My mother looked for answers everywhere: Was it this or that? Is the house out of alignment? Did we do something bad that the ancestors now say we have to pay for? Can we correct this through chemotherapy or through offering more sacrifices to the ancestors or by changing the direction of the wind that blows through our house? One way to survive is to resign yourself completely—to accept that there's nothing you can do, that this is what life dealt you.

Some people *have* to fight, they have to find a reason. It's behaviour that goes beyond survival. It's searching for meaning in life. When something devastating like that happens, the search itself is important—the search to discover whether or not these things are random bad luck or things you have control over, and to find some area where you have control over them. That's the feeling in *The Kitchen God's Wife*: a woman is dealt a life that's unbearable and wonders if it was her fault or if it was just fate. The fortune-teller dealt her this bad husband, and what can she do to survive?

WACHTEL You have a line: "If you can't change your fate, change your attitude."

TAN It's the Chinese way of thinking. There were so many people who couldn't change their life—whether or not it was fate—so the thing they could do was change their attitude. I think it also held for a lot of immigrants, who had to deal with the vast changes in their lives. You leave behind your language, your country, your family, your identity, your self-esteem. You go to a new country and you're not going to get those things back right away. You can either mourn them and become miserable or you can change your attitude. This was what many people had to do, not just Chinese people; I think it's typical of immigrants.

WACHTEL Your stories trace the incredible subtlety of emotional feeling and the degree of indirection that characterizes Chinese behaviour. Everything is implicit, coded, not so much understated as unstated. In one instance, a woman gives another woman her best embroidery needle. There are whole paragraphs interpreting this one gesture. This contrasts markedly with what we think of as American forthrightness or brashness. Which are you more comfortable with? And does it affect how you write?

TAN It really depends on the situation. If I'm dealing with some-body who needs that direct approach, that's what I will use. I'm very practical. I probably feel most comfortable with the Chinese approach, in which you know you have an understanding between you.

My writing is influenced by the Chinese way, in which you show more than you tell. But that's an old writer's axiom too, so this kind of Chinese thinking applies very well to fiction. Never generalize. Never say, "She's dishonest." Show what you mean by giving a sense of how you feel. I once wrote an essay called "The Language of Discretion." I always felt that Westerners have this view of Asians as "sneaky" and "inscrutable." Think about terms such as, "They're so polite." But it's simply that Westerners don't understand the rules, they don't have that level of understanding. If you say to someone, "Please take another scallop," they'd know immediately, through the context of the culture, what that really means.

WACHTEL It really means go home.

TAN Yes. "Would you like more tea?" You know the rules. There's nothing sneaky. It's just part of the culture.

There are things that are understood within language, within cultures, that are specific to those cultures. To interpret it from another point of view can lead to assumptions that people are sneaky or they're too brash and aggressive. I try to capture a little of this in my writing. But I hope that the reader can see, despite our different points of view, that the same emotions that every human being has are there, the same intensity and passions and feelings about friendship.

WACHTEL In some ways, *The Kitchen God's Wife* is a more "polit-ical" book than *The Joy Luck Club*, because of the context, the events it covers and its unusual perspective on the Second World War—from inside China, where we see war as a series of often quite confusing betrayals. What was it like for you, as an Amer-ican child of Chinese parents, to explore history from that perspective?

TAN I was fascinated by it. I finally had an excuse to look into that period of history in depth. I read periodicals like *National Geographic* and *Life* magazine that covered moments in history in China. Then I read books written in the last couple of years, revisionist accounts of the same events, the same period of time. It was so interesting to discover you could have all these differing accounts of what really happened—everything from numbers killed to whose fault it was, to which side the Americans, the British or the Japanese took.

I found these disturbing and contradictory fragments of history. There were glowing articles about Chiang Kai-shek in 1942, in which we Americans would call him our pal, and say how well they were taking care of these poor orphans. Then there were other accounts of the same period that saw things differently, reporting on how the Americans at the time were selling—I think it was gasoline—to the Japanese, selling them the means to continue to bomb China. Business interests still overrode the fact that we were saying the Nationalists were the ones we supported in the war. In the West we call it the Sino-Japanese war. The Chinese call it World War II; they consider that World War II started in China and that the Chinese helped end the war. What happened at Hiroshima was just excess force when the outcome had already been settled.

Perhaps it's not so important whose account is right as why these differences exist, and why we need to understand them, for within them are all the reasons why we have wars and the never-ending problems that follow them.

When I asked my mother about *her* experiences in the war, she said, "The war? Well, I wasn't affected." I thought, she was tucked away safely somewhere in free China. Lucky for her. Unlucky for me, because I didn't get to hear any interesting war stories. A little while later she was talking about what it was like living in Kunming. She said, "It was very boring. Although sometimes, two, three times a week, we had to run to the East Gate or the West Gate when the bombs started to fall."

I said, "The bombs? The bombs fell in Kunming?"

"Oh yeah, always in the morning. I don't know why they always fell in the morning. Maybe they liked to bomb Kunming first, then they'd fly to Chungking, and bomb over there."

"You went through these bombings?"

"Yes, although we didn't worry about it too much. We had dinners together, we laughed over things, and ate a thousand dumplings, with our friends."

"With your friends? How did they feel about these bombs?"

"I don't know, they were all dead the next week."

It would just grow and grow. I said, "Wait a minute. A while back you told me you weren't affected by the war." She looked at me with this exasperated-mother look, and said, "I wasn't. I wasn't killed."

My research into the history of this time is just a backdrop to help me understand and overlay my mother's account of the war. There are millions of accounts of what happened. This is just one of them.

WACHTEL *The Kitchen God's Wife* is really your mother's story. What does she think of the book?

TAN She loves it. I think, I *know* she's thrilled that I wrote this story that is her story. When I talked to her last night, she was telling me how a friend had just finished reading the book and said to her in Chinese, "Now I know what a bitterly hard life you lived and what a terrible husband you had." My mother said, "Yes! Now you know!" She was so happy! It had been a terrible secret that for so long she couldn't share with anybody. She was afraid that people would judge her harshly, accuse her of leaving her children or sharing the blame for this bad marriage. Instead, she's finding that people are interested in the story, that they cry for the narrator of the story. She almost feels like she wants to pull out other things from the past that have been too painful to tell and get rid of them too. Just say, "This is what the women in my family had to endure. Let's get rid of all that stuff now. Throw it out." She can laugh about certain things that happened. Telling me

more little, funny, subversive things she did during that time that I wish I'd known before because I would have put them in the book.
WACHTEL Tell me one.
TAN She had an unbearably horrible husband who would demand to sleep with her every night. He raped her at gunpoint. This happened to my mother. So she pretended she had contracted some terrible gastro-intestinal problem, and at night, just before he came to force her into bed, she would excuse herself and go to the bathroom and start flushing the toilet. For a month he had no desire for her. Now she can talk about this, and laugh at how subversive she was. Instead of going through the pain of remembering only the torture and the gun at her head and the threats to her children, she can remember these other things that she did. That's wonderful.

June 1991

interview prepared in collaboration
with Sandra Rabinovitch

Margaret Drabble

Margaret Drabble has been writing fiction for thirty years. She was twenty-four when her first novel, *A Summer Bird-Cage*, was published in 1963. Other early books, such as *The Garrick Year* (1964), *The Millstone* (1965) and *The Waterfall* (1969) are also about recognizably modern women—smart, attractive, educated—caught up in domestic lives centred on marriage and children, but with often submerged ambitions. For many women who came of age in the sixties and seventies, Margaret Drabble was a reliable companion.

But in the last ten years her writing has changed, her focus expanded to include a much wider, more crowded social canvas—nothing less than the moral and political condition of English society in the 1980s. This change in perspective is embodied in her ambitious trilogy of novels on Thatcher's England: *The Radiant Way* (1987), *A Natural Curiosity* (1989) and *The Gates of Ivory* (1991). Here Drabble blends the Victorian with the postmodern as she follows the lives—comfortable, middle-class but perplexed—of three women who appear and re-appear through the trilogy.

The Gates of Ivory extends Drabble's capacious vision to Southeast Asia by picking up the story of a writer, Stephen Cox, who travels to Cambodia to research a play on Pol Pot. His mysterious disappearance triggers the interest of his London friends.

I first spoke to Margaret Drabble when *A Natural Curiosity* was published. In March 1992 I met her for the first time in the CBC London studio, though I felt as if I already knew her. Her older sister is A.S. Byatt, and Drabble is married to the biographer Michael Holroyd, who had shown me a copy of *The Gates of Ivory* six months earlier in a taxicab in Toronto.

WACHTEL *The Gates of Ivory*, your latest novel and the final part in a trilogy, is about a writer who goes to Cambodia, the scene of one of the worst cases of genocide since the Second World War. It has been described as a kind of *Heart of Darkness*. In fact, many of your characters are reading Conrad during the course of the book. The first sentence is: "This is a novel—if novel it be—about Good Time and Bad Time." Why did you move the central moral action of your book outside of England—beyond the urban comfort zone, if you like, the location of most of your novels—to this other place, to the Bad Time?

DRABBLE I've always wanted to write a novel about Bad Time, a book that wasn't wholly based in Britain, but I hadn't really felt I'd had the experience or the knowledge to do it. While writing earlier novels I was aware that other writers, like Conrad and Hemingway, wrote the kinds of books that I myself had never attempted. So I suppose it was in part a challenge; though, of course, when one looks at the book, one sees that it is also quite closely anchored in Good Time, because I could not set a whole book abroad; I have to keep referring back. Also, I use parallels between the two. I'm writing about the Bad Times of Britain as well.

WACHTEL The novel credits the idea of Good Time and Bad Time to critic George Steiner.

DRABBLE Steiner uses it, I think, in one of his discussions of the Holocaust. He is talking about the nature of time and how in a Polish village next to a concentration camp, people just carried on their ordinary business, pretending not to know what was happening a mile down the road. He has this concept about loops in time and the connections between times. It's a concept that William Shawcross also uses in his books about Cambodia. I became fascinated by the fact that we in Britain, and no doubt in Canada too—in the Good Times of the West—can just switch on our telly and for entertainment look at people having a Bad Time.

WACHTEL More and more detachment.

DRABBLE And more and more media coverage. You could say that those Polish peasants who pretended not to know what was happening down the road were even more detached than we are. I think it is an open question whether increased media coverage makes us more or less detached, but it's a question I wanted to put.

WACHTEL The second book in the trilogy, *A Natural Curiosity*, features a serial killer, and essentially you were interested in what you called domestic murder. You said then that your next book would deal with mass murder, with political murder. Why is that a natural progression?

DRABBLE Well, it seems to me quite natural that if you're exploring what turns people into killers, you're interested equally in what turns them into the killers of people down the street and killers of a whole swathe of humanity. I suppose I'm asking myself whether there is any similarity between Pol Pot and my serial murderer.

WACHTEL Are you interested in murder because it's an extreme manifestation of human behaviour?

DRABBLE I don't think it's an unnatural interest. Almost everybody is interested in it. I reached the stage where I felt I had the confidence to address this very basic curiosity in myself about what it is that makes it possible for some people to kill while other people aren't able to kill a fly. Are these people of the same human flesh as us? That was very much the question asked in *A Natural Curiosity*. I suppose in *The Gates of Ivory* I'm trying to ask, Can a political ideology, can being part of a political movement, make you behave in ways that you wouldn't dream of behaving if you were not thus infected?

WACHTEL One of the questions you've posed concerns the relationship between an individual and society. Is the individual pure and innocent and corrupted by the environment, or is the individual's own greed tamed by the environment?

DRABBLE It's the perpetual struggle between nature and nurture. I have been wondering recently whether humankind is basically violent. This is a question that I do put to myself. I was brought up by Quakers to believe that the light of God was in every man, that we were all, at heart, good; something in me deeply wants to believe that. I act on that principle and I get better results than people who behave as though everybody was wicked. But I do think perhaps it overestimates human nature, this view that everybody's good, and I'm struggling with the relationship of these two philosophies. I think there's better in people than is ever allowed to show, but I think there is also something very violent and prim itive in us that we have not quite come to terms with.

WACHTEL Unlike Conrad's *Heart of Darkness*, in *The Gates of Ivory* you don't remain in the darkness. As you've said, you need to go back to the light, you need to shift back and forth between Cambodia and England. What do these worlds say to each other?

DRABBLE These worlds are much closer now than they were. In Conrad's day, if you were going into the heart of darkness you went on a boat. You started off in the Thames in a perfectly normal environment, then you sailed for several days, then you tramped, you went in little river boats and you walked. You really did make a very long physical journey. Now interpenetrations between one part of the world and another are terribly quick. It's not simply that you can watch it on the screen; you can be there physically within twenty-four hours. I suppose the very switching backwards and forwards in the book is an attempt to reflect the speed of communication, the speed of travel, the widening of our horizons for good or bad. But it means that we're very fragmented. Our brains aren't quick enough to process the information or to deal with the options we're presented with every hour of our lives.

WACHTEL But just in terms of the scope of your book, what do these two worlds say to each other?

DRABBLE That people in the West can be very, very smug about those in what we call the disadvantaged areas of the world. But also, I hope you can see that some of the people in the disadvantaged areas are perfectly normal human beings leading perfectly normal human lives, even in conditions of extreme stress, like a displaced persons' camp. These are people with very similar emotions, very similar motivations to ours. It's simply that their physical life is a great deal more unpleasant. I'm trying to say—or part of me is trying to say—that there is a common humanity. How does it work? Can we get in touch with it? Is it possible for one woman from London to meet somebody in a displaced persons' camp and have a proper conversation? This is where my belief in the good or the possible in every person comes out. I believe that we can communicate far more than we think we can. In that I am more optimistic than Conrad. He thought there was a heart of darkness where a savage, primitive terror would destroy civilization. I believe that you can make contact with cultures very, very remote indeed and have a sort of human conversation.

WACHTEL Your characters are reading Conrad but they don't much like him.

DRABBLE They disapprove of him rather, yes. But they're fascinated by him, as am I. However one thinks about Conrad, he's a very important writer, though pessimistic.

WACHTEL With this kind of novel, there seems to be an inevitability that the "hero" must die, as in Conrad's "Mistah Kurtz, he dead," and the movie *Apocalypse Now*. Death does seem to be what lies right at the heart of darkness.

DRABBLE That's true. And, of course, that death represents only one amongst one or two million deaths. In the last few years quite a few war reporters, journalists and cameramen have also been killed, so the writer Stephen is a symbol of that, of how it's not safe even for a man from the Good Time. You can get caught up in it; it can go wrong for you.

WACHTEL Is that a way of making death more real and immediate, the death of a man from the Good Time, a man whom we might recognize more easily?

DRABBLE Yes, though I would feel completely fraudulent writing from the point of view of a Cambodian soldier caught up in the strife, or a Cambodian terrorist. It's easier for me to observe it through the eyes of a Westerner. I did write from the point of view of some Cambodian characters, but not those actively involved in the warfare. I only wrote from the point of view of those who were hopeless, who were victims; I found this easier. The Cambodian characters I described are victims, and Stephen is also a victim. I couldn't find it in myself to write about the military or the murderous act.

I did talk to and read the testimony of people who had tramped through the mountains and whose families had died on the way. But I couldn't see the whole drama through the eyes of a Cambodian; I had to reflect it, using as a prism Stephen's vision of their suffering.

WACHTEL Pol Pot had some French education. Is there a sense in which Stephen, as a lapsed leftist, thinks that Western ideas, "the French disease," as he calls it, contributed to Pol Pot's becoming a mass murderer? Does Stephen feel guilty about that?

DRABBLE Yes, I think he does. An awful lot of people on the left do feel that they were fellow-travellers and that they should have known what was coming. There were many apologists for the Khmer Rouge; in fact, I've met one or two of them still going strong, which is interesting. There is something very honourable about them when they keep on saying, Yes, but I do believe in equality, I do believe in Year Zero, I do believe in the French Revolution. We hear very little of that now. Stephen went off hoping that it might not be as black as it was painted, hoping against hope that socialism or communism wasn't the disaster that it actually turns out to have been.

WACHTEL Is that the delusion invoked in your title? You quote a passage from Homer's *Odyssey* in which the gates of ivory are the gates of false dreams, and the gates of horn are where reality resides.

DRABBLE In fact, I started off calling this novel "The Gates of Horn," which could apply equally well. Stephen does go through the gates of horn. Death is about the only reality we can be certain of. Yes, I suppose it was the dream, the dream of socialism, the dream of a better life, the delusive dream. There's quite a lot of dreaming in the book. I'm interested in dreams, and some dreams tell you the truth.

WACHTEL Set against these Cambodian scenes in the novel are the London characters, some of whom are familiar from the earlier novels in the trilogy—often women, often eating posh lunches, living lives in various states of distraction. How do you feel about these women?

DRABBLE I feel about them as I feel about the people I know: I like them, and they irritate me, as I irritate myself. This is the life we lead. Sometimes it feels good, sometimes bad. Sometimes people annoy me; sometimes they seem wonderful and spirited and brave.

There is something ironic about our culture. We now live in a deeply relativist world where we're always comparing what we're doing with what we might have been doing or with what other people are doing in a city five miles away. This has become a natural way of looking at ourselves. We no longer say, "What I am is right and it's inevitable." We see all the options. Irony is a natural consequence of that. You cannot sit there having a nice lunch without being aware that there are other people who are having a horrid lunch or no lunch at all. On the other hand, you know perfectly well that your having no lunch isn't going to help anybody else, so you might as well have your lunch.

WACHTEL So, how do you think this affects us, to not be able to just...sit in absolute "lunchness"? It makes us uneasy, I would think.

DRABBLE It makes us uneasy. There's quite a lot of uneasiness in this novel—people feeling uneasy about themselves, about their way of life, about other people's ways of life. At the same time it's very important not to have false certainties. I try to suggest that some people, such as missionaries and nurses, who in the past would have been convinced they were doing the right thing were perhaps doing it for very odd reasons. We have to know that about ourselves—that we are driven by egotism and greed and all sorts of emotions. We can't pretend we're good when we're not. I suppose that's partly why there's so much irony.

WACHTEL There's a breed of novelists who write about lonely, alienated individuals; but your novels are about characters who are remarkably social. There are lots of interconnections. Is that the way you see the world?

DRABBLE I see the world as immensely interconnected, and I find that delightful and fascinating. I like the idea of people in conjunction. I like the idea of long-term friendships, sudden friendships. I'm interested in the way people get on with one another or don't get on with one another. Yet at the same time, being a writer, there is that solitary, reclusive side of me, which you must have or you'll never get down to work. In this novel I put this all into poor old Stephen and let the others go on having parties back home. But I think that's not unfair; life is a bit like that sometimes. Some people get landed with the solitary bit and other people enjoy, as I greatly enjoy, social life and all its oddities.

WACHTEL That also seems to be the source of optimism in this book—the renewal of connections and an almost heroic act of connectedness when Liz, Stephen's friend, goes to Cambodia to try to find him.

DRABBLE I simply cannot accept a view of society which sees us all as selfish, discrete particles. I prefer to think that what animates us is that we are part of one another. Sex is to do with being connected with people and creating new people, and friendship is to do with being connected with people and changing and altering and surviving and keeping one another going. And I think that, if we look at our social life, it's full of an amazing range of relationships.

WACHTEL At the end of the novel, you bring many of these interrelated people together, which makes for a nice, neat arc back to the beginning of the first book in the trilogy, *The Radiant Way*, which began with a New Year's Eve party. This one ends with a large memorial service, which may or may not be symbolic, but when you bring all these people together a certain sardonic quality slips in.

DRABBLE Yes, but I do so enjoy describing large gatherings of people. I sometimes think I'm expecting too much of the reader because there are a very large number of characters assembled at the end of this book but I just long to hear what they have to say to one another. I could have gone on writing that scene forever. There were all sorts of people who didn't get a chance to speak. As at any good party, they hadn't been introduced or they would certainly have had something to say. But I don't feel wholly sardonic about them at all. It was a funeral, but they were having a good time.

WACHTEL Your earlier novels were about individuals, mostly women, often struggling in a narrow orbit: domestic situations, marriages, children, that sort of thing. With this trilogy you move into much broader territory; you are concerned less with character and more with a broader social tapestry, if you like. In fact, when a couple of the characters from your 1972 novel, *The Needle's Eye*, wander into *The Gates of Ivory*, you dismiss them as belonging to the old-fashioned, Freudian, psychological novel. Why does that kind of novel no longer interest you?

DRABBLE I suppose it's a question of age. I've written some psychological novels—I've read an awful lot more than I've written myself—and I want to do something else. It doesn't mean that I'm not interested in those two characters, but I've lost patience with going through every phase of their thought processes. Perhaps it is a sort of greediness of middle age—of wanting to cram everything in rather than just dwelling on the inner thoughts of one or two characters. Mrs. Thatcher once said, "There is no such thing as society." I think she was wrong.

WACHTEL She was exalting the individual.

DRABBLE Yes, the individual and the family. She said there were just the people who make up society, and families who make up society. But I don't think this is true. I think society is absolutely engrossing as a spectacle.

WACHTEL But I suspect that you're chafing at even these expanded borders. There is a sense in which your subject is too big. It can't be contained in a novel, in a fiction. You even say at one point, "Look, I could have given you this or that conventional narrative and even a happy ending, but it won't do, it won't work here."

DRABBLE Yes, I do find it can be unsatisfying. And I also recognize—I wouldn't always recognize this, but I'm prepared to recognize it with you—that perhaps my form is too demanding, that I am actually trying to cram in things that make it very difficult for the reader. Some readers have told me there were too many characters, too many bits of plot, too much going on here; it isn't really a novel. I accept that some people do not like to read this kind of book, but it's the kind of book I want to write. It's possible that next time I write a work of fiction it will be completely different. I might go back to something very narrow, or I might go to something more like a sociological treatise.

WACHTEL You once said that your novels are halfway between fiction and sociology.

DRABBLE I think they are. I'm very interested in sociology. I'm very interested in us as representatives of social attitudes. In that, I have reacted slightly against the Freudian, everything being just an individual-lonely-in-their-family history. I think that we are lonely in our family history, but we are also connected with social history, class structure, nationality, even our place in the chronology of the universe. Here we are in 1992, thinking thoughts that we couldn't have thought a year ago and won't be able to hold valid in a year's time. That's fascinating. And that's not really to do with character, as it's generally considered in the novel. I have a great curiosity about what some people consider—my husband teases me greatly with this—the most boring sociological fact. For example, why is it that in the north of England people have far more washing machines than dishwashers? The dishwasher is still disapproved of in social brackets that ought to accept it in the north of England. That's the kind of thing that I find terribly interesting. And if I can squeeze that into a fictional scene, I know that a sociologist somewhere will pick it up and smile.

I'm interested in plying my way through social trends and asking myself why it is that we haven't all turned into uniform mashed potatoes yet, when we've been given every opportunity to do so. We are still quirky and peculiar, and sociology is one way of looking at that.

WACHTEL *The Gates of Ivory* takes a fairly bleak view of progress. Sixties idealism is supplanted by a kind of limitless greed and the primacy of money. What is your own view of change?

DRABBLE We've been through a very bleak decade from that point of view. All this monetarism and money talk has been very depressing. Even those who've made a lot of money have been depressed by the idea that money is an ultimate value. It's terribly depressing, the idea that capitalism is the ultimate life form. If that is the ultimate life form, then help us all. I suppose I now feel we're coming through that, that we've realized the limitations of that particular vision. The trilogy does end on a sobering note concerning change. But I hoped to suggest in the final sequence that things might open up again in some mysterious way, that next year you could go on a picnic, and something might happen that will make life quite different. And this is my optimistic bit.

We are told that we have come to the end of history, that capitalism has won and it's going to be mass-produced materialism for the rest of time. I don't believe that for a moment, but we can't yet see what the next vision will be. We're waiting for our prophet;

we're waiting for something wonderful to happen. I can't provide it, but I can certainly keep my characters with their hopes still intact.

March 1992

interview prepared in collaboration
with Richard Handler